TWENTIETH CENTURY VIEWS

The aim of this series is to present the best in contemporary critical opinion on major authors, providing a twentieth century perspective on their changing status in an era of profound revaluation.

Maynard Mack, *Series Editor*
Yale University

WHITMAN

WHITMAN

A COLLECTION OF CRITICAL ESSAYS

Edited by

Roy Harvey Pearce

Prentice-Hall, Inc., *Englewood Cliffs, N.J.*

Current printing (last digit):

12 11 10 9

LIBRARY OF CONGRESS CATALOG CARD NO.: 62-9310

Printed in the United States of America

94458-C

Table of Contents

INTRODUCTION—*Roy Harvey Pearce* 1

THE OPEN ROAD

WALT WHITMAN—*Ezra Pound* 8

WHITMAN—*D. H. Lawrence* 11

THE INTEGRITY OF *LEAVES OF GRASS*

LEAVES OF GRASS AND THE AMERICAN PARADOX —*John Kinnaird* 24

WHITMAN JUSTIFIED: THE POET IN 1860 —*Roy Harvey Pearce* 37

AMERICA'S EPIC—*James Miller, Jr.* 60

THE POET IN HIS ART

ONLY A LANGUAGE EXPERIMENT —*F. O. Matthiessen* 66

WHITMAN AS SYMBOLIST—*Charles Feidelson, Jr.* 80

WHITMAN'S STYLE: FROM MYSTICISM TO ART —*Roger Asselineau* 89

THE NEW ADAM: WHITMAN—*R. W. B. Lewis* 107

WHITMAN'S POETIC ENSEMBLES—*Walter Sutton* 119

DEMOCRATIC VISTAS

THE SHAPING OF THE AMERICAN CHARACTER —*Perry Miller* 132

AN ESSAY ON *LEAVES OF GRASS*
—William Carlos Williams 146

WALT WHITMAN AS AMERICAN SPOKESMAN
—Richard Chase 155

THE POETRY OF PRAISE—*Josephine Miles* 163

Chronology of Important Dates 177

Notes on the Editor and Contributors 179

Bibliography 181

Introduction

by Roy Harvey Pearce

During Whitman's lifetime, the great and immediate power of the man and his poems made any ordered assessment of his work virtually impossible. To read Whitman was to know a man who made himself out to be now visionary, now sage, now prophet, often all three at once—and only incidentally a poet. Or rather: to read him was to discover that poetry as traditionally conceived, mere poetry, no longer counted for much; it had to be made into a means whereby the "simple, separate person" might discover once and for all that he was bound up ecstatically in the "democratic," the community in which he might discover that he was one with all men, therefore one with God. Whitman said this again and again, most insistently after the Civil War, as here, in "A Backward Glance O'er Travel'd Roads" (1888):

> But it is not on "Leaves of Grass" distinctively *as literature,* or a specimen thereof, that I feel [it necessary] to dwell, or advance claims. No one will get at my verses who insists upon viewing them as a literary performance, or attempt at such performance, or as aiming mainly toward art or aestheticism.

In short, Whitman demanded of his readers not just the willing suspension of disbelief, but belief itself.

He proudly yielded to his own demand. He could be bold, furtive, devious, active, passive—for the sake of writing poems which would express all these capacities of man. He sacrificed himself to his own image—which he meant to be an all-inclusive image of man. He postured and posed, acted (sometimes behind the scenes) as his own public-relations man, sounded now a barbaric yawp, now a lyric cry, now an epic salutation, now a prayerful meditation, as his sense of the occasion demanded. He was ambivalent about most things because he had an amazing capacity to yield himself wholly to the moment—and then, as though he were quite another person, to seize himself in the moment of yielding. And so he changed, and through nine editions changed *Leaves of Grass* with himself. *Leaves of Grass was* himself—as he said on one occasion, an attempt "to put *a Person,* a human being (myself, in the latter half of the Nineteenth Century, in America) freely, fully and truly on record." The record would be so free and full (as he said on another occasion) that it would make possible an "aggregated, inseparable, unprecedented, vast, composite, electric *Democratic Nationality.*"

But of course the freedom and fullness of the record have posed a great problem, perhaps *the* great problem, for critics of Whitman: to decide upon the truth, the authentic version of *Democratic Nationality*—indeed, of Whitman. Initially, the problem is biographical; then it is artistic; then moral, or religious, or philosophical. The complete critic of Whitman (so far we have not had him) would have to be something of a philosophical anthropologist: one who could put together biography, critical analysis, and philosophical judgment in a single grand synthesis, centering upon an inclusive and definitive conception of man. Yet, if Whitman's life and work are to be comprehended, the idea of such a complete critic is impossible, since the life and work teach us that nothing is inclusive and definitive—above all, a conception of man. Thus, much of the earlier criticism of Whitman, which aimed at some kind of "completeness," was wrong-headed from the start. The criticism of the sort represented in this collection makes a more positive achievement because its makers assume there is more than one truth about Whitman and further that, it is possible to seize upon that truth, elucidate it, and, if necessary, show how it is superior to other truths. The difficult thing is to get used to the idea that one can never be sure.

The work of Emory Holloway and Gay Wilson Allen, Whitman's chief biographers, has done much to make this positive achievement possible. (Their relevant work is listed in the Bibliographical Note at the end of this book.) The record of Whitman's career was first set down by some of the disciples who flocked to him during the last stages of his career. To them, he was a prophet; and all his devious claims about his life and works were true, were a part of the synoptic gospel that was the final version of *Leaves of Grass.* Critical analysis, in effect considered irrelevant, was virtually impossible; synthesis was everything —the synthesis of the Whitmanian "system." Considerations of "art" and "aestheticism" were also in effect regarded as irrelevant. First Holloway in the 1920's and 1930's, then Allen in the 1940's and 1950's (Allen was aided by the work of Clifton J. Furness, who died before he could publish many of the results of his research), steadily accumulated the data which let them get straight the facts of Whitman's life and works. Their biographical studies are strongest when they are least interpretive. They make it quite clear that there are many Whitmans, not one; that the parts of his life and work can never be added up to a whole. In effect, their studies have freed critics of

Whitman to find a viable relationship between his work as it was taken to be and as it is, perhaps as it should be. Whitman fully expected this; for he wrote in 1891: "In the long run the world will do as it pleases with the book. I am determined to have the world know what I was pleased to do." Critics of Whitman now see clearly that their task is to justify their choice among the various truths about the life and works. If biographical study of Holloway's and Allen's sort is not represented in this collection, it must nonetheless be remembered that many of the essays here collected could not have been conceived, much less written, if such biographical study had not been so masterfully carried out.

In the years between his death and the 1920's, then, Whitman posed an exasperating problem for men of letters—above all, for the poets to whom he had looked forward:

> Poets to come! orators, singers, musicians to come!
> Not to-day is to justify me and answer what I am for,
> But you, a new brood, native, athletic, continental, greater than before known,
> Arouse! for you must justify me.
>
> I myself but write one or two indicative words for the future,
> I but advance a moment only to wheel and hurry back in the darkness.
> I am a man who, sauntering along without fully stopping, turns a casual look upon you and then averts his face,
> Leaving it to you to prove and define it,
> Expecting the main things from you.

The record of the "main things" is the record of American poetry since Whitman; Whitman has been the main force which the poets who have come have had to contend with. The year of Whitman's death, E. A. Robinson addressed a poem to Whitman in which he wondered if poetry were no longer possible except as Whitman had made it possible, if "the master songs" were once and for all "ended." Some years later Ezra Pound wrote a poem in which he made a "truce" with Whitman. (He later changed the word to "pact.") Having freed himself from an oppressively anti-poetic American milieu, Pound felt that he could counter Whitman—and he has been doing so ever since, most notably in the middle of the *Pisan Cantos,* in which he identifies his role with Whitman's: making the modern world possible for poetry. In one of his critical essays of the 1920's, T. S. Eliot attacked what he claimed to be Whitman's moon-mist ideas; yet the *Four Quartets* are charged with Whitmanian echoes and recollections. Hart Crane, attacking Eliot's "pessimism," made Whitman into a culture hero in *The*

Bridge. William Carlos Williams has recently discovered that Whitman was the pioneer who cleared the way for modern poetry, specifically "American" poetry of Williams' free-wheeling sort. Most recently, poets of the barbarian persuasion have discovered in Whitman the one Old Priest whose Grove they will not violate. Once more they look to the "great audience" as a necessary condition for "great poets." And so it goes. The record of American poetry since Whitman is the record of a series of confrontations like these.

The record is especially significant for this collection, because modern criticism has been so closely tied to the making of modern poetry. The modern critic has increasingly found that his task is defined by the achievement of modern poetry; his role has been to justify, in his own way, the poet's way with language and the modes of sensibility it projects, extends, and authenticates. His task, so far as Whitman is concerned, is to try to determine which Whitman (or, as I have said, which truth about Whitman) is the most "useful," which has the most bearing upon the possibilities of poetry in the modern age. Nor is this a matter of mere "art or aestheticism." For in an age whose language is increasingly vitiated by mass communications and all they entail, the possibility of making authentic poems is one with the possibility of speaking out honestly, fully, frankly, wholly—thus of being true to oneself as a simple separate person, yet democratic, en-masse. Whitman, then, was quite right, not only in what he wanted out of poetry, but in the frankly experimental, shape-shifting way he sought what he wanted. His modern critic must discriminate among the various Whitmans and his various truths, and must justify the discriminations with analysis and interpretation.

The essays collected here represent the great variety among such discriminations and the "methods" by which they are justified. I have put at the beginning the pronouncement of the young Ezra Pound and the not-so-young D. H. Lawrence; these essays in effect define the problem of Whitman as a problem at once in criticism and cultural history. They are egregious essays, but no less so than other comparable pieces —the chief examples of which are the essays by John Jay Chapman and George Santayana in the Bibliography cited at the end of this book. (Both the Chapman and the Santayana essays have been recently reprinted and are readily available.) These four writers, from the turn of the century through the early twenties, saw clearly that Whitman's promise was also a threat; that somehow Whitman's conception of man was one with his conception of poetry; and that at bottom the issue posed by Whitman's very existence was, as he himself had declared, the inviting yet dangerous vistas of art and belief open to a world in which democratic institutions gave the means but not the force whereby man might at long last achieve the dignity which was rightfully his. They saw that Whitman was whole-heartedly and compulsively, with no holds barred, the *modern* poet, for whom matters literary-artistic and socio-political had to be one and the same. Quite uncomfortably, they wanted to come to terms with Whitman—but not exactly on his terms.

Between them, the Pound and Lawrence essays define the boundaries of Whitman criticism. Pound's assessment of Whitman's importance has proved to be the enduring one—even for critics who would be unhappy to know how precisely Pound has announced their themes for them. Pound, in an age when Whitman's immediate disciples were still striving for their synoptic gospel, sees Whitman primarily as a poet's father-figure from whom he must free himself even while acknowledging that it is his father who has taught him that freedom is not only possible but necessary. (What Whitman in one of his later essays called that "ultimate vivification" which is at the heart of all genuine poetry, Pound came to call "making it new.") Yet for Pound—and this is the notion brilliantly and impatiently developed by Lawrence also—to see Whitman thus is not yet to see him as he saw himself: changing, growing, picking and choosing, teaching himself (and his readers) how to bear the burden of reality his poetry revealed. In the end his life was a series of *rites de passage,* his poems a series of ritual forms, none necessarily demanding the others.

It is on the whole a sense of freedom to choose among these forms, and thus among Whitman's varying identities, which marks the rest of the essays in this collection. In the section called "The Integrity of *Leaves of Grass,*" I have included essays which make out the integral Whitman to be he of the 1855, the 1860, and the 1892 (that is, the final) versions respectively. The word *integrity* is crucial here, for the different versions of the poem center on a sense of the wholeness and perfectibility of the idea of man from which derive an artistic wholeness and perfection signified by *integrity*. Thus Whitman's art and aestheticism is discovered to be bound up in various forms of his "personalism." The first essay in the group, by John Kinnaird, makes out in the boldest terms the case for the 1855 *Leaves of Grass*—arguing that Whitman was not the sort of poet, or man, to "improve" his spontaneous song of himself. The last essay in the group, that by James Miller, marks a recent tendency to try to recover the Whitman of the synoptic gospel, as though—because of the careful biographical and historical study which has been carried on since the 1920's—we were now in a position to accept Whitman at face value, the face being that of the prophet of cosmic consciousness. My own understanding of the problem urges me to argue against choosing this version of Whitman's "truth"—as it urges me to argue against the anti-intellectualism which demands of poetry that it do more than it can: "save" man. All this is implicit in my own essay—the second one in the group, which argues for the preeminence of the 1860 *Leaves of Grass.* (Because my essay is included, I do not venture here any "interpretation" of Whitman.) In any case, the three essays are there: representing three choices. If he is willing to suspend his disbelief, the reader can take them all. The question is: Is this to gainsay, or to deny, one Whitman at the expense of another?

The section called "The Poet in His Art" contains essays which deal with some of the principal topics in Whitman's work—politics, religion, language, the structure of poetic discourse. The reader will note that the critic, though he focuses on only one of these topics, must perforce deal with them all. Here the question is not so much deciding upon the "truest" Whitman, but seeing how the poet variously dealt with problems raised by his inquiries into himself, his culture, and his art.

A final section contains essays that do not deal exclusively with Whitman. I have followed him in calling this section "Democratic Vistas"—but have gone beyond him in allowing the vistas to open on the past as well as the future. The essays I have included here are rather occasioned by Whitman's life and work than centered upon them. But surely this is as Whitman wanted it. The poetry, in the end, was to occasion a reader's composing his own song of himself. These essays do not quite consist in this; but they do deal with the occasion of Whitman's poetry, its derivation from its own past and present, and its bearing upon not only the poets who have come, but also the readers. All of which is to say, the essays deal with what Whitman's poetry occasions. But then, as all the essays in this collection testify, the great use of Whitman's work—what pushes it beyond art and aestheticism—is that it would teach readers that they too must be poets, constantly composing their lives in a song, so to celebrate their highest humanity: the *possibility* of composing their songs of themselves and so creating something actual, "a *Person* . . . freely, fully and truly on record."

Do we yet know how to read Whitman? We have not yet sufficiently grasped the structure and quality of the several versions of *Leaves of Grass*—and therefore of Whitman's several identities. We have not yet sufficiently understood the role of the poet in nineteenth-century culture as Whitman's career shows it developing. We have not yet learned well enough to comprehend the "organic" structure of Whitman's poems, taken one by one. We still have not learned to do without the kind of perfection he eschewed. Too often we still ask the wrong questions of his verse. Or rather, we still insist that we cannot ask of it as many questions as we might. The range of the essays in this collection—which I think fairly represents the range of first-rate Whitman criticism—shows all this. Perhaps this is Whitman's greatest triumph: that we have not yet got used to him. And yet somehow the tone of our critical ventures seems to imply that we must at all costs *try* to get used to him, to domesticate the barbarian, to domesticate the barbarian in ourselves. Perhaps there *is* one truth about him—that he will always surprise us, catch us unawares, teach us to catch ourselves unawares. Above all in an Introduction, the final words (the last section of "Song of Myself") must be his:

> The spotted hawk swoops by and accuses me, he complains of my
>   gab and my loitering.
>
> I too am not a bit tamed, I too am untranslatable,
> I sound my barbaric yawp over the roofs of the world.
>
> The last scud of day holds back for me,
> It flings my likeness after the rest and true as any on the shadow'd
>   wilds,
> It coaxes me to the vapor and the dusk.
>
> I depart as air, I shake my white locks at the runaway sun,
> I effuse my flesh in eddies, and drift it in lacy jags.
>
> I bequeath myself to the dirt to grow under the grass I love,
> If you want me again look for me under your boot-soles.
>
> You will hardly know who I am or what I mean,
> But I shall be good health to you nevertheless,
> And filter and fibre your blood.
>
> Failing to fetch me at first keep encouraged,
> Missing me one place search another,
> I stop somewhere waiting for you.

The Open Road

"Years of the modern! years of the unperform'd!
Your horizon rise. . . ."

Walt Whitman

by Ezra Pound

From this side of the Atlantic I am for the first time able to read Whitman, and from the vantage of my education and—if it be permitted a man of my scant years—my world citizenship: I see him America's poet. The only Poet before the artists of the Carman-Hovey period, or better, the only one of the conventionally recognized "American Poets" who is worth reading.

He *is* America. His crudity is an exceeding great stench, but it *is* America. He is the hollow place in the rock that echoes with his time. He *does* "chant the crucial stage" and he is the "voice triumphant." He is disgusting. He is an exceedingly nauseating pill, but he accomplishes his mission.

Entirely free from the renaissance humanist ideal of the complete man or from the Greek idealism, he is content to be what he is, and he is his time and his people. He is a genius because he has vision of what he is and of his function. He knows that he is a beginning and not a classically finished work.

I honor him for he prophesied me while I can only recognize him as a forebear of whom I ought to be proud.

"Walt Whitman" (Original title: "What I Feel About Walt Whitman," dated 1 February 1909). First published from manuscript by Herbert Bergman in *American Literature, XXVII* (1955), 59-61. I have made a new transcription of the manuscript, which is in the Yale Collection of American Literature, and have silently corrected some of Pound's obvious first-draft slips. This essay is published by the permission of the Yale University Library and Dorothy Pound, Committee for Ezra Pound.—R.H.P.

In America there is much for the healing of the nations, but woe unto him of the cultured palate who attempts the dose.

As for Whitman, I read him (in many parts) with acute pain, but when I write of certain things I find myself using his rhythms. The expression of certain things related to cosmic consciousness seems tainted with this maramis.[1]

I am (in common with every educated man) an heir of the ages and I demand my birth-right. Yet if Whitman represented his time in language acceptable to one accustomed to my standard of intellectual-artistic living he would belie his time and nation. And yet I am but one of his "ages and ages' encrustations" or to be exact an encrustation of the next age. The vital part of my message, taken from the sap and fibre of America, is the same as his.

Mentally I am a Walt Whitman who has learned to wear a collar and a dress shirt (although at times inimical to both). Personally I might be very glad to conceal my relationship to my spiritual father and brag about my more congenial ancestry—Dante, Shakespeare, Theocritus, Villon, but the descent is a bit difficult to establish. And, to be frank, Whitman is to my fatherland (Patriam quam odi et amo for no uncertain reasons) what Dante is to Italy and I at my best can only be a strife for a renaissance in America of all the lost or temporarily mislaid beauty, truth, valor, glory of Greece, Italy, England and all the rest of it.

And yet if a man has written lines like Whitman's to the "Sunset breeze" one has to love him. I think we have not yet paid enough attention to the deliberate artistry of the man, not in details but in the large.

I am immortal even as he is, yet with a lesser vitality as I am the more in love with beauty (If I really do love it more than he did). Like Dante he wrote in the "vulgar tongue," in a new metric. The first great man to write in the language of his people.

Et ego Petrarca in lingua vetera scribo. And in a tongue my people understand not.

It seems to me I should like to drive Whitman into the old world I sledge, he drill—and to scourge America with all the old beauty (For Beauty *is* an accusation) and with a thousand thongs from Homer to

[1] [I do not know what this word means, and Mr. Pound has so far declined to answer my inquiries about it. His deep interest in medieval Romance literature (he had originally gone to Europe to do research and writing in the field) impels two guesses: 1. that this is his faulty recollection of a crux word in *Aucassin et Nicolette* (V, 4), "miramie"—which no one really understands but which some Romance scholars guess is a form of "merveille"—i.e., "marvelous things"; 2. that this is a faulty recollection and characteristically Poundian extension of the Spanish "marrano": "marranismo"—a "marrano" being a Jew converted to Christianity in order to save himself from persecution, and "marranismo," by extension, being the quality of protesting too much about religious matters. (The word "marranism," from "marranismo," exists in Renaissance English with roughly this meaning.)—R.H.P.]

Yeats, from Theocritus to Marcel Schwob. This desire is because I am young and impatient. Were I old and wise I should content myself in seeing and saying that these things will come. But now, since I am by no means sure it would be true prophecy, I [would] fain set my own hand to the labour.

It is a great thing, reading a man, to know, not "His Tricks are not as yet my Tricks, but I can easily make them mine" but "His message is my message. We will see that men hear it."

Whitman

by D. H. Lawrence

Post mortem effects?

But what of Walt Whitman?

The "good grey poet."

Was he a ghost, with all his physicality?

The good grey poet.

Post mortem effects. Ghosts.

A certain ghoulish insistency. A certain horrible pottage of human parts. A certain stridency and portentousness. A luridness about his beatitudes.

DEMOCRACY! THESE STATES! EIDOLONS! LOVERS, ENDLESS LOVERS!

ONE IDENTITY!

ONE IDENTITY!

I AM HE THAT ACHES WITH AMOROUS LOVE.

Do you believe me, when I say post mortem effects?

When the *Pequod* went down, she left many a rank and dirty steamboat still fussing in the seas. The *Pequod* sinks with all her souls, but their bodies rise again to man innumerable tramp steamers, and ocean-crossing liners. Corpses.

What we mean is that people may go on, keep on, and rush on, without souls. They have their ego and their will, that is enough to keep them going.

So that you see, the sinking of the *Pequod* was only a metaphysical tragedy after all. The world goes on just the same. The ship of the *soul* is sunk. But the machine-manipulating body works just the same: digests, chews gum, admires Botticelli and aches with amorous love.

I AM HE THAT ACHES WITH AMOROUS LOVE.

What do you make of that? I AM HE THAT ACHES. First generalization.

"Whitman." From *Studies in Classic American Literature* by D. H. Lawrence (New York, 1923), pp. 241-264. [The essay comes at the end of *Studies in Classic American Literature,* after a meditation on American "doom" as it is figured by the conclusion of *Moby Dick*. Thus Lawrence's opening words.—R.H.P.]

First uncomfortable universalization. WITH AMOROUS LOVE! Oh, God! Better a bellyache. A bellyache is at least specific. But the ACHE OF AMOROUS LOVE!

Think of having that under your skin. All that!

I AM HE THAT ACHES WITH AMOROUS LOVE.

Walter, leave off. You are not HE. You are just a limited Walter. And your ache doesn't include all Amorous Love, by any means. If you ache you only ache with a small bit of amorous love, and there's so much more stays outside the cover of your ache, that you might be a bit milder about it.

I AM HE THAT ACHES WITH AMOROUS LOVE.

CHUFF! CHUFF! CHUFF!

CHU-CHU-CHU-CHU-CHUFF!

Reminds one of a steam-engine. A locomotive. They're the only things that seem to me to ache with amorous love. All that steam inside them. Forty million foot-pounds pressure. The ache of AMOROUS LOVE. Steam-pressure. CHUFF!

An ordinary man aches with love for Belinda, or his Native Land, or the Ocean, or the Stars, or the Oversoul: if he feels that an ache is in the fashion.

It takes a steam-engine to ache with AMOROUS LOVE. All of it.

Walt was really too superhuman. The danger of the superman is that he is mechanical.

They talk of his "splendid animality." Well, he'd got it on the brain, if that's the place for animality.

> I am he that aches with amorous love:
> Does the earth gravitate, does not all matter, aching, attract all
> matter?
> So the body of me to all I meet or know.

What can be more mechanical? The difference between life and matter is that life, living things, living creatures, have the instinct of turning right away from *some* matter, and of blissfully ignoring the bulk of most matter, and of turning towards only some certain bits of specially selected matter. As for living creatures all helplessly hurtling together into one great snowball, why, most very living creatures spend the greater part of their time getting out of the sight, smell or sound of the rest of living creatures. Even bees only cluster on their own queen. And that is sickening enough. Fancy all white humanity clustering on one another like a lump of bees.

No, Walt, you give yourself away. Matter *does* gravitate, helplessly. But men are tricky-tricksy, and they shy all sorts of ways.

Matter gravitates because it *is* helpless and mechanical.

And if you gravitate the same, if the body of you gravitates to all you meet or know, why, something must have gone seriously wrong with you. You must have broken your mainspring.

You must have fallen also into mechanization.

Your Moby Dick must be really dead. That lonely phallic monster of the individual you. Dead mentalized.

I only know that my body doesn't by any means gravitate to all I meet or know. I find I can shake hands with a few people. But most I wouldn't touch with a long prop.

Your mainspring is broken, Walt Whitman. The mainspring of your own individuality. And so you run down with a great whirr, merging with everything.

You have killed your isolate Moby Dick. You have mentalized your deep sensual body, and that's the death of it.

I am everything and everything is me and so we're all One in One Identity, like the Mundane Egg, which has been addled quite a while.

"Whoever you are, to endless announcements——"
"And of these one and all I weave the song of myself."

Do you? Well, then, it just shows you haven't *got* any self. It's a mush, not a woven thing. A hotch-potch, not a tissue. Your self.

Oh, Walter, Walter, what have you done with it? What have you done with yourself? With your own individual self? For it sounds as if it had all leaked out of you, leaked into the universe.

Post mortem effects. The individuality had leaked out of him.

No, no, don't lay this down to poetry. These are post mortem effects. And Walt's great poems are really huge fat tomb-plants, great rank graveyard growths.

All that false exuberance. All those lists of things boiled in one pudding-cloth! No, no!

I don't want all those things inside me, thank you.

"I reject nothing," says Walt.

If that is so, one must be a pipe open at both ends, so everything runs through.

Post mortem effects.

"I embrace ALL," says Whitman. "I weave all things into myself."

Do you really! There can't be much left of *you* when you've done. When you've cooked the awful pudding of One Identity.

"And whoever walks a furlong without sympathy walks to his own funeral dressed in his own shroud."

Take off your hat then, my funeral procession of one is passing.

This awful Whitman. This post mortem poet. This poet with the private soul leaking out of him all the time. All his privacy leaking out in a sort of dribble, oozing into the universe.

Walt becomes in his own person the whole world, the whole universe, the whole eternity of time. As far as his rather sketchy knowledge of history will carry him, that is. Because to *be* a thing he had to know it. In order to assume the identity of a thing, he had to know that thing. He was not able to assume one identity with Charlie Chaplin, for example, because Walt didn't know Charlie. What a pity! He'd have done poems, pæans and what not, Chants, Songs of Cinematernity.

"Oh, Charlie, my Charlie, another film is done——"

As soon as Walt *knew* a thing, he assumed a One Identity with it. If he knew that an Esquimo sat in a kyak, immediately there was Walt being little and yellow and greasy, sitting in a kyak.

Now will you tell me exactly what a kyak is?

Who is he that demands petty definition? Let him behold me *sitting in a kyak.*

I behold no such thing. I behold a rather fat old man full of a rather senile, self-conscious sensuosity.

DEMOCRACY. EN MASSE. ONE IDENTITY.

The universe, in short, adds up to ONE.

ONE.

1.

Which is Walt.

His poems, *Democracy, En Masse, One Identity,* they are long sums in addition and multiplication, of which the answer is invariably MYSELF.

He reaches the state of ALLNESS.

And what then? It's all empty. Just an empty Allness. An addled egg.

Walt wasn't an esquimo. A little, yellow, sly, cunning, greasy little Esquimo. And when Walt blandly assumed Allness, including Esquimoness, unto himself, he was just sucking the wind out of a blown egg-shell, no more. Esquimos are not minor little Walts. They are something that I am not, I know that. Outside the egg of my Allness chuckles the greasy little Esquimo. Outside the egg of Whitman's Allness too.

But Walt wouldn't have it. He was everything and everything was in him. He drove an automobile with a very fierce headlight, along the track of a fixed idea, through the darkness of this world. And he saw Everything that way. Just as a motorist does in the night.

I, who happen to be asleep under the bushes in the dark, hoping a snake won't crawl into my neck; I, seeing Walt go by in his great fierce poetic machine, think to myself: What a funny world that fellow sees!

ONE DIRECTION! toots Walt in the car, whizzing along it.

Whereas there are myriads of ways in the dark, not to mention trackless wildernesses. As anyone will know who cares to come off the road, even the Open Road.

ONE DIRECTION! whoops America, and sets off also in an automobile.

ALLNESS! shrieks Walt at a cross-road, going whizz over an unwary Red Indian.

ONE IDENTITY! chants democratic En Masse, pelting behind in motor-cars, oblivious of the corpses under the wheels.

God save me, I feel like creeping down a rabbit-hole, to get away from all these automobiles rushing down the ONE IDENTITY track to the goal of ALLNESS.

"A woman waits for me——"

He might as well have said: "The femaleness waits for my maleness." Oh, beautiful generalization and abstraction! Oh, biological function.

"Athletic mothers of these States——" Muscles and wombs. They needn't have had faces at all.

> As I see myself reflected in Nature,
> As I see through a mist, One with inexpressible completeness, sanity, beauty,
> See the bent head, and arms folded over the breast, the Female I see.

Everything was female to him: even himself. Nature just one great function.

> This is the nucleus—after the child is born of woman, man is born of woman,
> This is the bath of birth, the merge of small and large, and the outlet again——

"The Female I see——"

If I'd been one of his women, I'd have given him Female. With a flea in his ear.

Always wanting to merge himself into the womb of something or other.

"The Female I see——"

Anything, so long as he could merge himself.

Just a horror. A sort of white flux.

Post mortem effects.

He found, like all men find, that you can't really merge in a woman, though you may go a long way. You can't manage the last bit. So you have to give it up, and try elsewhere. If you *insist* on merging.

In "Calamus" he changes his tune. He doesn't shout and thump and exult any more. He begins to hesitate, reluctant, wistful.

The strange calamus has its pink-tinged root by the pond, and it sends up its leaves of comradeship, comrades from one root, without the intervention of woman, the female.

So he sings of the mystery of manly love, the love of comrades. Over and over he says the same thing: the new world will be built on the love of comrades, the new great dynamic of life will be manly love. Out of this manly love will come the inspiration for the future.

Will it though? Will it?

Comradeship! Comrades! This is to be the new Democracy: of Comrades. This is the new cohering principle in the world: Comradeship.

Is it? Are you sure?

It is the cohering principle of true soldiery, we are told in *Drum Taps*. It is the cohering principle in the new unison for creative activity. And it is extreme and alone, touching the confines of death. Something terrible to bear, terrible to be responsible for. Even Walt Whitman felt it. The soul's last and most poignant responsibility, the responsibility of comradeship, of manly love.

> Yet you are beautiful to me, you faint-tinged roots, you make me think of death.
> Death is beautiful from you (what indeed is finally beautiful except death and love?)
> I think it is not for life I am chanting here my chant of lovers, I think it must be for death,
> For how calm, how solemn it grows to ascend to the atmosphere of lovers,
> Death or life, I am then indifferent, my soul declines to prefer
> (I am not sure but the high soul of lovers welcomes death most)
> Indeed, O death, I think now these leaves mean precisely the same as you mean——

This is strange, from the exultant Walt.

Death!

Death is now his chant! Death!

Merging! And Death! Which is the final merge.

The great merge into the womb. Woman.

And after that, the merge of comrades: man-for-man love.

And almost immediately with this, death, the final merge of death.

There you have the progression of merging. For the great mergers, woman at last becomes inadequate. For those who love to extremes. Woman is inadequate for the last merging. So the next step is the merging of the man-for-man love. And this is on the brink of death. It slides over into death.

David and Jonathan. And the death of Jonathan.

It always slides into death.

The love of comrades.

Merging.

So that if the new Democracy is to be based on the love of comrades, it will be based on death too. It will slip so soon into death.

The last merging. The last Democracy. The last love. The love of comrades.

Fatality. And fatality.

Whitman would not have been the great poet he is if he had not taken the last steps and looked over into death. Death, the last merging, that was the goal of his manhood.

To the mergers, there remains the brief love of comrades, and then Death.

> Whereto answering, the sea.
> Delaying not, hurrying not
> Whispered me through the night, very plainly before daybreak,
> Lisp'd to me the low and delicious word death,
> And again death, death, death, death.
> Hissing melodious, neither like the bird nor like my arous'd child's heart,
> But edging near as privately for me rustling at my feet,
> Creeping thence steadily up to my ears and laving me softly all over
> Death, death, death, death, death——

Whitman is a very great poet, of the end of life. A very great post mortem poet, of the transitions of the soul as it loses its integrity. The poet of the soul's last shout and shriek, on the confines of death. *Après moi le déluge.*

But we have all got to die, and disintegrate.

We have got to die in life, too, and disintegrate while we live.

But even then the goal is not death.

Something else will come.

"Out of the cradle endlessly rocking."

We've got to die first, anyhow. And disintegrate while we still live.

Only we know this much. Death is not the *goal*. And Love, and merging, are now only part of the death-process. Comradeship—part of the death-process. Democracy—part of the death-process. The new Democracy—the brink of death. One Identity—death itself.

We have died, and we are still disintegrating.

But IT IS FINISHED.

Consummatum est.

Whitman, the great poet, has meant so much to me. Whitman, the one man breaking a way ahead. Whitman, the one pioneer. And only Whitman. No English pioneers, no French. No European pioneer-poets. In Europe the would-be pioneers are mere innovators. The same in America. Ahead of Whitman, nothing. Ahead of all poets, pioneering into the wilderness of unopened life, Whitman. Beyond him, none. His wide, strange camp at the end of the great high-road. And lots of new little poets camping on Whitman's camping ground now. But none going really beyond. Because Whitman's camp is at the end of the road, and on the edge of a great precipice. Over the precipice, blue distances, and the blue hollow of the future. But there is no way down. It is a dead end.

Pisgah. Pisgah sights. And Death. Whitman like a strange, modern, American Moses. Fearfully mistaken. And yet the great leader.

The essential function of art is moral. Not æsthetic, not decorative, not pastime and recreation. But moral. The essential function of art is moral.

But a passionate, implicit morality, not didactic. A morality which changes the blood, rather than the mind. Changes the blood first. The mind follows later, in the wake.

Now Whitman was a great moralist. He was a great leader. He was a great changer of the blood in the veins of men.

Surely it is especially true of American art, that it is all essentially moral. Hawthorne, Poe, Longfellow, Emerson, Melville: it is the moral issue which engages them. They all feel uneasy about the old morality. Sensuously, passionally, they all attack the old morality. But they know nothing better, mentally. Therefore they give tight mental allegiance to a morality which all their passion goes to destroy. Hence the duplicity which is the fatal flaw in them; most fatal in the most perfect American work of art, *The Scarlet Letter*. Tight mental allegiance given to a morality which the passional self repudiates.

Whitman was the first to break the mental allegiance. He was the first to smash the old moral conception, that the soul of man is something "superior" and "above" the flesh. Even Emerson still maintained this tiresome "superiority" of the soul. Even Melville could not get over it. Whitman was the first heroic seer to seize the soul by the scruff of her neck and plant her down among the potsherds.

"There!" he said to the soul. "Stay there!"

Stay there. Stay in the flesh. Stay in the limbs and lips and in the belly. Stay in the breast and womb. Stay there, O Soul, where you belong.

Stay in the dark limbs of negroes. Stay in the body of the prostitute. Stay in the sick flesh of the syphilitic. Stay in the marsh where the calamus grows. Stay there, Soul, where you belong.

The Open Road. The great home of the Soul is the open road. Not heaven, not paradise. Not "above." Not even "within." The soul is neither "above" nor "within." It is a wayfarer down the open road.

Not by meditating. Not by fasting. Not by exploring heaven after heaven, inwardly, in the manner of the great mystics. Not by exaltation. Not by ecstasy. Not by any of these ways does the soul come into her own.

Only by taking the open road.

Not through charity. Not through sacrifice. Not even through love. Not through good works. Not through these does the soul accomplish herself.

Only through the journey down the open road.

The journey itself, down the open road. Exposed to full contact. On two slow feet. Meeting whatever comes down the open road. In company with those that drift in the same measure along the same way. Towards no goal. Always the open road.

Having no known direction, even. Only the soul remaining true to herself in her going.

Meeting all the other wayfarers along the road. And how? How meet them, and how pass? With sympathy, says Whitman. Sympathy. He does not say love. He says sympathy. Feeling with. Feel with them as they feel with themselves. Catching the vibration of their soul and flesh as we pass.

It is a new great doctrine. A doctrine of life. A new great morality. A morality of actual living, not of salvation. Europe has never got beyond the morality of salvation. America to this day is deathly sick with saviourism. But Whitman, the greatest and the first and the only American teacher, was no Saviour. His morality was no morality of salvation. His was a morality of the soul living her life, not saving herself. Accepting the contact with other souls along the open way, as they lived their lives. Never trying to save them. As leave try to arrest them and throw them in gaol. The soul living her life along the incarnate mystery of the open road.

This was Whitman. And the true rhythm of the American continent speaking out in him. He is the first white aboriginal.

"In my Father's house are many mansions."

"No," said Whitman. "Keep out of mansions. A mansion may be heaven on earth, but you might as well be dead. Strictly avoid mansions. The soul is herself when she is going on foot down the open road."

It is the American heroic message. The soul is not to pile up defenses round herself. She is not to withdraw and seek her heavens inwardly, in mystical ecstasies. She is not to cry to some God beyond, for salvation. She is to go down the open road, as the road opens, into the unknown, keeping company with those whose soul draws them near to her, accomplishing nothing save the journey, and the works incident to the journey, in the long life-travel into the unknown, the soul in her subtle sympathies accomplishing herself by the way.

This is Whitman's essential message. The heroic message of the American future. It is the inspiration of thousands of Americans today, the best souls of today, men and women. And it is a message that only in America can be fully understood, finally accepted.

Then Whitman's mistake. The mistake of his interpretation of his watchword: Sympathy. The mystery of SYMPATHY. He still confounded it with Jesus' LOVE, and with Paul's CHARITY. Whitman, like all the rest of us, was at the end of the great emotional highway of Love. And because he couldn't help himself, he carried on his Open Road as a prolongation of the emotional highway of Love, beyond Calvary. The highway of Love ends at the foot of the Cross. There is no beyond. It was a hopeless attempt, to prolong the highway of Love.

He didn't follow his Sympathy. Try as he might, he kept on automatically interpreting it as Love, as Charity. Merging.

This merging, en masse, One Identity, Myself monomania was a carry-over from the old Love idea. It was carrying the idea of Love to its logical physical conclusion. Like Flaubert and the leper. The decree of unqualified Charity, as the soul's one means of salvation, still in force.

Now Whitman wanted his soul to save itself, *he* didn't want to save it. Therefore he did not need the great Christian receipt for saving the soul. He needed to supersede the Christian Charity, the Christian Love, within himself, in order to give his Soul her last freedom. The highroad of Love is no Open Road. It is a narrow, tight way, where the soul walks hemmed in between compulsions.

Whitman wanted to take his Soul down the open road. And he failed in so far as he failed to get out of the old rut of Salvation. He forced his Soul to the edge of a cliff, and he looked down into death. And there he camped, powerless. He had carried out his Sympathy as an extension of Love and Charity. And it had brought him almost to madness and soul-death. It gave him his forced, unhealthy, post-mortem quality.

His message was really the opposite of Henley's rant:

> I am the master of my fate.
> I am the captain of my soul.

Whitman's essential message was the Open Road. The leaving of the soul free unto herself, the leaving of his fate to her and to the loom of the open road. Which is the bravest doctrine man has ever proposed to himself.

Alas, he didn't quite carry it out. He couldn't quite break the old maddening bond of the love-compulsion, he couldn't quite get out of the rut of the charity habit. For Love and Charity have degenerated now into habit: a bad habit.

Whitman said Sympathy. If only he had stuck to it! Because Sympathy means feeling with, not feeling for. He kept on having a passionate feeling *for* the negro slave, or the prostitute, or the syphilitic. Which is merging. A sinking of Walt Whitman's soul in the souls of these others.

He wasn't keeping to his open road. He was forcing his soul down an old rut. He wasn't leaving her free. He was forcing her into other people's circumstances.

Supposing he had felt true sympathy with the negro slave? He would have felt *with* the negro slave. Sympathy—compassion—which is partaking of the passion which was in the soul of the negro slave.

What was the feeling in the negro's soul?

"Ah, I am a slave! Ah, it is bad to be a slave! I must free myself. My soul will die unless she frees herself. My soul says I must free myself."

Whitman came along, and saw the slave, and said to himself: "That negro slave is a man like myself. We share the same identity. And he is bleeding with wounds. Oh, oh, is it not myself who am also bleeding with wounds?"

This was not *sympathy*. It was merging and self-sacrifice. "Bear ye one another's burdens."—"Love thy neighbour as thyself."—"Whatsoever ye do unto him, ye do unto me."

If Whitman had truly *sympathised,* he would have said: "That negro slave suffers from slavery. He wants to free himself. His soul wants to free him. He has wounds, but they are the price of freedom. The soul has a long journey from slavery to freedom. If I can help him I will: I will not take over his wounds and his slavery to myself. But I will help him fight the power that enslaves him when he wants to be free, if he wants my help. Since I see in his face that he needs to be free. But even when he is free, his soul has many journeys down the open road, before it is a free soul."

And of the prostitute Whitman would have said:

"Look at that prostitute! Her nature has turned evil under her mental lust for prostitution. She has lost her soul. She knows it herself. She likes to make men lose their souls. If she tried to make me lose my soul, I would kill her. I wish she may die."

But of another prostitute he would have said:

"Look! She is fascinated by the Priapic mysteries. Look, she will soon be worn to death by the Priapic usage. It is the way of her soul. She wishes it so."

Of the syphilitic he would say:

"Look! She wants to infect all men with syphilis. We ought to kill her."

And of another syphilitic:

"Look! She has a horror of her syphilis. If she looks my way I will help her to get cured."

This is sympathy. The soul judging for herself, and preserving her own integrity.

But when, in Flaubert, the man takes the leper to his naked body; when Bubu de Montparnasse takes the girl because he knows she's got syphilis; when Whitman embraces an evil prostitute: that is not sympathy. The evil prostitute has no desire to be embraced with love; so if you sympathise with her, you won't try to embrace her with love. The leper loathes his leprosy, so if you sympathise with him, you'll loathe it too. The evil woman who wishes to infect all men with her syphilis hates you if you haven't got syphilis. If you sympathise, you'll feel her hatred, and you'll hate too, you'll hate her. Her feeling is hate, and you'll share it. Only your soul will choose the direction of its own hatred.

The soul is a very perfect judge of her own motions, if your mind doesn't dictate to her. Because the mind says Charity! Charity! you don't have to force your soul into kissing lepers or embracing syphilitics. Your lips are the lips of your soul, your body is the body of your soul; your own single, individual soul. That is Whitman's message. And your soul hates syphilis and leprosy. Because it *is* a soul, it hates these things which are against the soul. And therefore to force the body of your soul into contact with uncleanness is a great violation of your soul. The soul wishes to keep clean and whole. The soul's deepest will is to preserve its own integrity, against the mind and the whole mass of disintegrating forces.

Soul sympathises with soul. And that which tries to kill my soul, my soul hates. My soul and my body are one. Soul and body wish to keep clean and whole. Only the mind is capable of great perversion. Only the mind tries to drive my soul and body into uncleanness and unwholesomeness.

What my soul loves, I love.

What my soul hates, I hate.

When my soul is stirred with compassion, I am compassionate.

What my soul turns away from, I turn away from.

That is the *true* interpretation of Whitman's creed: the true revelation of his Sympathy.

And my soul takes the open road. She meets the souls that are passing, she goes along with the souls that are going her way. And for one and all, she has sympathy. The sympathy of love, the sympathy of hate, the sympathy of simple proximity: all the subtle sympathisings of the incalculable soul, from the bitterest hate to the passionate love.

It is not I who guide my soul to heaven. It is I who am guided by my own soul along the open road, where all men tread. Therefore, I must accept her deep motions of love, or hate, or compassion, or dislike, or indifference. And I must go where she takes me. For my feet and my lips and my body are my soul. It is I who must submit to her.

This is Whitman's message of American democracy.

The true democracy, where soul meets soul, in the open road. Democracy. American democracy where all journey down the open road. And where a soul is known at once in its going. Not by its clothes or appearance. Whitman did away with that. Not by its family name. Not even by its reputation. Whitman and Melville both discounted that. Not by a progression of piety, or by works of Charity. Not by works at all. Not by anything but just itself. The soul passing unenhanced, passing on foot and being no more than itself. And recognized, and passed by or greeted according to the soul's dictate. If it be a great soul, it will be worshipped in the road.

The love of man and woman: a recognition of souls, and a communion of worship. The love of comrades: a recognition of souls, and a communion of worship. Democracy: a recognition of souls, all down the open road, and a great soul seen in its greatness, as it travels on foot among the rest, down the common way of the living. A glad recognition of souls, and a gladder worship of great and greater souls, because they are the only riches.

Love, and Merging, brought Whitman to the Edge of Death! Death! Death!

But the exultance of his message still remains. Purified of MERGING, purified of MYSELF, the exultant message of American Democracy, of souls in the Open Road, full of glad recognition, full of fierce readiness, full of joy of worship, when one soul sees a greater soul.

The only riches, the great souls.

The Integrity of *Leaves of Grass*

"I resist anything better than my own diversity."

Leaves of Grass and the American Paradox

by John Kinnaird

At once the most personal and impersonal of modern poets, only rarely does Whitman confess any anxieties that might belie his pragmatic faith ("What I assume you shall assume") that all human contradictions are but phases of counterpoint in some ultimate music of hope. One of these rare moments occurs in an early poem, "The Sleepers"—a passage the vatic Whitman later deleted from his book—when almost imperceptibly the thematic major wavers, and a half-muted troubled undertone is heard:

> Pier that I saw dimly last night when I looked from the windows,
> Pier out from the main, let me catch myself with you and stay . . .
> I will not chafe you;
> I feel ashamed to go naked about the world,
> And am curious to know where my feet stand . . . and what is this flooding me, childhood or manhood . . . and the hunger that crosses the bridge between.

"*Leaves of Grass* and the American Paradox" (Original title: "Whitman: The Paradox of Identity"). From *Partisan Review,* XXV (Summer, 1958), 380-405. Copyright 1958 by *Partisan Review.* Revised by John Kinnaird for publication in this volume, and reprinted by his permission and that of the editors of the *Partisan Review.*

Nothing else that remained in *Leaves of Grass* suggests so much of the original existential Whitman that criticism must continue to recover and understand, particularly since this is the first poet who ever insisted that his book was in reality no book: "Who touches this touches a man." "Childhood or manhood"—presumably the emotions of the bachelor Whitman never crossed the phallic bridge between them; and perhaps his book, like *The Bridge* of Hart Crane, a poet with similar conflicts, should be regarded as his imaginary marriage of worlds: in Whitman's case, a kind of spiritual Brooklyn Ferry (he once called ferries "streaming, never-failing, living poems") on which he could both "stand" in the eternity of imagination and yet move in time, a man like any other, toward a more fully human significance. This would seem to be the first secret of his pose: he is *poised*, perfectly balanced as he moves between possibility and the past—always with the illusion of change as progress, yet never surrendering his freedom to return—between the Long Island shore of his childhood ("Paumanok") and the world of manly ego across the bay, the "Mannahatta" and the American continent that were always for Whitman the waiting and inescapable realities.

Whitman's uncertainty, as the imagery here suggests, was always sexual. The biographical evidence, in itself inconclusive, does seem to confirm what anyone may intuit from the poems: that Whitman was predominantly homosexual in his elementary responses, but never, it seems, in overt conduct and perhaps never in his private relations. But the most important fact is still that ambiguity itself, his uncertainty of sexual will, and this in itself indicates—as seems evident from the autoeroticism in "The Song of Myself"—a suspension, possibly life-long, in some childhood phase of introversion that may never have reached complete inversion. This eroticism, moreover, was further complicated, as Mark Van Doren has noted, by a condition of chronic sensory excitability known technically as *erethisia*. Whitman had an abnormal susceptibility to touch: nearly everyone who knew him well remarked that the skin on his rather large and languorous body seemed unusually soft and pink; in him, as he himself liked to say, was "the flush of the universe." By day he must have felt himself to be, as we have come to know him, the glowing epitome of health—in the American grand manner he established; but by night this same sensuous vitality might easily have abandoned him to an abysmal sense of deprivation, and in such moments, we may conjecture, he became not unlike the wandering sleeper of his poem, lost in an unknown inner "flood" of feeling, a relentless but nameless and impotent longing. This seems to have been the darker necessity animating this secretly lonely and anomalous "caresser of life": as he once confessed in a poem, "I had to let flame from me the fires that were threatening to consume me."

Whitman's adolescence seems almost wholly characterized by indolence and impressionability—a passivity of mind that produced in his youth a motley and unthinking imitation of the worldly conventions available to him, and inwardly (we remember his authorship of a temperance novel) a similarly lazy moral conformity with the great "They" of society across the bay. In his twenties, for instance, he seems to have taken up the fashionable role of Broadway dandy, sporting a cane and a boutonnière; and as such this shabby-genteel journalist may have found a satisfying but transient sense of identity in the cameraderie of work, in the Broadway crowds, at the opera, in debating societies, in Tammany meetings and rallies—and then in 1846 (the beginnings of his great change) in the confident stance he develops as the militant "Free Soil" editor of the Brooklyn *Eagle*. But perhaps all this while—until the seven obscure years, 1847-55, when *Leaves* began to materialize in his notebooks—Whitman never knew his latent sexual identity; and if it is true, as Malcolm Cowley thinks, that what provoked Whitman's poetic metamorphosis was some first fully satisfying—or profoundly disturbing—sexual experience, then what we encounter may be the crucial anomaly in a life that seems almost definable as a reversal of the normal development of self-consciousness. For perhaps it was only after reaching maturity in the world that Whitman discovered that sexual illumination of the life-processes normally experienced—without, of course, a correspondingly awakened mind—in late adolescence. This discovery of what might have seemed to him a kind of renascent innocence would have been received, again paradoxically, by a mind of experience; and the images it evoked in the release that became the poetry were not primarily, therefore, those of some long-lost adolescent enchantment (as with Sherwood Anderson, perhaps) but those from the public world itself, from the commonplace life of a petit bourgeois "failure" already well on in his thirties, his hair already beginning to gray. And coming, moreover, so late in life, this revelation of sexual fulfillment would almost certainly have been conjoined with the first intimations of death. Thus it was, perhaps, that it became forever impossible for Whitman to dissociate mind from flesh, sex and death, experience and psyche, body and soul, one's temporal from one's immortal identity—associations, in fact, so extreme in Whitman that while they intensify his luminous feeling for death they nevertheless limit, by their emotional oversimplification, his vision of death as personal mortality. Only, I think, by assuming some such strangely revolutionary experience, possessing Whitman with an almost religious intensity—and bringing with it, however bitter the shock, its own joy and power of redemption—can one account for that extreme identification of the spiritual essence of life with the organic modes of its birth and dissolution (and for his view, too, of the poetic imagination as, to quote Richard Chase, "a mode of the sense of death") that lies at the heart of his sensibility and which gives his verse its universality of appeal—even to temperaments so distant as the Latin or the Catholic mind: his sense, namely, of an infinite promise in the body, his belief in the flesh as the sacred and definitive human substance.

"I cannot understand the mystery," Whitman had written in his notebook in 1847, "but I am always conscious of myself as two—as my soul and I—and I reckon it is the same with all men and women." This, the ambivalence Whitman had always known—of "childhood and manhood," of private "soul" and worldly "I"—ceased to be a mute and paralytic conflict and became his lyrical dialogue, his antiphonal "song of myself," when he felt and could express their unconscious struggle as the rhythmic energy of Eros, as not only the human but the elementary organic mystery of change and possibility in the world. And so strong was his sense of power in at last being able to find in images of non-self a relativity for his mystery, that at first it seems to have been enough for Whitman simply to "celebrate" his inward paradox:

> I am satisfied—I see, dance, laugh, sing:
> As God comes a loving bedfellow and sleeps at my side all night and close on the peep of day,
> And leaves for me baskets covered with white towels bulging the house with their plenty,
> Shall I postpone my acceptation and realization and scream at my eyes,
> That they turn from gazing after and down the road,
> And forthwith cipher and show me to a cent,
> Exactly the contents of one, and exactly the contents of two, and which is ahead?

Here and in most of "The Song of Myself" Whitman was content to let even such obscurely troubled questions as this stand rhythmically as their own answers: he would exult in the self as he did in the universe—as perfect and joyous *because* they were insoluble: "the depths are fathomless and therefore calm." But if the divine "touch" of Eros "quivers" him, as he wrote elsewhere in the poem, "to a new identity"—what, then, did his lyrical "acceptation and realization" of this new and otherwise unintelligible "self" mean to the world? In a sense, the thematic problem Whitman now faced was not unlike that of the religious novice: having been converted to the mystery whose integrity 'passeth all understanding,' he must now serve his faith, and he can only communicate it to and with others (and even to himself) as an articulate idea or ritual—which, of course, the original mystery was not. This is the inescapable irony of meaning in the paradox Whitman celebrates; and his peculiarly modern greatness in "The Song" is that he recognizes with an instinctive honesty his enigma for what it is. In his sheer lyrical momentum he is able to play happily with his mystery as both irony and unity; at times he seems even to suggest that human happiness, like his own comic happiness, is revealed by and is even to be saved by this sense of the ambiguity of reality, this cosmic joke about the self-sufficiency of our cosmic ignorance—a joke he directed expressly, perhaps (as R. W. Flint has recently suggested) at the theological high priest of his new faith, at Emerson.

Whitman, however, was never consciously prepared to welcome the ambiguities of poetry as their own justification; and if the joke of his divine comedy was aimed at Emerson, this was so because it was chiefly he who gave Whitman the means of resolving his manifold "identity" problem. "Acceptation," being "enough for myself"—this freedom of sensibility was now the necessity of his "soul"; but Puritan America had imbedded in Whitman a conscience far more conventional—in matters of practical prudence—than this Quakerish Bohemian ever cared to admit, and an ego conditioned in the Jacksonian age of his youth still felt the need to satisfy whatever it sensed to be the more consciously masculine norms, both in ideology and in conduct, of the paternal American "Mannahatta." Whitman both needed and wished to return to the 'unreal city' of his experience, even though this return meant having somehow to find or create, to "assume," a new and—however vicarious—more personalized relation with the American authority across the bay that had heretofore offered his secret individuality no means of mediation or self-knowledge. His rebellion, therefore, had to be both an act of love and an exorcism of his old *alter ego*—a revolt against American society only in the name of its own ideal culture. And so it was that when Whitman had his phrenological bumps read—and learned that he was a manly specimen after all; when he read Emerson and George Sand and Carlyle and found in them moral and intellectual confirmation for his mysterious "self": when he discovered in these and other sources a way to extend magically and mythologically his rhythmic fantasies of "my soul and I" into an embrace of America—then, we may conclude, the poet of the notebooks had found a way of ordering his mystery and was ready and willing to publish.

What Whitman's mythical "assumption" was we may begin to understand, not by appealing at once to Democracy or Transcendentalism or Panpsychism, but by looking closely at the great structural paradox of the first *Leaves of Grass*. We find our revealing clue, I think, in the simple and astonishing fact that in the verse itself such words as *America* and *democracy* and *en masse* occur only very rarely—at most once or twice: we find them acquiring their first significance as determining concepts only in the famous prose Preface, where Whitman heraldically announces the coming of the Cosmic Democratic Poet. This fact is symptomatic of a disparity between the Preface and the earliest poetry that has never been duly recognized—probably because, like Emerson (who saw himself in the Preface) and like all readers since, we begin to read the poetry with elaborate preconceptions of what Whitman the poet means—a preconditioning Whitman himself was the first to establish. If, however, we read the poetry with an uncommitted eye, we find that we are really never in a consciously American world, but always within the purely magical universe of Whitman's "self" and its strange visitations.[1] Whitman reintroduces us kaleidoscopically to what seems *all* the phenomena of the world, yet now somehow all transfigured: we visit the grass, the sea, oxen, beetles, buzzards, stallions, molluscs, stars; suicides and murders and childbirths and shipwrecks; mechanics, sopranos, trappers, prostitutes, slaves, Indians, and Broadway buses and their drivers--but though the creatures of this world may often as it happens be Americans, we are always within a timeless and "primeval" democracy; we never find ourselves transported to transcendental realms called "America" or the "New World": we are never in a world of nationalism and ideology. It is only in the Preface that we encounter the familiar prophetic utterance we had been led to expect; only there are we told that "the United States themselves are the greatest poem," only there do we meet Whitman in the public phase of his new identity—as the would-be national bard.

This is not to say, of course, that the animus of the Preface differs radically from the spirit and style of the poetry; but the shift in focus and intention is clearly there, and indicates the duality of poetic motive that soon reveals itself as the dialectic of Whitman's career. For it is always, I think, the habitual *prose* Whitman—the aggressive editor, the would-be potent male, "of Manhattan the son"—who compulsively wills his meanings into ideology, who "promulges" vast generalizations, who "strikes up for a New World" and in doing so compensates for his ego in the real America. This was the Whitman who by printing his book accomplished his personal "realization"; but the sensibility with which it came into being belongs to the anonymous woman and child in him, to the lonely spirit of "Paumanok," of the earth and the sea and the darkened beach: the "soul" who "accepts" and "is satisfied," who sympathizes and particularizes and remembers, who knows only dumb rhythmic images and mutely caresses them. It would be wrong, however, to identify this recessive self as essentially "the poet" in Whitman; on the contrary, his poetry owes its expression, and even, in a sense, its imagination—its unity of word and image—precisely to the tendencies of his prosaic "I" to dominate with his pragmatic will in language, as he did politically in the Preface, this otherwise indeterminate lyricism of his "soul." Whitman, we remember, once called his book a "language

[1] Two of the twelve poems in the first edition—later entitled "Europe" and "A Boston Ballad"—constitute exceptions to this statement. Only in verse form, however —not in character and subject-matter—can they be said to be integral with the rest of the volume. I should add that much of what I say here of the early poems is true of them only as they first appeared—not as later revised by Whitman, which is, unfortunately, the variant of the text almost always reprinted today.

experiment"; and like all successful revolutions in the language of verse —like the stilnovists' and Dante's, like the Elizabethans', like Dryden's and Wordsworth's—Whitman's represented a new and necessary assimilation of the modes of poetry and prose: a marriage of mythopoeic or symbolic motives with the trafficking language of the ordinary world. And *Leaves of Grass* was just such a success because it "celebrated" a functionally similar marriage within Whitman: between the compensatory imagination of ego and the dream-fantasies of his unconscious "soul." The result was to create in the style the figure that was nominally its author—the novel *persona* or "mask" that gave Whitman his conscious continuity in conceiving the whole of the first edition: a representative "Walt Whitman," in which "soul" and "I" had found a more than public, a more than private, "identity"; an idea of himself expressible only as a self-dramatic image, but which, in being dramatic yet unitary as an image, was also a mythical idea of the world.

In understanding this *persona* at least three dramatic components must always be distinguished—as Whitman himself suggests when, bowing into his book for the first time (which, we remember, was otherwise anonymous), it takes him three distinct phrases to properly introduce himself:

> Walt Whitman, an American, one of the roughs, a kosmos

The first of these faces we may readily identify as the Whitman of Manhattan, the democratic ideologue of the Preface; the second we recognize as his compensatory masculine image of himself—the cocky, indolent young workingman of the anonymous daguerrotype frontispiece (actually, and intentionally so, Whitman here seems much more "rough" in his costume than in his pose or looks); while the third, the "kosmos," is the most functionally mythical aspect of the *persona* —the furthest from worldly ego and the closest to his dream life— the fantastic, serio-comic mask of godhead whereby Whitman resolved in imagination the contradictions of his conscious identity into a divinely free and conventionally lawless unity of opposites. This cosmic "self" suggests, of course, his debt to Emerson; but the stylistic life of Whitman's "kosmos" suggests also a rebellious conspiracy against the romantic transcendentalism from which it derives. Actually we find this and other Emersonian ideas serving Whitman as little more than conscious "motifs," while beneath this surface the value of the divine mask lies precisely in the power it gave Whitman to escape from Emerson's divine solemnities—from Platonic notions of the divine; and for a poet this meant a necessary freedom to transcend the received logic of his metaphors. With part of his mind, of course, Whitman took Emersonian mysticism seriously, but here again the value to the poetry lay in his having found a philosophical authority for regarding the contradictory depths in himself as a microcosm, not of human nature only, but of all reality: he was thus able to accept as an elemental power the essentially androgynous demands of his imagination. Thus assured of an absolute anonymity, his "soul" could now freely wander forth in the infinitudes of imagination, not only as a spirit "maternal as well as paternal, a child as well as a man," but as the vagabond "touch" of Eros and death, as the dynamic Itself of the universe. Now, too, with such a universal soul in its body, the "rough" male *persona*—the incarnate "I" of this "kosmos"—was free to vicariously love and caress not only its own but all bodies and all souls. And if the prose ideologue in Whitman was still troubled by this monstrous indulgence—and the self-defense of the Preface indicates that he was—there was always, as an ultimate justification, the glorious image of the Poet that the intoxicated humanism of the time afforded him. The Poet, wrote the Scottish poet, Alexander Smith—some of whose lines Whitman once quoted as a "grand announcement"—must "reflect our great humanity," must "sprout fragrantly green leaves" like the life-giving Spring, must "sphere the world" with his "heart of love": and in *Leaves of Grass,* thanks to the literalism of Whitman's imagination, this romantic rhetoric became amazingly incarnate—so much so, in fact, that most of Whitman's humanist contemporaries never recovered from their shock of recognition and were never to avow this giant bred by their own idealism.

However much indebted to the existing tradition for his messianic image of the poet-prophet, Whitman knew that he could never adapt the diction and manner of the contemporary romanticism to the vast expressive needs of his "kosmos"—necessities that proved revolutionary enough to overthrow ultimately in English literary culture the pious notion of poetry as a ritual dedicated to an absolute Protestant Good and its ministering angel of Beauty. The literary liberation of Whitman's "soul" became complete—and his *persona* may be said to have properly come into being—when his generalized reaction to conventionality still inchoately represented in the compensatory *imago* of the "rough" ("Washes and razors for foofoos—for me freckles and a bristling beard") joined with his ideological compulsions in willing the act of phallic boldness, the "oath of procreation," that became the metaphor of his "language experiment": "This day I am jetting the stuff of far more arrogant republics."

That seminal "stuff" for Whitman was the potency of the American vernacular, and especially the idiom of the new popular culture filtering in from the West—not so much its monstrosities of diction (he preferred his own "kosmos words") but its flair and grotesquerie and the genius of its slang for symbolic "indirection." Out of the same Jacksonian zeitgeist that had produced in American humor what Constance Rourke calls "the gamecock of the Western wilderness," Whitman fashioned his primitive "rough" *persona,* and like the gamecock, the proof of his *charisma* was his ability to talk big, to swagger with words. "I like limber, lasting, fierce words," he wrote in his *American Primer,* ". . . strong, cutting, beautiful, rude words. To the manly instincts of the People they will forever be welcome." And so, then, of course, *he* would, too: inevitably his egoistic motive recognizes its opportunity. "Words follow character," he wrote; and if he was to show himself a "a great user of words," was he not then giving proof that he really had as the phrenologists assured him, these "natural propensities in himself"? But when he wrote his first poetry—before, like a ventriloquist, he had fashioned the visual dummy of the frontspiece for the 'character' of the voice he was able to 'throw'—Whitman was primarily interested in accomplishing the anonymous release of his "soul": his *persona* was still only the unembarrassed voice of his "kosmos"—"gross, hankering, mystical, nude":

> Flaunt of the sunshine I need not your bask—lie over!
>
> I too am not a bit tamed—I too am untranslatable
>
> The last scud of day holds back for me,
> It flings my likeness after the rest and true as any on the shadowed wilds,
> It coaxes me to the vapor and the dusk.
>
> I believe a leaf of grass is no less than the journey-work of the stars,
> And the pismire is equally perfect, and a grain of sand, and the egg of the wren,
> And the tree-toad is a chef d'oeuvre for the highest,
> And the running blackberry would adorn the parlors of heaven . . .

Such lines as these were not, however, mere somersaults of verbal bravado, a witty indemnification for a sentimental pantheism or a mindless anarchic innocence—"a wild soft laughter," as Carl Sandburg would have it. The more we attend to them, in fact, the more we observe that they represent in their tonal inference nothing less than the meaning Whitman has found for the contradictions of the world. What the playful irony of his voice establishes for us as we read is the medium of feeling that Whitman imagines as existing between all beings in the world; for in line after line we learn that what it primarily means to have being of any kind—to have any sort of identity, animate or inanimate—is to be a manifest challenge, a "mocking taunt" to all other identities. This irony, however, remains playful because it expresses not only the oblique point of view of identity, of "each," but the loving irony of the poet who, from the omniscient vantage of the "all," represents the experience of being in all its continuity. From the point of view of each identity, existence is essentially ironical: there is nothing quite like itself in the whole world. But although there is a constant chaos and struggle of identities—and consequently suffering, death and defeat (which do *not* go unrepresented in Whitman's world)—the "mocking taunt" is not finally ironic because no identity, whether destroyed or destroying, "countervails" another. Everything has its *thereness,* is "in its place"; has its own body, its own involvement with itself, its own perfection, and is therefore "great." And in having absolute joy or possession of itself, in being individual, it obeys the common "law of perfections": that law of "precision and balance," as he says in the Preface, which was Whitman's own way of enjoying himself and which became, therefore, his principle of perception—the ontology of his vision and the individualistic aesthetic of his "free verse."

What is it, then, to be a self in such a universe? Like all animate identities, Whitman's self finds its positive life in the "dilation and pride" of being, in the will to power; and even love, having its roots, like all emotion, in sexual energy, partakes of this challenge "to be master." The human self, however, is itself a microcosm of struggling identities, in which "body" and "soul" and all the contradictory powers of Whitman's being contend and conspire to woo the secret and elusive beloved, "the Me myself." But the self always escapes from itself as from all other impinging identities, and when it does, the roles are soon reversed: then Whitman's "I" is the pursuer of the miraculous secret of power and love, the mystery whose "mocking taunt" winks back at him from the manifold interplay of the universe. (Here we glimpse the ironic relation that obtains in the poetry between Whitman *in propria persona* and his "kosmos" of Eros, which can only be imagined as existing in the world, and yet when felt or experienced becomes a mystery again by passing into his feeling, into "myself.") The secret thus turns out to be the joy and the style of its pursuit: unlike the romantic secret in *Faust,* the secret may only be sought and felt and loved *as* a secret, for all beings may only share the secret they can never know—the miracle of "touch" or "urge" that "quivers" them all to "identity." To have the self-experience of "identity," then, is not only to imitate the universal life in its expression of energy, but to imitate the universe in its secret balance, to recoil from all extremes and repose upon one's self as a secret, exactly as the body does. (Perhaps this helps to explain, too, Whitman's imagination of death as the perfection of "identity.") Whitman's irony, therefore, being inevitably a self-expression, rises and falls as only a phase of his balance, and must finally yield to the higher paradox of love that Whitman as the poet recognizes. For if "precision and balance" is the law of the body, then there is hope that the power of Eros may also order itself as a self-redemptive law in the world ("a kelson of the creation is love"), exactly as it does in his poetry.

This, then, insofar as it yields to analysis, is what I take to be Whitman's vision of the organic democracy of all things—and it will be seen at once how radically American this view of the world is. But the very intensity of Whitman's awareness of his vision seems to have bred a confusion of values and of the planes of thought and being, especially when the same voice modulated into the proselytic will of the Preface attempted to translate a poet's love into the democratic ethos of "sympathy and pride" and poetic "laws of perfection" into an evolutionary American "fruition." The irony of the "untranslatable" mystery begins to disappear in the very year of publication, for in the performance of 1856 Whitman has already begun to lose the delicate balance of his paradox. The first *Leaves of Grass,* the actual book, seems to have served Whitman as a kind of mirror, in which the *persona,* having acquired objective reality, saw itself for the first time; and from that moment, as it were, Whitman's love was less for his democratic mystery than for its American image. It is almost as if Whitman had looked too long at his own frontispiece, and had then begun primping to make good on his specifications for an "athletic bard," forgetting that this new "self" was not its own reality but an attitude, an imaginative way of speaking, a "language experiment." What was happening, of course, was what Nietzsche describes as the "typical velleity" of the artist: "tired to the point of despair of the eternal 'unreality' and falseness of innermost being," he is tempted to think that he actually *is* the object he is able to represent, imagine or express; and then, attempting to have real existence, he "trespasses on the forbidden ground" of actuality. Almost from the moment of his first creativity—in his attempt to somehow convert his "mystery" into a reclamation of ego; in his effort to put on the musical power of his imaginative experience and *be* the "personality" of his liberating Eros; in his necessity to find an epic American significance for his rebellious lyrical impulses—almost at once Whitman's career begins confirming the truth of Nietzsche's warning.

This American self-consciousness, first stylistically apparent in 1856, in the third (1860) edition became overwhelming. The writer of most of these new poems is trying manfully to be the poet of his Preface; and Whitman was, in fact, so enamoured of the Preface that one of the new additions, "Poem of Many in One" (later retitled "By Blue Ontario's Shore"), is almost literally a paraphrase of it—a poem filled with almost nothing but self-exhortations. This poem really inaugurates a change in Whitman's style and intention that has never been sufficiently remarked; for in almost all the new poems, even when not explicitly. "Chants Democratic," some form of incantation has become the dominant stylistic mode. The difference between Whitman's voice in the later editions and the "I" of the first *Leaves* might be described as the difference between a speaker on a platform—or an operatic soloist intoning a recitative (Whitman's own perilous analogy)—and a solitary "soul" standing up to speak in the silence of a Quaker meeting, and whose impassioned speech may, as "the spirit moves," modulate into rhapsodic rhythms of song. The first poems, moreover, had been written almost conversationally, addressed as an intimate letter to a personal and private "you"; but Whitman's "you" had now become essentially plural, the collective democratic conscience of America. And motivating this new "vocalism" was a change in Whitman's conception of his book: it was no longer simply the testament of an individual "modern," but "the new Bible"—a democratic missal and *vade mecum* for the entire nation, but especially for teachers, "mediums," "savans," "oratists." And since the "leader of leaders" was, as the prose Whitman had written, the native bard, he was now being true to his word:

> Chanter of Personality, outlining a history yet to be,
> I project the ideal man, the American of the future.

Throughout the nineteenth century much of the impulse to poetry was by way of overt or secret reaction to an abstract humanism or to bourgeois rationalism; and when he began *Leaves of Grass,* Whitman, too, had been reacting to an overexposure to ideology: like Wordsworth, like Mill and Carlyle, his "soul" had protested: "But where am I in all this?" Yet in seeking a freedom from the slavery of abstractions, his "soul" sought also to satisfy its craving for love; and by 1860 Whitman had found a way to anneal both his biological and his ideological compulsions into the single programmatic purpose of creating an American "Stock-Personality," a national comradeship, a "One Identity" for "ye partial, diverse lives." And so intense was this will that Whitman remained unaware that, in substance if not in form, his poetry was slowly receding to his habitual prose—an attrition of imaginative power that might, in fact, be demonstrated almost wholly in terms of the progressive socialization of his once unconscious "soul."

But in the great poems of 1855-56, Whitman remained true to his instinct for that descriptive law of our literature that Mark Twain similarly confirmed in our fictional prose—the truth, namely, that since no "classic" American tradition exists, there can be no significant idiom in our literature that is not a personal voice bearing a personalized vision; and conversely, there can be no personal voice—no way of even communicating with ourselves—that is not an individuation of American *speech,* which is incessantly dynamic for this very reason. "Speech," said Whitman in "The Song of Myself," "is the twin of my vision"; and if his later folly lay in confounding self-consciously his vision and his American *persona* of speech as the identical "I" of his American "personality," the wisdom of principle in that failure lay in his recognition that the democratic idiom and the personal vision of poetry must live together and cohere dialectically, as they are born together, in the same creative consciousness. If not—if an awareness of modern contradictions is allowed to overcome this sense of our original paradox, then, as is proverbially said of all twins, idiom or vision may cease to be itself when the other dies—and this, as it was Whitman's burden of truth, was also his fate as a poet.

Whitman Justified: The Poet in 1860

by Roy Harvey Pearce

Where are we going, Walt Whitman? The doors close in an hour.
Which way does your beard point tonight?
(Allen Ginsberg, "A Supermarket in California")

My title comes from the fourteenth of the "Chants Democratic" in the 1860 *Leaves of Grass*. (This is the poem which finally became "Poets to Come.") The first two stanzas read:

Poets to come!
Not to-day is to justify me, and Democracy, and what we are for,
But you, a new brood, native, athletic, continental, greater than before known,
You must justify me.

Indeed, if it were not for you, what would I be?
What is the little I have done, except to arouse you?

Whitman is, he concludes, "the bard" of a "future" for which he writes only "one or two indicative words."

The vision is utopian, of course—and became increasingly so in the 1870's and 80's, when he was calling for, even guaranteeing, a state of things whereby poems would work so as eventually to make for the withering away of poetry. In a preface of 1872 he could claim:

The people, especially the young men and women of America, must begin to learn that Religion, (like Poetry,) is something far, far different from what they supposed. It is, indeed, too important to the power and perpetuity of the New World to be consigned any longer to the churches, old or new, Catholic or Protestant—Saint this, or Saint that. . . . It must be con-

"Whitman Justified: The Poet in 1860." From *The Minnesota Review,* I (1961), 261-294. Copyright 1961 by *The Minnesota Review.* Reprinted by permission of the editors.

> signed henceforth to Democracy *en masse,* and to Literature. It must enter into the Poems of the Nation. It must make the Nation.

And by 1888 (in "A Backward Glance O'er Travel'd Roads") he could claim that, contrary to European critical opinion, verse was not a dying technique.

> Only a firmer, vastly broader, new area begins to exist—nay, is already form'd—to which the poetic genius must emigrate. Whatever may have been the case in years gone by, the true use for the imaginative faculty of modern times is to give ultimate vivification to facts, to science, and to common lives, endowing them with glows and glories and final illustriousness which belongs to every real thing, and to real things only. Without that ultimate vivification—which the poet or other artist alone can give—reality would seem to be incomplete, and science, democracy, and life itself, finally in vain.

These two statements (and they are quite typical) sum up Whitman's growing sense of the power of poetry, and thus of the poet: Religion, operating as poetry—and *only* as poetry—can make the nation, vivify it: or, in the language of a late poem like "Passage to India," "eclaircise" it.

"In the prophetic literature of these states," he had written in 1871 (in *Democratic Vistas*), ". . . Nature, true Nature, and the true idea of Nature, long absent, must, above all, become fully restored, enlarged, and must furnish the pervading atmosphere to poems . . ." And later in the same essay: "The poems of life are great, but there must be poems of the purports of life, not only in itself, but beyond itself." Life beyond life, poetry beyond poetry: This idea came to count for more and more in Whitman's conception of his vocation, and accordingly, of that of the poets who were to come. The last edition (1892) of *Leaves of Grass* is surely the testament of the sort of "divine literatus" whom he had earlier prophesied. Indeed, he had not only prophesied himself but made the prophecy come true. But, as he acknowledged, this was not the only form of his testament. For, when he wrote of the last edition, "I am determined to have the world know what *I* was pleased to do," he yet recognized: "In the long run the world will do as it pleases with the book." The question remains: How may we use the book so as to know what we please to do with it? And more: What does the book, in its structure and function, in its growth, teach us about the vocation of poet in the modern world? And more: How may it help the poets who yet are to come discover, and so define, their vocation?

The hard fact—so it seems to me—is that Whitman fails as prophetic poet, precisely because he was such a powerfully *humane* poet. The adjective makes us flinch, perhaps: but only because, like Whitman, we have found the beliefs it implies so difficult to hold to that we have come—if not to seek for the prophetic utterances which will offer us something in their stead, then to discount them as disruptive of the high sense of our private selves on which we ground our hopes for the lives we live. Still, it might be that a close reading of Whitman, the poet of 1860—for it is he whom I suggest we must recover—will teach us what it might be like once more to hold to them. Be that as it may, the record of Whitman's life would suggest that his own power, his own humanity, was at the end too much for him. In any case, when he tried to write prophetic poetry, he came eventually to sacrifice man—that finite creature, locked in time and history, at once agonized and exalted by his humanity—for what he has encouraged some of his advocates again to call cosmic man—the cosmic man of, say, these lines from "Passage to India":

> Passage, immediate passage! the blood burns in my veins!
> Away O soul! hoist instantly the anchor!
> Cut the hawsers—haul out—shake every sail!
> Have we not stood here like trees in the ground long enough?
> Have we not grovel'd here long enough, eating and drinking like
> mere brutes?
> Have we not darken'd and dazed ourselves with books long enough?
>
> Sail forth—steer for the deep waters only,
> Reckless O soul, exploring, I with thee, and thou with me,
> For we are bound where mariner has not yet dared to go,
> And we will risk the ship, ourselves and all.
>
> O my brave soul!
> O farther farther sail!
> O daring joy, but safe! are they not all the seas of God?
> O farther, farther, farther sail!

It is the idea of that "daring joy, but safe"—everywhere in the poem—which prevents one from assenting to this passage and all that comes before it. The passage of a soul, whether it is everyman's or a saint's, is not "safe," however "joyful." So that Whitman cannot focus the poem on the sort of *human* experience to which one might assent, because one could acknowledge its essential humanity. The figures in the passage proliferate farther and farther out from whatever center in which they have originated, until one wonders if there ever was a center. Probably not, because the experience of the protagonist in this poem is that of cosmic man, who, because he is everywhere, is nowhere; who, because he can be everything, is nothing. *This* Whitman, I believe, is he who mistakes vivification for creation, the ecstasy of cadence for the ecstasy of belief, efficient cause for final cause, poet for prophet. Which is not, I emphasize, the same as conceiving of the poet *as* prophet.

Whitman's genius was such as to render him incapable of the kind of discipline of the imagination which would make for the genuine sort of prophetic poetry we find in, say, Blake and Yeats: of whom we *can* say that they were poets *as* prophets; for whom we can observe that poetry is the vehicle for prophecy, not its tenor. Whitman is at best, at *his* best, *visionary,* and sees beyond his world to what it might be—thus, what, failing to be, it is. Blake and Yeats are at best, at *their* best, *prophetic,* and see through their world to what it really is—thus, what, pretending not to be, it might be. Visionary poetry projects a world which the poet would teach us to learn to acknowledge as our own; it comes to have the uncanniness of the terribly familiar. Prophetic poetry projects a world which the poet would teach us is alien to our own yet central to our seeing it as it really is—a world built upon truths we have hoped in vain to forget. We say of the visionary world that we could have made it—at least in dream—work. We say of the prophetic world that we could not possibly have made it, for it was there already. The ground of visionary poetry is indeed dream—work and magical thought; the ground of prophetic poetry, revelation and mythical thought. Thus the special language of prophetic poetry—one of its most marked formal characteristics—must, by the definition of its purpose, be foreign to us (for it reveals a world, and the strange things in it, hidden from us); yet, by the paradox of prophecy, it is a language native to us (for the things it reveals, being universal—out of the realm of day to day time, space, and conception—put all of us, all of our "actual" world, under their aegis). We can "understand" that language because its grammar and syntax are analogous to our own; understanding it, we assent to—and perhaps believe in—the metaphysical system which its structure and vocabulary entail; trying to account for its origin, we agree with the poet that he has been, in some quite literal sense, "inspired."

Now, when the mood came over him—as it did increasingly—perhaps Whitman did claim to have been "inspired" in this literal sense. But even so, his later work fails as prophetic poetry (for that is what it is meant to be) precisely because, like the earlier work, it projects not a world to which the poet stands as witness, but one to which he stands as maker. Yet he asks of the world projected in the later work that, in accordance with the requirements of prophetic poetry, it have the effect of revelation; that its language be at once of and not of our workaday world; that it imply what in *Democratic Vistas* he called a "New World metaphysics." Yet the editions of *Leaves of Grass* from 1867 on fail of the centrality and integrity of properly prophetic poetry: fail, I think, because the poet mistakenly assumes that poetry, when it is made to deal with the universe at large, *becomes* prophecy. For all his revisions and manipulations of his text, for all his enlargement of his themes, the later Whitman is but a visionary poet. And, since he asks more of it than it can properly yield, the vision, and consequently the poetry, even the conception of the poet, get increasingly tenuous. A certain strength is there, of course. But it is the strength of an earlier Whitman, who perhaps prophesied, but could not bring about, his own metamorphosis from poet to prophet. His genius was too great to let him forget that, after all, it was *poets* who were to come.

True enough, he wrote, toward the end of "A Backward Glance O'er Travel'd Roads":

> But it is not on "Leaves of Grass" distinctively as *literature,* or a specimen therefor, that I feel to dwell, or advance claims. No one will get at my verses who insists upon viewing them as a literary performance, or attempt at such performance, or as aiming mainly toward art or aestheticism.

One says: How right, how sad, how wasteful! For, ironically enough, Whitman's words characterize the *failure* of the 1892 *Leaves of Grass.* And one turns to the earlier Whitman, I daresay the authentic Whitman, whose verses did aim mainly toward art and aestheticism: toward a definition of the vocation of the poet in that part of the modern world which was the United States.

For me, then, the most important edition of *Leaves of Grass* is the 1860 edition; and its most important poem is "A Word out of the Sea" (which, of course, became "Out of the Cradle Endlessly Rocking" in later editions.) Here Whitman may be best justified: as a poet. The burden of this essay will be to justify Whitman's way with poetry in the 1860 volume; to show how the structure and movement of this volume and of some of the principal poems in it (above all, "A Word out of the Sea") are such as to furnish a valid and integral way for a poet dedicated to saving poetry for the modern world, thus—as poet, and only as poet—dedicated to saving the modern world for poetry. The Whitman of the 1860 *Leaves of Grass* would be a sage, a seer, a sayer. But he speaks of only what he knows directly and he asks of his speech only that it report fully and honestly and frankly, only that it evoke other speeches, other poems, of its kind. The poems in this volume do justify Whitman's claims for poetry in general—but in terms of what he may in fact give us, not of what he would like, or even need, to give us. The strength of the major poems in the volume is that they somehow resist *our* need for more than they present, and make us rest satisfied—or as satisfied as we ever can be—with what they give. Above all, this is true of "A Word out of the Sea"—as it is less true, and so characteristic of the later Whitman, the poet of "Out of the Cradle Endlessly Rocking."

The 1855, 1856, and 1860 *Leaves of Grass* make a complete sequence—one in which the poet invents modern poetry, explores its possibility as an instrument for studying the world at large and himself as somehow vitally constitutive of it, and comes finally to define, expound, and exemplify the poet's vocation in the modern world. The sequence, in brief, is from language to argument; and it is controlled at all points by a powerful sense of the ego which is struggling to move from language to argument and which must come to realize the limits of its own humanity, which are the limits of argument. If, as we well know, the poet as envisaged in the 1855 and 1856 *Leaves of Grass* is the counterpart of him of whom Emerson wrote in "The Poet" (1844), the poet envisaged in the 1860 *Leaves of Grass* is the counterpart of him of whom Emerson wrote in his essay on Goethe in *Representative Men* (1850): Not Shakespeare, not Plato, not Swedenberg would do for the modern world, which yet "wants its poet-priest, a reconciler . . ." Goethe was one such: "the writer, or secretary, who is to report the doings of the miraculous spirit of life that everywhere throbs and works. His office is a reception of the facts into the mind, and then a selection of the eminent and characteristic experiences." Note: just a "writer"—(what John Holloway in an important book of a few years ago called the *Victorian Sage*: a philosopher of a kind, but one who constructs his argument according to a grammar of assent). Emerson had concluded:

> The world is young: the former great men call to us affectionately. We too must write Bibles, to unite again the heavens and the earthly world. The secret of genius is to suffer no fiction to exist for us; to realize all that we know; in the high refinement of modern life, in arts, in sciences, in books, in men, to exact good faith, reality and a purpose; and first, last, midst and without end, to honor every truth by use.

The 1860 *Leaves of Grass,* as one of Whitman's notebook entries indicates, was to be a Bible too: "The Great Construction of the New Bible. . . . It ought to be ready in 1859." It was to offer a "third religion," Whitman wrote. And in a way it does; but, for well and for ill, that religion is a religion of man—man as he is, locked in his humanity and needing a religion, yet not claiming to have it by virtue of needing it; not hypnotizing himself into declaring that he has it. (For Whitman a little cadence was a dangerous, if exciting, thing, much cadence, disastrous.) The Whitman of the 1860 *Leaves of Grass* is, *par excellence,* Emerson's "secretary," reporting "the doings of the miraculous spirit of life that everywhere throbs and works." To accept a miracle, to live in its presence, even to try to comprehend it—this is not the same as trying to work one, even claiming to have worked one. And—as the poets who have come after him have variously testified in their puzzled, ambiguous relation to him—Whitman's way with the language of poetry, going against the grain of mass communications and "positivism," may well teach us how to recognize and acknowledge miracles. It cannot teach us how to work them; or even how to earn them. One can well imagine how hard it must be for a poet to go so far with language, only to discover that he can go no farther. Such a discovery constitutes the principal element of greatness in the 1860 *Leaves of Grass,* perhaps the principal element of greatness in Whitman's poetry as a whole.

I have said that in 1855 Whitman "invented" modern poetry. By this I mean only that, along with other major poets of the middle of the century, he participated—but in a strangely isolated way—in the development of romanticist poetics toward and beyond its symbolist phase. (*To invent* may mean, among other things, "to stumble upon.") I do not mean to claim too much for the word *symbolist* here; I use it only generally to indicate that Whitman too came to realize that a poet's vocation was fatefully tied to the state of the language which constituted his medium. He discovered with Baudelaire—although without Baudelaire's (and incidentally Emerson's) overwhelming sense of the problem of "correspondences," that, as regards language, "tout vit, tout agit, tout se correspond." The medium thus had a "life" of its own, and so might generate "life"—the "life" of poetry. Poetry, on this view, thus became *sui generis,* a unique mode of discourse; and the role of the poet became more and more explicitly to be that of the creator: one who might "free" language to "mean"—a creator in a medium, pure and simple. We have in Whitman's early work a version of that conception of poet and poetry with which we are now so familiar: To whom was the poet responsible? Not to whom, the reply ran, but to what? And the answer: to language. And language as such was seen to be the sole, overriding means to establish, or reestablish community. The perhaps inevitable drift—not only in Whitman's work but of that of his contemporaries and of the poets who have come—was toward an idea of poetry as a means of communion, perhaps modern man's sole means of communion, his religion. Professor Abrams (in *The Mirror and the Lamp*) concludes his account of these developments thus:

> It was only in the early Victorian period, when all discourse was explicitly or tacitly thrown into the two exhaustive modes of imaginative and rational, expressive and assertive, that religion fell together with poetry in opposition to science, and that religion, as a consequence, was converted into poetry, and poetry into a kind of religion.

Professor Abrams is speaking about developments in England. In the United States, conditions were somewhat simpler and, withal, more extreme. From the beginning, that is to say, Whitman was sure that the imaginative and rational might well be subsumed under a "higher" category, which was poetry. So that—as I have indicated in my remarks on Whitman and prophetic poetry—for him there was eventually entailed the idea that the New Bible might be just that, a total and inclusive account of cosmic man, of man as one of an infinitude of gods bound up in Nature. It is a nice question whether or not the "symbolist" dedication to the idea of language-as-communion must *inevitably* lead to a search for a metalinguistic structure of analogies and correspondences and then to an idea of poetry as religion and religion as poetry. And it is a nicer question whether or not "symbolist" poetics—with its emphasis on medium as against matrix, language per se as against language–in–culture—is characterized by a certain weakness in linguistic theory. Whitman's work raises these questions; and a full critique of his work would entail a critique of his theory of poetry, thus of his theory of language, thus of his theory of culture. But this is not the place to speak of critics to come, much less to prophesy them.

In any case, we must grant Whitman his special kind of "unmediated vision." But we are not by that token obliged to grant, or claim for him a "mysticism"—or for that matter, "an inverted mysticism"; or to declare that, *ecce,* his poetry is at once *"mystical and irreligious";* or to see in the Whitman of 1855 a good (prematurely) grey *guru.* (I cite here the recent claims for this Whitman of James Miller, Karl Shapiro, and Malcolm Cowley—who confuse, or conflate, this poet with the one who presided at Camden. And I think of the question, put with such sweet craziness, by Allen Ginsberg in the line I have used as epigraph.) At its most telling, Whitman's earlier poetry manifests what has been called (by Erich Kahler) an "existential consciousness," but of a mid-nineteenth-century American sort—its key term, its center of strength and weakness, being not anguish but joy. Or rather, the key term is triumph—as suffering, the poet endures, and rejoices: seeing that it is his vocation as poet to teach men that they can endure. The freedom which ensues is wonderful, not dreadful.

Thus I take the 1855 and 1856 editions of *Leaves of Grass,* which most freshly project this mode of consciousness, as stages on the way to the 1860 edition. In 1855 and 1856 Whitman shows that he has learned to report truthfully what he has seen; in 1860, that he has learned to measure its significance for the poet taken as the "secretary"—the archetypal man. He strove to go beyond this, but in vain. The movement from the 1855 to the 1856 editions is the movement from the first "Song of Myself" and the first "The Sleeper" (both originally untitled) to the first "Crossing Brooklyn Ferry (called, in 1856, "Sun-Down Poem"): the poet first learns to discipline himself into regressing deeply into his own pre-conscious; then, with his new-found sense of himself as at once subject and object in his world, he learns to conceive in a new way of the world at large; he is, as though for the first time, "in" the world. The crucial factor is a restoration of the poet's vital relationship to language. A good, powerfully naïve account of this discovery is that in Whitman's prose *American Primer,* written in the 1850's, but not published until after his death:

What do you think words are? Do you think words are positive and original things in themselves? No: Words are not original and arbitrary in themselves.—Words are a result—they are the progeny of what has been or is in vogue.—If iron architecture comes in vogue, as it seems to be coming, words are wanted to stand for all about iron architecture, for all the work it causes, for the different branches of work and of the workman. . . .

A perfect user of words uses things—they exude in power and beauty from him—miracles in his hands—miracles from his mouth. . . .

A perfect writer would make words sing, dance, do the male and female act, bear children, weep, bleed, rage, stab, steal, fire cannon, steer ships, sack cities, charge with cavalry or infantry, or do anything, that man or woman or the natural powers can do.

[Note the insistence on "natural"—not "supernatural" powers.]

Likely there are other words wanted.—Of words wanted, the matter is summed up in this: When the time comes for them to represent any thing or state of things, the words will surely follow. The lack of any words, I say again, is as historical as the existence of words. As for me, I feel a hundred realities, clearly determined in me, that words are not yet formed to represent. . . .

These sentiments generally, and some of these phrasings particularly, got into Whitman's prose meditations. More important, from the beginning they inform the poems. They derive much from Emerson's "The Poet," of course; but they are not tied to even Emerson's modestly transcendental balloon. The power which Whitman discovers is the power of language, fueled by the imagination, to break through the categories of time, space, and matter and to "vivify" (a word, as I have said, he used late in his life—so close to Pound's "Make it new") the persons, places, and things of his world, and so make them available to his readers. In the process—since the readers would, as it were, be using words for the first time—he would make them available to themselves; as poets in spite of themselves.

It is as regards this last claim—that the reader is a poet in spite of himself—that the 1860 *Leaves of Grass* is all-important. For there Whitman most clearly saw that the poet's power to break through the limiting categories of day-to-day existence is just that: a poet's power, obtaining only insofar as the poem obtains, and limited as the poem is limited. In 1860, that is to say, Whitman saw that his Bible was to be a poet's Bible, and had to be built around a conception of the poet's life: his origins, experience, and end; his relation with the persons, places, and things of his world. The 1855 and 1856 *Leaves of Grass* volumes are but *collections* of poems—their organization as rushed and chaotic as is the sensibility of the writer of the *American Primer*. *Within* individual poems, there is form, a form which centers on the moment in the poet's life which they project. But the 1860 *Leaves of Grass* is an articulated whole, with an *argument.* The argument is that of the poet's life as it furnishes a beginning, middle, and end to an account of his vocation. The 1860 volume is, for all its imperfections, one of the great works in that romantic mode, the autobiography. Or, let us give the genre to which it belongs a more specific name: archetypal autobiography. The 1860 volume is autobiographical as, say, *Moby Dick* and *Walden* are autobiographical; for its hero is a man in the process of writing a book, of writing himself, of making himself, of discovering that the powers of the self are the stronger for being limited. The hero who can say No! in thunder discovers that he can say Yes! in thunder too—but that the thunderation is his own and no one else's.

Now, to say that the 1860 *Leaves of Grass* is quintessentially autobiographical is to say what has been said before: most notably by Schyberg, Asselineau, and Allen. But I mean to say it somewhat differently than they do. For they see in the volume a sign of a crisis in Whitman's personal life; and this is most likely so. Yet I think it is wrong to read the volume as, in this *literal* sense, personal—that is, "private." (The Bowers edition of the surviving manuscript of the 1860 edition clearly shows that Whitman—naturally enough, most often in the "Calamus" poems—wanted to keep the book clear of too insistently and privately personal allusions. He was, I think, not trying to "conceal"—much less "mask"—his private personality but to transmute it into an archetypal personality. I think that it is a mistake to look so hard, as some critics do, for the "private" I.) Thus I should read the volume as not a personal but archetypal autobiography: yet another version of that compulsively brought-forth nineteenth-century poem which dealt with the growth of the poet's mind. (Well instructed by our forebears, we now have a variety of names for the form—all demonstrating how deeply, and from what a variety of non-literary perspectives, we have had to deal with the issues which it raises for us: *rite de passage,* quest for identity, search for community, and the like.) Whitman's problem, the poet's problem, was to show that integral to the poet's vocation was his life cycle; that the poet, having discovered his gifts, might now use them to discover the relevance of his life, his *lived* life, his *Erlebnis,* his *career,* to the lives of his fellows. It is the fact that his newly discovered use of poetry is grounded in his sense of a life lived-through: it is this fact that evidences Whitman's ability here, more than in any version of *Leaves of Grass,* to contain his gift and use it, rather than be used by it. Of *this* volume Whitman said: "I am satisfied with *Leaves of Grass* (by far the most of it), as expressing what was intended, namely, to express by sharp-cut self assertion, One's Self and also, or may be still more, to map out, to throw together for American use, a gigantic embryo or skeleton of Personality,—fit for the

West, for native models." Later, of course, he wanted more. But he never had the means beyond those in the 1860 edition to get what he wanted. And that has made all the difference.

The 1860 *Leaves of Grass* opens with "Proto-Leaf" (later, much revised, as "Starting from Paumanok.") Here Whitman announces his themes and, as he had done before, calls for his new religion; but he gives no indication that it is to be a religion of anything else but the poet's universalized vocation. (My misuse of the word *religion* is his. I mean neither to be victimized nor saved by following him here.) It might yet, on this account, be a precurser to a religion, in the more usual (and I think proper) sense, as well as a substitute for it. "Whoever you are! to you endless announcements," he says. There follows "Walt Whitman," a somewhat modified version of the 1855 poem which became "Song of Myself." It is still close to the fluid version of 1855; strangely enough, it is so over-articulated (with some 372 sections) that it does not have the rather massive, and therefore relatively dogmatic, articulation of the final version. In all, it gives us an account of the poet's overwhelming discovery of his native powers. Then in the numbered (but not separately titled) series of poems called "Chants Democratic," the poet—after an apostrophic salutation to his fellows (it ends "O poets to come, I depend on you!")—celebrates himself again, but now as he conceives of himself in the act of celebrating his world. The chief among these poems—as usual, much modified later—became "By Blue Ontario's Shore," "Song of the Broad Axe," "Song for Occupations," "Me Imperturbe," "I Was Looking a Long While," and "I Hear America Singing." Following upon "Walt Whitman," the "Chants Democratic" sequence successfully establishes the dialectical tension between the poet and his world—the tension being sustained as one is made to realize again and again that out of the discovery of his power for "making words do the male and female act" in "Walt Whitman," has come his power to "vivify" his world in the "Chants Democratic."

The transition to "Leaves of Grass," the next sequence—again the poems are numbered, but not separately titled—is natural and necessary. For the poet now asks what it is to make poems in the language which has been precipitated out of the communal experience of his age. The mood throughout is one of a mixture of hope and doubt, and at the end it reaches a certitude strengthened by a sense of the very limitations which initially gave rise to the doubt. The first poem opens—and I shall presently say more about this—with two lines expressing doubt; later—when the prophetic Whitman couldn't conceive of doubting—the lines were dropped in the poem, which became "As I Ebb'd with the Ocean of Life." The second poem is a version of an 1855 poem, "Great Are the Myths"; and it was finally rejected by Whitman as being, one guesses, too certain in its rejection of the mythic mode toward which he later found himself aspiring. The third poem, which, combined with the sixth later became "Song of the Answerer" opens up the issue of communication as such. The fourth, a version of an 1856 poem which eventually became "This Compost," conceives of poetry as a kind of naturalistic resurrection. It moves from "Something startles me where I thought I was safest"—that is, in the poet's relation to the materials of poetry—to a simple acknowledgment at the end that the earth "gives such divine materials to men, and accepts such leavings from them at last." The fifth (later "Song of Prudence") considers the insight central to the poet's vocation. To the categories of "time, space, reality," the poet would add that of "prudence"—which teaches that the "consummations" of poetry are such as to envisage the necessary relationship of all other "consummations": The imagination's law of the conservation of energy. The sixth (which, as I have said, later became part of "Song of the Answerer") develops an aspect of the theme of the fourth and fifth; but now that theme is interpreted as it is bound up in the problem of language: "The words of poems give you more than poems, They give you to form for yourself poems, religions, politics, war, peace, behavior, histories, essays, romances, and everything else." At this depth of discovery there is no possibility of any kind of logically continuous catalogue of what words "give you to form for yourself." Poetry is a means of exhausting man's powers to know the world, and himself in it, as it is. Beyond this, poems

> . . . prepare for death—yet they are not the finish, but rather the onset,
> They bring none to his or her terminus, or to be content and full;
> Whom they take, they take into space, to behold the birth of stars, to learn one of the meanings,
> To launch off with absolute faith—to sweep through the ceaseless rings, and never to be quiet again.

In the seventh poem (later "Faith Poem"), the poet discovers that he "needs no assurance"; for he is (as he says in the eighth poem, later "Miracles") a "realist" and for him the real (by which he means *realia*) constitute "miracles." The poet is led, in the ninth poem (later "There Was a Child Went Forth"), to a recollection of his first discovery of the miraculousness of the real: a discovery he only now understands; this poem, taken in relation to the rest of the sequence, properly anticipates "A Word out of the Sea." The tenth poem opens, in a passage dropped from the later version, "Myself and Mine,"—but one which is essential as a transition in the sequence:

> It is ended—I dally no more,
> After today I inure myself to run, leap, swim, wrestle, fight . . .

Simply enough: the poet, having accepted his vocation and its constraints, is now free—free *through* it; and he must now teach this freedom to others:

> I charge that there be no theory or school founded out of me,
> I charge you to leave all free, as I have left all free.

The rest of the sequence, some fourteen more poems, celebrates aspects of the poet's new freedom as it might be the freedom of all men. (I forebear giving their later titles.) It is the freedom to rejoice in the miraculousness of the real, and has its own costs. The greatest is a terrible passivity, as though in order to achieve his freedom, man had to offer himself up as the victim of his own newly vivified sensibility. Being as he is, the poet sees (in 12) "the vast similitude/which/interlocks all . . ."; yet he must admit (in 15) "that life cannot exhibit all to me—" and "that I am to wait for what will be exhibited by death." He is (in 17) the man who must "sit and look out upon all the sorrows of the world, and upon all oppression and shame"; and he must "See, hear,/be/silent," only then to speak. He declares (in 20); ". . . whether I continue beyond this book, to maturity/ . . . /Depends . . . upon you/ . . . you, contemporary America." Poem 24, wherein the poet completes his archetypal act, and gives himself over to his readers, reads:

> Lift me close to your face till I whisper,
> What you are holding is in reality no book, nor part of a book,
> It is a man, flushed and full-blooded—it is I—So long!
> We must separate—Here! take from my lips this kiss,
> Whoever you are, I give it especially to you;
> *So long*—and I hope we shall meet again.

I quote this last poem entire, because I want to make it clear that the lapses into desperate sentimentality—and this poem is a prime example—are intrinsically a part of Whitman's autobiographical mode in the 1860 *Leaves of Grass,* as they are of the mode, or genre, which they represent. It will not do to explain them away by putting them in a larger context, or considering them somehow as masked verses—evidences of Whitman the shape-shifter. (Speaking through a *persona,* the poet perforce hides behind it.) Confronting the agonies and ambiguities of his conception of the poet, Whitman too often fell into bathos or sentimentalism. Yet bathos and sentimentalism, I would suggest, are but unsuccessful means—to be set against evidence of successful means—of solving the archetypal autobiographer's central problem: at once being himself and seeing himself; of bearing witness to his own deeds. If what he is, as he sees it, is too much to bear; if he is incapable of bearing it; if his genius is such as not to have prepared him to bear it—why then, his miraculism will fail him precisely because he cannot stand too much reality.

Bathos and sentimentalism—and also anxious, premonitory yearnings for something beyond mere poetry—inevitably mar the rest of the 1860 *Leaves of Grass*: but not fatally, since they are the by-products of its total argument. At some point, most foxes want to be hedgehogs. Whitman is a poet who must be read at large. And I am claiming that Whitman can be best read at large in the 1860 *Leaves of Grass*. When he can be read in smaller compass—as in "A Word out of the Sea"—it is because in a single poem he manages to recapitulate in little what he was developing at large. I should guess—as I shall presently try to show—that the large poem, the 1860 volume, is a necessary setting for the little poem, "A Word out of the Sea." That poem (later, I remind my reader, "Out of the Cradle . . .") is one of Whitman's greatest. And I shall want to show that it is even greater than we think. So I must carry through, however cursorily, my glance o'er the 1860 *Leaves of Grass*. There comes next a series of poems ("A Word out of the Sea" is one of them) in which the poet meditates the sheer givenness of the world his poems reveal; he is even capable of seeing himself as one of the givens. But then he must specify in detail the nature of his kind of givenness: which includes the power to give, to bring the given to a new life. Here—after "Salut au Monde," "Poem of Joys," "A Word out of the Sea," 'A Leaf of Faces," and "Europe,"—there is first the "Enfants d'Adam" sequence, and then, after an interlude of generally celebrative poems, the "Calamus" sequence. I want to say of these two sequences only that they are passionate in a curiously objective fashion; I have suggested that the proper word for their mood and tone is neither personal nor impersonal, but archetypal. In contrast, they furnish analogues—directly libidinal analogues, as it were—for the poet's role, seen now not (as in the earlier sequences) from the point of view of a man telling us how he has discovered his gift, put it to use, and measured the cost of using it properly; but seen rather from the point of view of the reader. The *I* of these poems, I suggest, is meant to include the reader—as at once potential poet and reader of poems. So that the "Enfants d'Adam" sequence tell us how it is—what it means, what it costs—to be a maker of poems and the "Calamus" sequence how it is to be a reader of poems—in the first instance the analogue is procreation; in the second it is community. And if Whitman's own homosexuality led him to write more powerfully in the second vein than in the first, we should be mindful of the fact that, in his times as in ours, it seems to be easier to make poems, good poems, even to publish them, than to get readers for them.

Indeed, Whitman announces in the next-to-last of the "Calamus" sequence that we are to be ready for his most "baffling" words, which come in the last poem of the sequence, later "Full of Life Now":

When you read these, I, that was visible, am become invisible;
Now it is you, compact, visible, realizing my poems, seeking me,
Fancying how happy you were, if I could be with you, and become
your lover;
Be it as if I were with you. Be not too certain but I am with you
now.

Later Whitman changed *lover* to *comrade*—mistakenly, I think; for, as their function in the 1860 volume shows, the "Calamus" poems were to carry through to completion the poet's conception of his painfully loving relation with his readers.

Having, in the "Enfants d'Adam" and "Calamus" sequences, defined the poetic process itself, as he had earlier defined the poet's discovery of that process, Whitman proceeds variously to celebrate himself and his readers at once under the aegis of the "Enfants d'Adam" and the "Calamus" analogue. (As Lorca said in his "Oda," "Este es el mundo, amigo . . .") Much of the power of the poems, new and old, derives from their place in the sequences. In "Crossing Brooklyn Ferry" and the series of "Messenger Leaves" there are addresses to all and sundry who inhabit Whitman's world, assurances to them that now he can love them for what they are, because now he knows them for what they are. There is then an address to Manahatta—which returns to the problem of naming, but now with an assurance that the problem has disappeared in the solving: "I was asking for something specific and perfect for my city, and behold! here is the aboriginal name!" Then there is an address in "Kosmos" to the simple, separate persons—to each of his readers who is "constructing the house of himself or herself." Then there is "Sleep Chasings" (a version of the 1855 "The Sleepers"), now a sublime poem, in which the poet can freely acknowledge that the source of his strength is in the relation of his night- to his day-time life, the unconscious and the conscious:

I will stop only a time with the night, and rise betimes
I will duly pass the day, O my mother, and duly return to you.

And "Sleep Chasings" is the more telling for being followed by "Burial" (originally an 1855 poem which eventually became "To Think of Time"). For in his incessant moving between night and day, the poet manages to make poems and so proves immortal. He makes men immortal in his poems, as he teaches them to make themselves immortal in their acts:

To think that you and I did not see, feel, think, nor bear our part!
To think that we are now here, and bear our part!

This poem comes nearly at the end of the 1860 volume. Only an address to his soul—immortal, but in a strictly "poetic" sense—and "So Long!" follow. In the latter we are reminded once again:

> This is no book,
> Who touches this book, touches a man,
> (Is it night? Are we done?)
> It is I you hold, and who holds you,
> I spring from the pages into your arms—decease calls me forth.

We are reminded thus, to paraphrase a recent Whitmanian, that in the flesh of art we are immortal: which is a commonplace. We are reminded also that in our age, the role of art, of poetry, is to keep us alive enough to be capable of this kind of immortality: which is not quite a commonplace.

The central terms in the argument of the 1860 *Leaves of Grass*, I suggest, run something like this: first, in the poems which lead up to "A Word out of the Sea"—self-discovery, self-love, rebirth, diffusion-of-self, art; and second, in the poems which follow "A Word out of the Sea"—love-of-others, death, rebirth, reintegration-of-self, art, immortality. The sequence is that of an ordinary life, extraordinarily lived through; the claims are strictly humanistic. The child manages somehow to achieve adulthood; the movement is from a poetry of diffusion to a poetry of integration. Immortality is the *result* of art, not its origin, nor its cause. The humanism is painful, because one of its crucial elements (centering on "death" as a "clew" in "A Word out of the Sea") is an acknowledgment of all-too-human limitations and constraints. So long as Whitman lived with that acknowledgment, lived *in* that acknowledgment—even when living with it drove him (as it too often did) toward bathos and sentimentalism—, he managed to be a poet, a "secretary," a "sage," a seer, a visionary. His religion was the religion of humanity: the only religion that a work of art can *directly* express, whatever other religion it may confront and acknowledge. *Indirectly,* it can confront religion in the more usual and more proper sense; for it can treat of man in his aspiration for something beyond manhood, even if it cannot claim—since its materials are ineluctably those of manhood—to treat directly of that something-beyond. The burden—someone has called it the burden of incertitude; Keats called it "negative capability"—is a hard one to bear. Whitman, I am suggesting, bore it most successfully, bore it most successfully for us, in the 1860 *Leaves of Grass.*

Which brings me to the most important of the poems first collected in this volume, "A Word out of the Sea."[1] It was originally published separately in 1859, as *A Child's Reminiscence.* Thus far, I have tried to suggest the proper context in which the poem should be read: as part of the volume for which it was originally written; as a turning point in the argument of that book. Note that "A Word out of the Sea" comes about mid-way in the book after "Walt Whitman," the "Chants Democratic," "Leaves of Grass," "Salut au Monde," and "Poem of Joys"—that is, after those poems which tell us of the poet's discovery of his powers as poet and of his ability to use those powers so to "vivify" his world, and himself in it: after his discovery that it is man's special delight and his special agony to be at once the subject and object of his meditations; after his discovery that consciousness inevitably entails self-consciousness and a sense of the strengths and weaknesses of self-consciousness. Moreover, "A Word out of the Sea" comes shortly before the "Enfants d'Adam" and "Calamus" sequences—that is, shortly before those poems which work out the dialectic of the subject-object relationship under the analogue of the sexuality of man as creator of his world and of persons, places, and things as its creatures. I cannot but think that Whitman knew what he was doing when he placed "A Word out of the Sea" thus. For he was obligated, in all his autobiographical honesty, to treat directly of man's fallibilities as well as his powers, to try to discover the binding relationship between fallibilities and powers: to estimate the capacity of man to be himself and the cost he would have to pay. The poems which came before "A Word out of the Sea" have little to do with fallibilities; they develop the central terms of the whole argument only this far: self-discovery, self-love, rebirth, art. Theirs is the polymorph perverse world of the child. In them, death only threatens, does not promise; power is what counts. The turning-point in the poet's life can come only with the "adult" sense of love and death, the beginning and the end of things: out of which issues art, now a mode of immortality. In "A Word out of the Sea" the 1860 volume has its turning-point. Beyond this poem, we must remember, are the "Enfants d'Adam" and "Calamus" sequences, and also "Crossing Brooklyn Ferry" and the "Messenger Leaves" sequence.

The 1860 poem begins harshly: "Out of the rocked cradle." The past participle, unlike the present participle in the later versions, implies no continuing agent for the rocking; the sea here is too inclusive to be a symbol; it is just a fact of life—life's factuality. Then comes the melange of elements associated with the "sea." They are among the

[1] The complete text of "A Word out of the Sea" is given in the issue of *The Minnesota Review* in which this essay was originally printed, pp. 273-280, and in a facsimile edition of the 1860 *Leaves of Grass* published by the Cornell University Press, 1961.—R.H.P.

realities whose miraculousness the poet is on his way to understanding. Note the third line (omitted in later versions) which clearly establishes the autobiographical tone and makes the boy at once the product of nature at large and a particular nature: "Out of the boy's mother's womb, from the nipples of her breasts." All this leads to a clear split in point of view, so that we know that the poet-as-adult is making a poem which will be his means to understanding a childhood experience. Initially we are told of the range of experiences out of which this poem comes: the sea as rocked cradle seems at once literally (to the boy) and metaphorically (to the poet) to "contain" the song of the bird, the boy's mother, the place, the time, the memory of the brother, and the as yet unnamed "word stronger and more delicious than any" which marks a limit to the meaning of the whole. This is quite explicitly an introduction. For what follows is given a separate title, "Reminiscence," as though the poet wanted to make quite plain the division between his sense of himself as child and as adult. Then we are presented with the story of the birds, the loss of the beloved, and the song sung (as only *now* the poet knows it) to objectify this loss, so make it bearable, so assure that it can, in *this* life, be transcended. Always we are aware that the poet-as-adult, the creative center of the poem seeks that "word stronger and more delicious" which will be his means finally to understand his reminiscences and—in the context of this volume (I emphasize: in the context of *this* volume)—serve to define his vocation as poet: at once powerful and fallible. The points of view of bird, child, and adult are kept separate until the passage which reads:

> Bird! (then said the boy's Soul,)
> Is it indeed toward your mate you sing? or is it mostly to me?
> For I that was a child, my tongue's use sleeping,
> Now that I have heard you,
> Now in a moment I know what I am for—I awake,
> And already a thousand singers—a thousand songs, clearer louder,
>   more sorrowful than yours,
> A thousand warbling echoes have started to life within me,
> Never to die.

The boy, even as a man recalling his boyhood, does not, as in later versions, at first address the bird as "Demon." He is at this stage incapable of that "or"—in the latter reading "Demon or bird." Even though his soul speaks, he is to discover—some lines later—his special "poetic" relation to the bird. Moreover, as "boy," he holds toward death an attitude half-way between that of the bird—who is merely "instinctive" and that of the man—who is "reflective," capable of "reminiscence." Yet the points of view begin to be hypnotically merged

—*after* the fact. In the boy's "soul" the poet discovers a child's potentiality for adult knowledge; but he keeps it as a potentiality, and he never assigns it to the bird, who (or which) is an occasion merely. Yet having seen that potentiality as such, he can "now," in the adult present, work toward its realization, confident that the one will follow necessarily in due course from the other. Now, in the adult present, he can ask for "the clew," "The word final, superior to all," the word which "now" he can "conquer." I cannot emphasize too much that it is a *"word"* —that the poet is translating the sea (and all it embodies) as prelinguistic fact into a word, knowledge of which will signify his coming to maturity. "Out of," in the original title, is meant quite literally to indicate a linguistic transformation. In the record of the growth of his mind, he sees *now* that the word will once and for all precipitate the meaning he has willed himself to create, and in the creating to discover. And it comes as he recalls that time when the sea, manifesting the rhythm of life and death itself,

> Delaying not, hurrying not,
> Whisper'd me through the night, and very plainly before daybreak,
> Lisp'd to me the low and delicious word DEATH,
> And again Death—ever Death, Death, Death

(Not *Death,* merely repeated four times as in later versions—but *ever,* beyond counting. The prophetic Whitman was bound to drop that *ever,* since for him nothing was beyond counting.)

The merging of the points of view occurs as not only past and present, child and adult, but subject and object (i.e., "The sea . . . whisper'd me"—not "*to* me") are fused. The poet now knows the word, because he has contrived a situation in which he can control its use; he has discovered (to recall the language of the *American Primer* notes) another reality, one that words until *now* had not been formed to represent. He has, as only a poet can, *made* a word out of the sea—for the duration of the poem understood *"sea"* as it may be into *"death"*—*"ever death."* His genius is such as to have enabled us to put those quotation marks around the word—guided by him, to have "bracketed" this portion of our experience with language; and we discover that as language binds in the poet's time, so it is bound in human time.

If the end of the poem is to understand cosmic process as a continual loss of the beloved through death and a consequent gain of death-in-life and life-in-death—if this is the end of the poem, nonetheless it is gained through a creative act, an assertion of life in the face of death, and a discovery and acknowledgment of the limits of such an assertion. And this act is that of the very person, the poet, whom death would deprive of all that is beloved in life. Moreover, the deprivation is quite literally that and shows the poet moving, in high honesty, from the "Enfant d'Adam" sequence to "Calamus." In the 1860 volume, "A Word out of the Sea" entails the "Calamus" sequence. (What if Whitman had, in "A Word out of the Sea," written *comrade* instead of *brother*?)

In any case, at this stage of his career, Whitman would not yield to his longing for such comfort as would scant the facts of life and death. There is, I repeat, that opening *rocked,* not *rocking* cradle; there is the quite naturalistic acknowledgment of the "boy's mother's womb." And there is stanza 31 (the stanzas in the 1860 poem are numbered, as the stanzas of the final version are not):

> O give me some clew!
> O if I am to have so much, let me have more!
> O a word! O what is my destination?
> O I fear it is henceforth chaos!
> O how joys, dreads, convolutions, human shapes, and all shapes, spring as from graves around me!
> O phantoms! you cover all the land, and all the sea!
> O I cannot see in the dimness whether you smile or frown upon me;
> O vapor, a look, a word! O well-beloved!
> O you dear women's and men's phantoms!

In the final version, the equivalent stanza reads only:

> O give me the clew (it lurks in the night here somewhere,)
> O if I am to have so much, let me have more!

The difference between "some clew" and "the clew" marks the difference between a poet for whom questions are real and one for whom questions are rhetorical. The later Whitman was convinced that the lurking clew would find him—and to that degree, whatever else he was, was not a poet. The earlier Whitman, in all humility, feared that what might issue out of this experience was "phantoms"—a good enough word for aborted poems. And often—but not too often—he was right.

Finally, there is not in "A Word out of the Sea" the falsely (and, in the context of the poem, undeservedly) comforting note of "Or like some old crone rocking the cradle swathed in sweet garments, bending aside." Indeed, the sentimentality and bathos of this too-much celebrated line, as I think, is given away by the fact that it is the only simile, the only *like* clause, in the poem. And, in relation to the total effect of the poem, the strategic withdrawal of the *Or* which introduces the line is at least unfortunate, at most disastrous.

I make so much of the kind of disaster, as I think it is, because it became increasingly characteristic of Whitman's way with poetry after the 1860 *Leaves of Grass*. Probably there are poems, written later, which show him at his best; and probably some of his revisions and rejections are for the best. But I more and more doubt it, as I doubt that he had reached his best in 1855 and 1856. I do not mean to take the part of Cassandra; but I think it as inadvisable to take the part of Pollyanna. The facts, as I see them, show that Whitman, for whatever reason, after 1860 moved away from the mode of archetypal autobiography toward that of prophecy. He worked hard to make, as he said, a cathedral out of *Leaves of Grass*. He broke up the beautifully wrought sequence of the 1860 volume; so that, even when he let poems stand unrevised, they appear in contexts which take from them their life-giving mixture of tentativeness and assurance, of aspiration, and render them dogmatic, tendentious, and overweening.

In Lawrence's word, Whitman "mentalized" his poems. To give a few examples of "mentalizing" revisions of 1860 poems: The opening of the third "Enfants d'Adam" poem reads in the 1860 text:

> O my children! O mates!
> O the bodies of you, and of all men and women, engirth me, and I engirth them.

In the 1867 version the lines read:

> I sing the body electric,
> The Armies of those I love engirth me and I engirth them.

Another example: the opening line of the fourteenth poem of the same sequence—reads in the 1860 version: "I am he that aches with love"; and becomes in 1867: "I am he that aches with amorous love." (This is the *amorous* which so infuriated Lawrence.) And another example: the opening lines of the fifteenth poem in the sequence—read in the 1860 version: "Early in the morning,/ Walking . . ."; and became in 1867: "As Adam early in the morning,/ Walking . . ." Small examples surely. But note the unsupported and unsupportable claims of "body electric," "armies," "amorous," and the Old Testament "Adam."

A larger—but still characteristic—example is Whitman's revision of the first of the 1860 "Leaves of Grass" sequence, which became "As I Ebb'd with the Ocean of life." The 1860 poem opens thus:

> Elemental drifts!
> O I wish I could impress others as you and the waves have just been impressing me.
>
> As I ebbed with an ebb of the ocean of life,
> As I wended the shores I know.

In the poem as it appears in the 1892 edition of *Leaves of Grass*, the first two lines—expressing doubt, as I have pointed out—are missing; the third has been simplified to "As I ebb'd with the ocean of life"—so that the poet is no longer conceived as part of an "ebb." And the fourth line stands as we have it now. Later in the seventh line of the 1892 version, the poet says that he is "Held by the electric self out of the pride of which I utter poems." In the 1860 version he says that he is "Alone, held by the eternal self of me that threatens to get the better of me, and stifle me." And so it goes—all passion beyond spending (unless vivified by a kind of cosmic electroshock), all poetry beyond the mere writing, all life beyond the mere living—since the poet's tactic, however unconscious, is to claim to have transcended that which must have been hard to live with: his extraordinarily ordinary self and the ordinarily extraordinary death that awaits him. Granting the mood and movement of the later editions of *Leaves of Grass*, it is only proper that Whitman would have rejected the eighth poem in the 1860 "Calamus" sequence—which begins "Long I thought that knowledge alone would suffice me—O if I could but obtain knowledge!" and ends, as the poet is brought to confront the readers to whom he would offer his poems, "I am indifferent to my own songs—I will go with him I love . . ."

One more example: this one not of a revision but of an addition to a sequence originating in the 1860 volume. In the 1871 *Leaves of Grass*, Whitman, now wholly committed to making of his poem a series of prophetic books, placed in the "Calamus" sequence the woolly "Base of All Metaphysics," the last stanza of which reads:

> Having studied the new and antique, the Greek and Germanic
> systems,
> Kant having studied and stated, Fichte and Schelling and Hegel,
> Stated the lore of Plato, and Socrates greater than Plato,
> And greater than Socrates sought and stated, Christ divine having
> studied long.
> I see reminiscent to-day those Greek and Germanic systems,
> See the philosophies of all, Christian churches and tenets see,
> Yet underneath Socrates clearly see, and underneath Christ the
> divine I see,
> The dear love of man for his comrade, the attraction of friend to
> friend,
> Of the well-married husband and wife, of children and parents,
> Of city for city and land for land.

Whitman stuck by this poem until the end, and it went unchanged into the 1892 edition of *Leaves of Grass*, contributing its bit to the "mentalizing" of the whole. And it is only too typical of additions to the book made from 1867 on.

This Whitman begins to take over *Leaves of Grass* in the 1867 edition and is fully in command by the time of the 1871 edition. It is, unhappily, he whom he knew best and he with whom our poets have tried to make their pacts and truces—but, as I think, so that during the uneasy peace they might come to know another (and, as I have tried to show, earlier) Whitman: whose way with the poetry they seem to sense but can never quite get to. The way to that Whitman is not impassable, although working with the Inclusive Edition of *Leaves of Grass* (upon whose variant readings I have depended) is tedious. But there is yet a more direct way: reading the 1860 *Leaves of Grass.*

Meantime we must bring ourselves to say of the Whitman of 1892, the literatus, that he was driven to claim prophetic powers, not to put poetry to their service. Nothing could hold this Whitman back, not even the facts of a poet's life. Indeed, life—his own and life in general—became less "factual," less "real" for him. And—since justification consists in deriving the necessary from the real, of tracing the necessary back to its roots in the real, of showing that the real is necessary—he no longer had a need to justify himself. Well: In this our world, where we too find it increasingly hard to assent to the factually real, where we have got so far as to call the factually real the "absurd," we find it increasingly difficult to hold ourselves back: as do our poets, acting on our behalf. Thus I daresay we need to recover the Whitman of 1860—with his heroic sense of grounding the necessary in the real. He gave us permission to. I am suggesting that we *need* the poet of 1860, the poet of "A Word out of the Sea." I mean to say thereby that our poets need him too. And justifying the need, we must justify him who contrived that his need be archetypal of ours.

America's Epic

by James Miller, Jr.

Did Whitman write the epic for modern America? There have been many who contend that *Leaves of Grass* is merely a collection of lyric poetry, some good, some bad, all of it of a peculiarly personal nature that disqualifies its attitudes and philosophy generally. There have been others who have defended Whitman's book as the embodiment of the American reality and ideal, as a superb fulfilment of all the genuine requirements of the national epic.[1]

What did Whitman believe? The answer may be found in a number of prose works, beginning with the 1855 Preface. It is clear in this early work that Whitman desired *Leaves of Grass* to bear a unique relationship with America: "Here [in America] at last is something in the doings of man that corresponds with the broadcast doings of the day and night. . . . It awaits the gigantic and generous treatment worthy of it." [2] It is generally recognized that the entire Preface is a veiled account of Whitman's concept of his own role as poet. Certainly he includes himself in the category when he asserts: "The poets of the kosmos advance through all interpositions and coverings and turmoils and stratagems to first principles." [3] Although Whitman does not use the term, it is clear throughout the 1855 Preface that he believes his book to have the basic nature and general scope of the traditional national epic.

In *Democratic Vistas,* in the same indirect manner, Whitman again reveals his concept of the nature of his poetry: "Never was anything more wanted than, to-day, and here in the States, the poet of the modern is wanted, or the great literatus of the modern. At all times, perhaps, the central point in any nation, and that whence it is itself really sway'd the

"America's Epic." From *A Critical Guide to Leaves of Grass,* pp. 174-186, by James Miller, Jr., by permission of The University of Chicago Press.

[1] See Fern Nuhn, "Leaves of Grass Viewed as an Epic," *Arizona Quarterly,* VII (Winter, 1951), 324-38.

[2] Facsimile of 1855 text of *Leaves of Grass* (New York: Columbia University Press, 1939), p. iii.

[3] *Ibid.,* p. ix.

most and whence it sways others, is its national literature, especially its archetypal poems" (V, 54-55).[4] Whitman was by this time (1871) acutely aware that America had not accepted his book as he had planned and hoped. There can be little doubt that he conceived *Leaves of Grass* as an "archetypal" poem produced and offered to America at its "central point"—a book "sway'd" by the nation and written to sway others. Such a work as Whitman calls for in *Democratic Vistas* is surely the epic of America. And, basically, it is his own work which he desires to be recognized as such.

In "A Backward Glance o'er Travel'd Roads" (1888), summing up the contribution of his own work, Whitman again emphasizes the need of the nation for a commensurate poetry. But no longer is he evasive; his claim is direct: "As America fully and fairly construed is the legitimate result and evolutionary outcome of the past, so I would dare to claim for my verse." The Old World, as the poet points out, "has had the poems of myths, fictions, feudalism, conquest, caste, dynastic wars, and splendid exceptional characters," but the "New World needs the poems of realities and science and of the democratic average and basic equality." And, instead of the "splendid exceptional characters" of the Old World epics, the New World epic will portray simply—man: "In the centre of all, and object of all, stands the Human Being, towards whose heroic and spiritual evolution poems and everything directly or indirectly tend, Old World or New" (V, 54).

Should there be any doubts about the ambition of Whitman to write America's epic, the opening pages of *Leaves of Grass* should dispel them. In "Inscriptions" and "Starting from Paumanok" there are innumerable indications of the epic nature of the work. In the very opening poem, Whitman uses the construction, "I Sing," characteristic of the epic in introducing themes—"One's-Self I Sing," "The Female equally with the Male I sing," "The Modern Man I sing." In this first poem, too, the Muse is mentioned—"Not physiognomy alone nor brain alone is worthy for the Muse, I say the Form complete is worthier far"; but it is not until the second poem, "As I Ponder'd in Silence," that the Muse is invoked, addressed, and reassured. As the poet considers his work, he is visited by the Old World Muse:

> A Phantom arose before me with distrustful aspect,
> Terrible in beauty, age, and power,
> The genius of poets of old lands [I, 1].

This Muse is skeptical, for all past epics countenanced by the "haughty shade" have had as their subject the "theme of War, the fortune of

[4] Whitman quotations are where possible identified in the text by volume and page number of *The Complete Writings of Walt Whitman,* ed. Richard M. Bucke *et al.* (New York: G. P. Putnam's Sons, 1902).

battles, / The making of perfect soldiers." The poet welcomes the challenge and assures the Muse that he, too, sings of "war, and a longer and greater one than any." In the poet's war, the field is the world, the battle "For life and death, for the Body and for the eternal Soul." The central point of this key "Inscriptions" poem is that the poet's book qualifies as an epic, even under the Old World definition, if sufficient liberality is allowed in interpreting the terms.

There are other instances in *Leaves of Grass* in which Whitman calls attention to the epic nature of his book. In "Starting from Paumanok" he outlines his plan for encompassing in his poetry the entire nation—"Solitary, singing in the West, I strike up for a New World." The poems of *Leaves of Grass* are to constitute "a programme of chants" for "Americanos." The poet advises:

> Take my leaves America, take them South and take them North,
> Make welcome for them everywhere, for they are your own offspring [I, 18].

Whitman's insistence on an intimate and unique relation between his book and his country appears no more frequently than his appeal to the Muse. In "Song of the Exposition," the form is epic if the tone is comic:

> Come Muse migrate from Greece and Ionia,
> Cross out please those immensely overpaid accounts [I, 238].

If in this poem the Muse loses some of her dignity as the poet instals her amid the drainpipes, artificial fertilizers, and the kitchen ware, in "By Blue Ontario's Shore" the Muse is transfigured into a "Phantom gigantic superb, with stern visage," who commands the poet:

> *Chant me the poem,* it said, *that comes from the soul of America, chant me the carol of victory,*
> *And strike up the marches of Libertad, marches more powerful yet,*
> *And sing me before you go the song of the throes of Democracy* [II, 107].

It is characteristic of Whitman that he would reverse the Old World epic practice by which the poet called upon the Muse for help and would place the Muse in the position of pleading with the poet to continue his writing so that vital themes would not go unsung.

It is clear from both external and internal evidence that Whitman thought of his work in epic terms. The extent to which he fulfilled his epic ambitions, however, may be measured only in terms of his final achievement. The answer that achievement provides is impressive.

For the hero of his epic, Whitman created the archetypal personality for the New World (the modern man of "One's-Self I Sing"), a man both individual and of the mass. This hero, unlike the hero of past epics, discovers his heroic qualities not in superman characteristics but in the *selfhood* common to every man. Every man in America, according to Whitman, is potentially an epic hero, if he is sufficiently aware of the potentiality of his selfhood, if he celebrates his vital procreative role, and if he is capable of depth of feeling in spiritually complex attachments. In doing and being all these things, the New World epic hero sings the song of himself, acknowledges the parentage of Adam, and finds spiritual fulfilment in "Calamus" comradeship. He accepts, moreover, his New World place in space and position in time. He relishes his home on the rolling earth, and he finds that his appointed position in the unfolding of mystic evolution places him where all time past converges and all time future originates.

Having created his epic hero by broad, free strokes in the first part of *Leaves of Grass,* Whitman next engages him in the usual trial of strength in a great and crucial war on which the national destiny depends. As Whitman's modern man of the New World represents above all a reconciliation of the paradoxically opposed ideals of democracy—individuality and equality (separateness and "en-masse")—so his epic hero paradoxically exemplifies both traits in war. "Drum-Taps" demonstrates the triumph of the American epic hero "en-masse." No individual is singled out from the rest for heroic deeds, but, throughout, the emphasis is on the ranks, the large mass of men welded together in comradeship and a common national purpose. The poet at one point asserts that America has too long "learn'd from joys and prosperity only":

> But now, ah now, to learn from crises of anguish, advancing, grappling with direst fate and recoiling not,
> And now to conceive and show to the world what your children en-masse really are,
> (For who except myself has yet conceiv'd what your children en-masse really are?) [II, 77].

But, as the Civil War proved the heroic quality on an epic scale of America's "children en-masse," the same national crisis also demonstrated democracy's ability to produce individuality of epic proportions. "Drum-Taps" gives way to "Memories of President Lincoln" and that magnificent threnody, "When Lilacs Last in the Dooryard Bloom'd." But the traits of this epic hero are not different from but similar to the traits of the soldiers "en-masse." He is the "powerful western fallen star"; he is the captain of the ship whose loss is universally mourned;

he is the "dear commander" of the soldiers; but he is above all the "departing comrade" who possessed an infinite capacity for love.

In the latter part of *Leaves of Grass,* the mythological background of the epic hero of the New World is completed as he is related to the "resistless gravitation of spiritual law." The entire section of the book from "Proud Music of the Storm" through "Whispers of Heavenly Death" not only presents the New World hero with "religious" convictions and impresses him with the reality of the spiritual world but also provides him with his immortality. Even the gods (like the heroes) in this New World epic are conceived in democratic terms. At the climactic point in "Passage to India" the poet exclaims:

> Surrounded, copest, frontest God, yieldest, the aim attain'd,
> As fill'd with friendship, love complete, the Elder Brother found,
> The Younger melts in fondness in his arms [II, 196].

God is the "final" comrade, the perfect embodiment of those ideal traits earlier invested in the New World epic hero. The relationship to God is not the relationship of a subject to his superior but the relationship of the ideal brotherhood, the perfectly fulfilled comradeship.

In a very complicated way, Whitman's epic embodies at the same time that it creates America's image of itself—the American dream, the American vision, as it reached its climactic elaboration during the nineteenth century. If in retrospect Whitman's faith in science and democracy seems naïve, we must remember that our perspective is a bit jaded. And Whitman's faith was the American faith, his naïveté the American naïveté. In insisting on being the poet of science and democracy and, above all, of "religion," Whitman was not clinging to personal attitudes but was rather defining the nineteenth century's view of the universe and itself and reflecting it in his epic, as the epic poets of the past—Homer, Vergil, Dante, and Milton—reflected their own times in order to become epic spokesmen for their ages. Whitman embraced the modern "myth" of science, democracy, religion, and much more. The question of the "truth" of these nineteenth-century beliefs and attitudes is as irrelevant as the question of the "truth" of Homer's gods or Milton's devils. The relevant fact is that these views were held by an entire culture and the people lived and acted in the simple faith that their beliefs were true.

Leaves of Grass has just claim as America's epic. No attempt before it (and there were many) succeeded in becoming more than awkward imitations of the epics of the past. No book after it can ever again achieve its unique point of view. Coming shortly after the birth of the nation, embodying the country's first terrible trial by fire, prophesying the greatness to be thrust upon these states, *Leaves of Grass* possesses a position of intimate relationship with America that no other work can now ever assume. For better or worse, *Leaves of Grass* is America's, a reflection of her character and of her soul and of her achievements and her aspirations. If *Leaves of Grass* transfigures what it reflects, that is because its poet wanted to dwell not on the reality but on the ideal. If *Leaves of Grass* has its shortcomings and defects, so, surely, does the culture it attempted to embody. But after all the reservations are stated and the qualifications noted, we must confess that the book does measure up. If Whitman's vision exceeded his achievement, the scope of his achievement was still sufficient to win him just claim to the title of America's epic poet.

The Poet in His Art

"I am determined to have the world know what I was pleased to do. . . . In the long run the world will do as it pleases with the book."

Only a Language Experiment

by F. O. Matthiessen

One aspect of Whitman's work that has not yet received its due attention is outlined in *An American Primer,* notes for a lecture that he seems to have collected mainly between 1855 and 1860, using the paper covers of the unbound copies of the first edition of *Leaves of Grass* for his improvised sheets. This lecture, which, as he says, "does not suggest the invention but describes the growth of an American English enjoying a distinct identity," remained, like most of Whitman's lectures, undelivered and unpublished at his death. But he often talked to Traubel about it in the late eighteen-eighties, telling him that he never quite got its subject out of his mind, that he had long thought of making it into a book,[1] and adding: "I sometimes think the *Leaves* is only a language experiment." It will be interesting, therefore, to begin by seeing how much we can learn about Whitman just by examining his diction.

He understood that language was not "an abstract construction" made by the learned, but that it had arisen out of the work and needs, the joys and struggles and desires of long generations of humanity, and that it had "its bases broad and low, close to the ground." Words were not arbitrary inventions, but the product of human events and customs, the

[1] It was issued as a separate book by Traubel in 1904.

progeny of folkways. Consequently he believed that the fresh opportunities for the English tongue in America were immense, offering themselves in the whole range of American facts. His poems, by cleaving to these facts, could thereby release "new potentialities" of expression for our native character. When he started to develop his conviction that "a perfect user of words uses things," and to mention some of the things, he unconsciously dilated into the loose beats of his poetry: "they exude in power and beauty from him—miracles from his hands—miracles from his mouth . . . things, whirled like chain-shot rocks, defiance, compulsion, houses, iron, locomotives, the oak, the pine, the keen eye, the hairy breast, the Texan ranger, the Boston truckman, the woman that arouses a man, the man that arouses a woman."

He there reveals the joy of the child or the primitive poet just in naming things. This was the quality in Coleridge that made Whitman speak of him as being "like Adam in Paradise, and almost as free from artificiality"—though Whitman's own joy is far more naïve and relaxed than anything in Coleridge. Whitman's excitement carries weight because he realized that a man cannot use words so unless he has experienced the facts that they express, unless he has grasped them with his senses. This kind of realization was generally obscured in the nineteenth century, partly by its tendency to divorce education of the mind from the body and to treat language as something to be learned from a dictionary. Such division of the individual's wholeness, intensified by the specializations of a mechanized society, has become a chief cause of the neurotic strain oppressing present-day man, for whom the words that pour into him from headlines so infrequently correspond to a concrete actuality that he has touched at first hand. For Whitman it was axiomatic that the speakers of such words are merely juggling helplessly with a foreign tongue. He was already convinced by 1847—as he recorded in the earliest of his manuscript notebooks that has been preserved—that "a man only is interested in anything when he identifies himself with it." When he came to observe in the *Primer* that "a perfect writer would make words sing, dance, kiss . . . or do any thing that man or woman or the natural powers can do," he believed that such a writer must have realized the full resources of his physical life, and have been immersed in the evolving social experience of his own time.

Thus instinctively, if crudely, he reached the conviction that "only the greatest user of words himself fully enjoys and understands himself," a conviction surprisingly close to Eliot's, that Racine and Baudelaire, the two chief French "masters of diction are also the greatest two psychologists" among French poets. Whitman thought that all the talk in Racine was "on stilts," and his sole mention of Baudelaire was to quote one of the few beliefs they shared, "The immoderate taste for beauty and art leads men into monstrous excesses." Noting that *Les Fleurs du Mal* appeared only two years after *Leaves of Grass,* Eliot has asked whether any age could have produced "more heterogeneous leaves and flowers?" But his pronouncement that there was for Whitman "no chasm between the real and the ideal, such as opened before the horrified eyes of Baudelaire," did not blind him to Whitman's prodigious faculty "in making America as it was . . . into something grand and significant," "of transmuting the real into an ideal."

Feeling that he had discovered the real America that had been hidden behind the diction of a superficial culture which hardly touched native life, Whitman exclaimed with delight: "Monongahela—it rolls with venison richness upon the palate." He pursued the subject of how "words become vitaliz'd, and stand for things" in an essay in his late *November Boughs* called "Slang in America" (1885). He grasped there the truth that language is the "universal absorber and combiner," the best index we have to the history of civilization. In the *Primer* his cognizance that English had assimilated contributions from every stock, that it had become an amalgamation from all races, rejecting none, had led him to declare that he would never allude to this tongue "without exultation." In the few pages of his printed essay there is more exultation than clarity, particularly in his conception of slang. His starting point is straightforward enough, the statement that "slang, profoundly consider'd, is the lawless germinal element, below all words and sentences, and behind all poetry, and proves a certain perennial rankness and protestantism in speech." But when he equates slang with "indirection, an attempt of common humanity to escape from bald literalism, and express itself illimitably," we are reminded of Emerson's use of the term "indirection" and need recourse to other passages in Whitman for the elusive connotations that he associated with this word.

When he said in his 1855 Preface that the expression of the American poet was to be "transcendent and new," "indirect and not direct or descriptive or epic," he had just been enumerating the kinds of things the poet must incarnate if he was to be commensurate with his people: the continent's geography and history, the fluid movement of the population, the life of its factories and commerce and of the southern plantations. He appears to have thought that the expression of this surging newness must be "indirect" in the sense that it could not find its voice through any of the conventional modes, but must wait for the poet who "sees the solid and beautiful forms of the future where there are now no solid forms." Here Whitman's belief in the way in which the organic style is called into being is seen to converge with his similar understanding of the origin of words. He might have had in mind either or both in his account of the creative process, in another early notebook: "All truths lie waiting in all things.—They neither urge the opening of themselves nor resist it. For their birth you need not the obstetric forceps of the surgeon. They unfold to you and emit themselves more fragrant than roses from living buds, whenever you fetch the spring sunshine moistened with summer rain.—But it must be in yourself.—It shall come from your soul.—It shall be love."

Living speech could come to a man only through his absorption in the life surrounding him. He must learn that the final decisions of language are not made by dictionary makers but "by the masses, people nearest the concrete, having most to do with actual land and sea." By such a route, illogical as it may be, Whitman came to think of slang as indirection, as the power to embody in a vibrant word or phrase "the deep silent mysterious never to be examined, never to be told quality of life itself." When he tried to make his meaning plainer by giving examples of how many "of the oldest and solidest words we use, were originally generated from the daring and license of slang," he showed that what he was really thinking of was something very like Emerson's first proposition about language—that words are signs of natural facts. Whitman's examples are almost identical with those in *Nature:* "Thus the term *right* means literally only straight. *Wrong* primarily meant twisted, distorted. *Integrity* meant oneness. *Spirit* meant breath, or flame. A *supercilious* person was one who rais'd his eyebrows. To *insult* was to leap against. If you *influenc'd* a man, you but flow'd into him." Moreover, as Whitman continued, he expanded into Emerson's next proposition—that natural facts are symbols of spiritual facts—by launching from the word *prophesy* into an enunciation of the transcendental view of the poet: "The Hebrew word which is translated *prophesy* meant to bubble up and pour forth as a fountain. The enthusiast bubbles up from the Spirit of God within him, and it pours forth from him like a fountain. The word prophecy is misunderstood. Many suppose that it is limited to mere prediction; that is but the lesser portion of prophecy. The greater work is to reveal God. Every true religious enthusiast is a prophet."

In such a passage you come up against one of the most confusing aspects of Whitman, the easy-hearted way he could shuttle back and forth from materialism to idealism without troubling himself about any inconsistency. Thinking of "Children of Adam" or of what Lawrence cared for in Whitman, "the sheer appreciation of the instant moment, life surging itself at its very wellhead," we tend to deny that his bond with transcendentalism could have been strong. But it is significant that his earliest quotation from one of Emerson's "inimitable lectures," in a notice for *The Brooklyn Eagle* in 1847, is from "Spiritual Laws" and begins, "When the act of reflection takes place in the mind, when we look at ourselves in the light of thought, we discover that our life is embosomed in beauty." Whitman's response to this kind of idealism was more than fleeting, as we may judge from his marginal note on an unidentified essay on "Imagination and Fact," which Bucke dated to the early fifties. The sentence that struck the poet reads: "The mountains, rivers, forests and the elements that gird them round about would be only blank conditions of matter if the mind did not fling its own divinity around them." Whitman commented: "This I think is one of the most indicative sentences I ever read."

The idealistic strain also runs through his conception of language. Although he asks in his "Song of the Banner at Daybreak":

> Words! book-words! what are you?

and affirms in "A Song of the Rolling Earth":

> The substantial words are in the ground and sea,

nevertheless he proclaims on the first page of his *Primer:* "All words are spiritual—nothing is more spiritual than words." This is the Whitman who could say, "The words of my book nothing, the drift of it everything," the Whitman so concerned with the idea rather than the form that he could take flight into the vaguest undifferentiated generalizations about "Democracy, ma femme," or could write on occasion even of "the body electric" with no sensuous touch of his material:

> O for you whoever you are your correlative body! O it, more than all else, you delighting!

This is the Whitman who has seemed to linguists as though he was trying to get beyond the limits of language altogether. In the view of Sapir, subscribed to by Ogden and Richards, he sometimes is moving so entirely in terms of abstractions that he appears to be "striving for a generalized art language, a literary algebra." In this quality of his work Sapir regarded him as an extreme example of the transcendental drift, an artist whose "expression is frequently strained, it sounds at times like a translation from an unknown original—which, indeed, is precisely what it is." We recall that Emerson's most idealized passages of verse struck Chapman in much the same way.

Thus Whitman seems to show the very dichotomy between the material and the ideal, the concrete and the abstract that we observed in Emerson's remarks on language. Nevertheless, when we look at their poems, it is obvious that Whitman often bridged the gap in a way that Emerson could not. The whole question of the relation of Whitman's theory and practice of art to Emerson's is fascinating, since, starting so often from similar if not identical positions, they end up with very different results. The extent of Emerson's influence has been obscured by Whitman's desire in his old age not to appear to have been too indebted to anyone. In his open letter to Emerson, which appeared in the second (1856) edition, though not subsequently, Whitman did not hesitate to address him as "Master." Speaking of "that new moral

American continent without which, I see, the physical continent remained incomplete," he said: "Those shores you found. I say you have led the States there—have led me there." Long afterwards he told his disciples that he was referring to the experience of having read Emerson after receiving his tribute to the first edition of the *Leaves,* but a more likely account would seem to be the one he gave to J. T. Trowbridge. In this version, based on a conversation in 1860—though not printed until after Whitman's death—the poet "freely admitted that he could never have written his poems if he had not first 'come to himself,' and that Emerson helped him to 'find himself.' I asked him if he thought he would have come to himself without that help. He said, 'Yes, but it would have taken longer.' " Here Whitman dated the fecund reading to the summer of 1854 when he had been working at his trade of carpenter and had carried a book with him in his lunch pail. One day it "chanced to be a volume of Emerson; and from that time he took with him no other writer." As we know, he had been at least acquainted with Emerson's ideas for some years before that, and their working in him may well have been a slower fermentation. He gave his own characteristic expression to the process: "I was simmering, simmering, simmering; Emerson brought me to a boil."

It is not hard to find, for what they are worth, passages in Whitman running parallel to most of Emerson's major convictions about the nature of art. But it would always be salutary to head them with these two from "Self-Reliance" and "Song of Myself": "Suppose you should contradict yourself; what then? . . . With consistency a great soul has simply nothing to do"; and

> Do I contradict myself?
> Very well then I contradict myself,
> (I am large, I contain multitudes.)

At the end of a long paragraph of appreciation of Emerson that Bucke places around eighteen-fifty, Whitman had already observed that "there is hardly a proposition in Emerson's poems or prose which you cannot find the opposite of in some other place." Nevertheless, the main contours of Emerson's doctrine of expression, as we have seen it develop, are unmistakable, and unmistakably Whitman's as well. They can both compress it into headlines: Emerson, "By God, it is in me, and must come forth of me"; Whitman, "Walt you contain enough, why don't you let it out then?" Again, whole essays of Emerson's, notably that on "The Poet," speak eloquently about the very things from which Whitman made his poetry. The two share the same view of the poet as inspired seer, of his dependence for his utterance upon his moments of inner illumination. Yet looking back over forty years, though Whitman reaffirmed that his last word would be "loyal, loyal," he admitted that Emerson's work had latterly seemed to him "pretty thin," always a *make,* never an unconscious *growth,*" and "some ways short of earth."

Whitman's language is more earthy because he was aware, in a way that distinguished him not merely from Emerson but from every other writer of the day, of the power of sex. In affirming natural passion to be "the enclosing basis of everything," he spoke of its sanity, of the sacredness of the human body, using specifically religious terms: "we were all lost without redemption, except we retain the sexual fibre of things." In defending his insistence on this element in his poems (1856), he made clear his understanding of its immediate bearing upon a living speech: "To the lack of an avowed, empowered, unabashed development of sex (the only salvation for the same), and to the fact of speakers and writers fradulently assuming as always dead what every one knows to be always alive, is attributable the remarkable non-personality and indistinctness of modern productions in books." Continuing in this vein he made almost the same observations about conventional society as were later to be expressed by Henry Adams, who, incidentally, found Whitman to be the only American writer who had drawn upon the dynamic force of sex "as every classic had always done." Both were agreed, though the phrasing here is Whitman's, that particularly among the so-called cultivated class the neuter gender prevailed, and that "if the dresses were changed, the men might easily pass for women and the women for men."

Emerson never gave up deploring the want of male principle in our literature, but one reason why it remained remote from his own pages is contained in his pronouncement (1834): "I believe in the existence of the material world as the expression of the spiritual or real." The continuation of his thought reveals the difference of his emphasis from that of the poet of "Crossing Brooklyn Ferry": "and so look with a quite comic and condescending interest upon the show of Broadway with the air of an old gentleman when he says, 'Sir, I knew your father.' Is it not forever the aim and endeavor of the real to embody itself in the phenomenal?" No matter how happily inconsistent Emerson might be on other matters, this basic position of the idealist was one from which he never departed. Whitman was far less consistent in his consideration of the relation between body and soul. He was impressed by a line of John Sterling's, which was also a favorite of Emerson's, "Still lives the song tho' Regnar dies." Whitman added this gloss to it: "The word is become flesh." Just what he implied in talking about language as incarnation, and how he diverged from Emerson, can be followed most briefly in his own words.

In the manuscript draft for the opening section of "Song of Myself," he announced the equalitarian inclusiveness that was destined always to be part of his desire:

> And I say that the soul is not greater than the body,
> And I say that the body is not greater than the soul.

However, that arbitrary equilibrium between the two is far less characteristic of his accents of most intimate discovery than his exultant reckless feeling in "Children of Adam" that the body "includes and is the soul,"

> And if the body were not the soul, what is the soul?

But in different moods, as in "A Song of Joys," he veers towards the other pole and seems loosely to approximate Blake in saying that the real life of his senses transcends his senses and flesh, that it is not his material eyes that finally see, or his material body that finally loves. However, he does not pursue this strain very long, and says more usually that the soul achieves its "identity" through the act of observing, loving, and absorbing concrete objects:

> We realize the soul only by you, you faithful solids and fluids.

This particular kind of material ideality, suggestive in general of Fichte's, remains his dominant thought, so it is worth observing how he formulated it in one of his notebooks: "Most writers have disclaimed the physical world and they have not over-estimated the other, or soul, but have under-estimated the corporeal. How shall my eye separate the beauty of the blossoming buckwheat field from the stalks and heads of tangible matter? How shall I know what the life is except as I see it in the flesh? I will not praise one without the other or any more than the other."

In commenting on the mixture of his heritage, Whitman once remarked that "like the Quakers, the Dutch are very practical and materialistic . . . but are terribly transcendental and cloudy too." That mixture confronts and tantalizes you throughout his poetry. He is at his firmest when he says that "imagination and actuality must be united." But in spite of his enthusiasm for the natural sciences as well as for every other manifestation of progress, he never came very close to a scientific realism. When he enunciated, in the eighteenth-seventies, that "body and mind are one," he had then been led into this thought by his reading of—or about—the German metaphysicians. And he declared that "only Hegel is fit for America," since in his system "the human soul stands in the centre, and all the universes minister to it." Following the Civil War, and increasingly during the last twenty years of his life, he kept saying that in his *Leaves,* "One deep purpose underlay the others—and that has been the religious purpose." He often posed variants of the question, "If the spiritual is not behind the material, to what purpose is the material?" Yet, even then, his most natural way of reconciling the dichotomy between the two elements, "fused though antagonistic," was to reaffirm his earlier analogy: "The Soul of the Universe is the Male and genital master and the impregnating and animating spirit—Physical matter is Female and Mother and waits . . ."

No arrangement or rearrangement of Whitman's thoughts on this or any other subject can resolve the paradoxes or discover in them a fully coherent pattern. He was incapable of sustained logic, but that should not blind the reader into impatient rejection of the ebb and flow of his antithesis. They possess a loose dialectic of their own, and a clue of how to find it is provided by Engels' discussion of Feuerbach: "One knows that these antithesis have only a relative validity; that that which is recognized now as true has also its latent false side which will later manifest itself, just as that which is now regarded as false has also its true side by virtue of which it could previously have been regarded as true." Whitman's ability to make a synthesis in his poems of the contrasting elements that he calls body and soul may serve as a measure of his stature as a poet. When his words adhere to concrete experience and yet are bathed in imagination, his statements become broadly representative of humanity:

> I am she who adorn'd herself and folded her hair expectantly,
> My truant lover has come, and it is dark.

When he fails to make that synthesis, his language can break into the extremes noted by Emerson when he called it "a remarkable mixture of the *Bhagvat-Geeta* and the *New York Herald*." The incongruous lengths to which Whitman was frequently carried in each direction shows how hard a task he undertook. On the one hand, his desire to grasp American facts could lead him beyond slang into the rawest jargon, the journalese of the day. On the other, his attempts to pass beyond the restrictions of language into the atmosphere it could suggest often produced only the barest formulas. His inordinate and grotesque failures in both directions throw into clearer light his rare successes, and the fusion upon which they depend.

The slang that he relished as providing more fun than "the books of all 'the American humorists' " was what he heard in the ordinary talk of "a gang of laborers, rail-road men, miners, drivers, or boatmen," in their tendency "to approach a meaning not directly and squarely" but by the circuitous routes of lively fancy. This tendency expressed itself in their fondness for nicknames like Old Hickory, or Wolverines, or Suckers, or Buckeyes. Their inventiveness had sowed the frontier with many a Shirttail Bend and Toenail Lake. Current evasions of the literal transformed a horsecar conductor into a "snatcher," straight whisky into "barefoot," and codfish balls into "sleeve buttons." But even though Whitman held such slang to be the source of all that was poetical in human utterance, he was aware that its fermentation was often hasty and frothy, and, except for occasional friendly regional epithets like Hoosiers or Kanucks, he used it only sparingly in his poems. Indeed, in some notes during the period of the gestation of his first *Leaves*, he advised himself to use "common idioms and phrases—Yankeeisms and vulgarisms—cant expressions, when very pat only." In consequence, the diction of his poetry is seldom as unconventional as that in the advice he gave himself for an essay on contemporary writing: "Bring in a sockdolager on the Dickens-fawners." He gave examples of "fierce words" in the *Primer—skulk, shyster, doughface, mean cuss, backslider, lickspittle*—and sometimes cut loose in the talk that Traubel reported. But only on the rare occasions when he felt scorn did he introduce into his poems any expressions as savagely untrammelled as

> This now is too lamentable a face for a man,
> Some abject louse asking leave to be, cringing for it,
> Some milk-nosed maggot blessing what lets it wrig to its hole.

By contrast his most characteristic colloquialisms are easy and relaxed, as when he said "howdy" to Traubel and told him that he felt "flirty" or "hunkydory," or fell into slang with no self-consciousness, but with the careless aplomb of a man speaking the language most natural to him:

> I reckon I am their boss, and they make me a pet besides.

> And will go gallivant with the light and air myself.

> Shoulder your duds, dear son, and I will mine.

> Earth! you seem to look for something at my hands,
> Say, old top-knot, what do you want?

One of Whitman's demands in the *Primer* was that words should be brought into literature from factories and farms and trades, for he knew that "around the markets, among the fish-smacks, along the wharves, you hear a thousand words, never yet printed in the repertoire of any lexicon." What resulted was sometimes as mechanical as the long lists in "A Song for Occupations," but his resolve for inclusiveness also produced dozens of snap-shot impressions as accurate as

> The butcher-boy puts off his killing-clothes, or sharpens his knife at
> the stall in the market,
> I loiter enjoying his repartee and his shuffle and break-down.

Watching men in action called out of him some of his most fluid phrases, which seem to bathe and surround the objects they describe—as this, of the blacksmiths:

> The *lithe sheer* of their waists plays even with their massive arms.

Or this,

> The negro holds firmly the reins of his four horses, the block *swags underneath* on its tied-over chain.

Or a line that is itself a description of the very process by which he enfolds such movement:

> In me the caresser of life wherever moving, backward as well as forward *sluing*.

At times he produced suggestive coinages of his own:

> The blab of the pave, tires of carts, sluff of boot-soles, talk of the promenaders.

Yet he is making various approaches to language even in that one line. *Blab* and *sluff* have risen from his desire to suggest actual sounds, but *promenaders,* which also sounds well, has clearly been employed for that reason alone since it does not belong to the talk of any American folk. *Pave* instead of *pavement* is the kind of bastard word that, to use another, Whitman liked to "promulge." Sometimes it is hard to tell whether such words sprang from intention or ignorance, particularly in view of the appearance of *semitic* in place of *seminal* ("semitic muscle," "semitic milk") in both the 1855 Preface and the first printing of "A Woman Waits for Me." Most frequently his hybrids take form of the free substitution of one part of speech for another—sometimes quite effectively ("the soothe of the waves"), sometimes less so (she that "birth'd him").

Although it has been estimated that Whitman had a vocabulary of more than thirteen thousand words, of which slightly over half were used by him only once,[2] the number of his authentic coinages is not very large. Probably the largest group is composed of his agent-nouns, which is not surprising for a poet who was so occupied with types and classes of men and women. Unfortunately these also furnish some of the ugliest-sounding words in his pages, *originatress, revoltress, dispensatress,* which have hardly been surpassed even in the age of the realtor and the beautician. He was luckier with an occasional abstract noun like *presidentiad,* though this is offset by a needless monstrosity like *savantism.* The one kind of coinage where his ear was listening sensitively is in such

[2] The reported figures, 13,447 and 6,978, are those of W. H. Trimble's unpublished concordance. The most useful work that has been done on Whitman's diction are several articles by Louise Pound, particularly "Walt Whitman's Neologisms" (*American Mercury,* February 1925) and "Walt Whitman and the French Language" (*American Speech,* May 1926).

compounds as "the transparent green-shine" of the water around the naked swimmer in "I Sing the Body Electric," or that evoking the apples hanging "indolent-ripe" in "Halcyon Days."

His belief in the need to speak not merely for Americans but for the workers of all lands seems to have given the impetus for his odd habit of introducing random words from other languages, to the point of talking about "the ouvrier class"! He took from the Italian chiefly the terms of the opera, also *viva, romanza,* and even *ambulanza.* From the Spanish he was pleased to borrow the orotund way of naming his countrymen "Americanos," while the occasional circulation of Mexican dollars in the States during the eighteen-forties may have given him his word *Libertad.* His favorite *camerado,* an archaic English version of the Spanish *camarada,* seems most likely to have come to him from the pages of the Waverley novels, of which he had been an enthusiastic reader in his youth. But the smattering of French which he picked up on his trip to New Orleans, and which constituted the most extensive knowledge that he ever was to have of another tongue, furnished him with the majority of his borrowings. It allowed him to talk of his "amour" and his "eleves," of a "soiree" or an "accoucheur," of "trottoirs" and "feuillage" and "delicatesse"; to say that his were not "the songs of an ennuyeed person," or to shout, "Allons! from all formules! . . . Allons! the road is before us!" Frequently he was speaking no language, as when he proclaimed himself "no dainty dolce affetuoso." But he could go much farther than that into a foreign jargon in his desire to "eclaircise the myths Asiatic" in his "Passage to India," or to fulfil "the rapt promises and luminè of seers." He could address God, with ecstatic and monumental tastelessness, as "thou reservoir."

Many of these are samples of the confused American effort to talk big by using high-sounding terms with only the vaguest notion of their original meaning. The resultant fantastic transformations have enlivened every stage of our history, from the frontiersman's determination to twist his tongue around the syllables of the French settlement at Chemincouvert, Ark., which ended up with the name being turned into Smackover, down to Ring Lardner's dumb nurse who thought people were calling her "a mormon or something." In Whitman's case, the fact that he was a reader and so could depend upon letters as well as upon sounds overheard kept him from drifting to such gorgeous lengths. His transformations retain some battered semblance of the original word, which, with the happy pride of the half-educated in the learned term, he then deployed grandly for purposes of his own. Often the attraction for him in the French words ran counter to the identification he usually desired between the word and the thing, since it sprang from intoxication with the mere sound. You can observe the same tendency in some of the jotted lists of his notebooks, *Cantaloupe. Muskmelon. Cantabile. Cacique City,* or in his shaping such a generalized description of the earth as "O vast rondure swimming in space." When caught up by the desire to include the whole universe in his embrace, he could be swept far into the intense inane, chanting in "Night on the Prairies" of "immortality and peace":

> How plenteous! how spiritual! how resumé!

The two diverging strains in his use of language were with him to the end, for he never outgrew his tendency to lapse from specific images into undifferentiated and lifeless abstractions, as in the closing phrase of this description of his grandfather: "jovial, red, stout, with sonorous voice and characteristic physiognomy." In some of his latest poems, "Sands at Seventy," he could still be satisfied with the merest rhetoric:

> Of ye, O God, Life, Nature, Freedom, Poetry.

In his fondness for all his *Leaves,* he seems never to have perceived what we can note in the two halves of a single line,

> I concentrate toward them that are nigh, I wait on the door slab,

—the contrast between the clumsy stilted opening and the simple close. The total pattern of his speech is, therefore, difficult to chart, since it is formed both by the improviser's carelessness about words and by the kind of attention to them indicated in his telling Burroughs that he had been "searching for twenty-five years for the word to express what the twilight note of the robin meant to him." He also engaged in endless minute revisions of his poems, the purpose of which is often baffling. Although sometimes serving to fuse the syllables into an ampler rhythm, as in the transformation of

> Out of the rocked cradle

into one of his most memorable opening lines; they seem almost as likely to add up to nothing more than the dozens of minor substitutions in "Salut au Monde," which leave it the flat and formless catalogue that it was in the beginning.

In a warm appreciation of Burns in *November Boughs,* Whitman said that "his brightest hit is his use of the Scotch patois, so full of terms flavor'd like wild fruits or berries." Thinking not only of Burns he relished a special charm in "the very neglect, unfinish, careless nudity," which were not to be found in more polished language and verse. But his suggested comparison between the Scotch poet and himself would bring out at once the important difference that Whitman is not using anything like a folk-speech. Indeed, his phrasing is generally remote from any customary locutions of the sort that he jotted down as notes for one unwritten poem. This was to have been based on a free rendering of local native calls, such as "Here goes your fine fat oysters—Rock Point oysters—here they go." When put beside such natural words and cadences, Whitman's usual diction is clearly not that of a countryman but of what he called himself, "a jour[neyman] printer." In its curious amalgamation of homely and simple usage with half-remembered terms he read once somewhere, and with casual inventions of the moment, he often gives the impression of using a language not quite his own. In his determination to strike up for a new world, he deliberately rid himself of foreign models. But, so far as his speech is concerned, this was only very partially possible, and consequently Whitman reveals the peculiarly American combination of a childish freshness with a mechanical and desiccated repetition of book terms that had had significance for the more complex civilization in which they had had their roots and growth. The freshness has come, as it did to Huck Finn, through instinctive rejection of the authority of those terms, in Whitman's reaction against what he called Emerson's cold intellectuality: "Suppose his books becoming absorb'd, the permanent chyle of American general and particular character—what a well-wash'd and grammatical, but bloodless and helpless race we should turn out!"

Yet the broken chrysalis of the old restrictions still hangs about Whitman. Every page betrays that his language is deeply ingrained with the educational habits of a middle-class people who put a fierce emphasis on the importance of the written word. His speech did not spring primarily from contact with the soil, for though his father was a descendant of Long Island farmers, he was also a citizen of the age of reason, an acquaintance and admirer of Tom Paine. Nor did Whitman himself develop his diction as Thoreau did, by the slow absorption through every pore of the folkways of a single spot of earth. He was attracted by the wider sweep of the city, and though his language is a natural product, it is the natural product of a Brooklyn journalist of the eighteen-forties who had previously been a country schoolteacher and a carpenter's helper and who had finally felt an irresistable impulse to be a poet.

Whitman as Symbolist

by Charles Feidelson, Jr.

"No one will get at my verses," Whitman declared, "who insists upon viewing them as a literary performance, or attempt at such performance, or as aiming mainly toward art or aestheticism." In his conscious literary theory literature is subordinate to sociology, "the United States themselves are essentially the greatest poem," the poet must "tally" the American scene, and the function of poetry is the creation of heroic citizens. Yet it is obvious that a larger principle governs both his poetic and his sociological doctrine; no one will get at his verses who insists upon viewing them as a sociological performance. Whitman intimates that the link between his poems and American life is actually a new method exemplified by both:

> One main contrast of the ideas behind every page of my verses, compared with establish'd poems, is their different relative attitude towards God, towards the objective universe, and still more (by reflection, confession, assumption, &c.) the quite changed attitude of the ego, the one chanting or talking, towards himself and towards his fellow-humanity. It is certainly time for America, above all, to begin this readjustment in the scope and basic point of view of verse; for everything else has changed.

The distinctive quality of Whitman's poetry depends on this change of standpoint. In his effort "to articulate and faithfully express . . . [his] own physical, emotional, moral, intellectual, and aesthetic Personality, in the midst of, and tallying, the momentous spirit and facts of its immediate days," his interest is not so much in the Personality or the environment *per se* as in the "changed attitude of the ego." The new method is better defined in the poems themselves than in the critical prose. The ego appears in the poems as a traveler and explorer, not as

"Whitman as Symbolist." Reprinted from *Symbolism and American Literature*, pp. 16-27, by Charles Feidelson, Jr., by permission of The University of Chicago Press. The title has been supplied by the editor. [Mr. Feidelson's essay is reprinted here, with his permission, without the notes which buttress and expand his argument. They are to be found on pp. 235-240 of *Symbolism and American Literature*.—R.H.P.]

a static observer; its object is "to know the universe itself as a road, as many roads, as roads for traveling souls." The shift of image from the contemplative eye of "establish'd poems" to the voyaging ego of Whitman's poetry records a large-scale theoretical shift from the categories of "substance" to those of "process." Whitman's "perpetual journey" is not analogous to a sight-seeing trip, though his catalogues might give that impression; the mind and the material world into which it ventures are not ultimately different in kind. Instead, what seems at first a penetration of nature by the mind is actually a process in which the known world comes into being. The "child who went forth every day, and who now goes, and will always go forth every day," is indistinguishable from the world of his experience: "The first object he look'd upon, that object he became, / And that object became part of him." The true voyage is the endless becoming of reality:

> Allons! to that which is endless as it was beginningless,
> To undergo much, tramp of days, rests of nights,
> To merge all in the travel they tend to, and the days and nights they
> tend to,
> Again to merge them in the start of superior journeys. . . .

Here there is no clear distinction among the traveler, the road, and the journey, for the journey is nothing but the progressive unity of the voyager and the lands he enters; perception, which unites the seer and the seen, is identical with the real process of becoming. God, in this context, is a "seething principle," and human society is a flow of "shapes ever projecting other shapes." Whitman's "readjustment in the scope and basic point of view of verse" is actually a transmutation of all supposed entities into events.

A poem, therefore, instead of referring to a completed act of perception, constitutes the act itself, both in the author and in the reader; instead of describing reality, a poem is a realization. When Whitman writes, "See, steamers steaming through my poems," he is admonishing both himself and his audience that no distinction can be made among themselves, the steamers, and the words. Indeed, no distinction can be made between the poet and the reader: "It is you talking just as much as myself, I act as the tongue of you." His new method was predicated not only on the sense of creative vision—itself a process which renders a world in process—but also, as part and parcel of that consciousness, on the sense of creative speech. The *I* of Whitman's poems speaks the world that he sees, and sees the world that he speaks, and does this by *becoming* the reality of his vision and of his words, in which the reader also participates. Most of Whitman's poems, more or less explicitly, are "voyages" in this metaphysical sense. This was Whitman's genre, his "new theory of literary composition for imaginative works." Even in the most personal lyrics of "Children of Adam" and "Calamus," the "one chanting or talking" is not simply the poet; the chant is neither pure self-expression nor pure description; what is talked about is oddly confused with the talker and the talking; and the audience is potentially both the subject and the writer. "Song of Myself," though it breathes the personal egotism of Whitman, makes sense as a whole only when the self is taken dramatically and identified with "the procreant urge of the world."

Consider the last four sections of "Starting from Paumanok"—the entire poem being the "Song of Myself" in miniature. Here at the end of the poem it appears that to start from Paumanok is to start far back of the speaker's birth in the opening line. The beginnings (of the speaker, of America, and of the world) are "aboriginal," as typified by the Indian name; the beginnings, indeed, by a leap of thought, become the perpetual genesis of "a world primal again," announced by the poet's voice. In the following section, with its images of incessant motion, the announcement itself is the genesis of the world; the voice is equated with the becoming of reality. Retrospectively, one sees that the preliminary statement of the poem—"Solitary, singing in the West, I strike up for a New World"—has ushered in a song which not only is addressed to and descriptive of America but also is the vehicle, at once product and creator, of a metaphysical "newness." In the course of the poem the solitary voice of the individual poet has expanded into the presence of an all-inclusive Word—"a word to clear one's path ahead endlessly." And the speaker's union with his hearer is imaged in the final section as the love relationship of "camerados" on the journey. The method of "Starting from Paumanok" does not palliate Whitman's diffuseness and arbitrary choice of material; rather, by depriving him of a static point of view, it is the immediate cause of these defects. Yet the principle behind this poem, the exploitation of Speech as the literary aspect of eternal process, is the source of whatever literary value resides in *Leaves of Grass.*

"This subject of language," Whitman confided to Horace Traubel, "interests me—interests me: I never quite get it out of my mind. I sometimes think the Leaves is only a language experiment." *An American Primer,* Whitman's fragmentary lecture on language, reveals a mind that fed upon words: "*Names* are magic.—One word can pour such a flood through the soul." The sense of language as inherently significant is his meeting ground with Hawthorne, for whom a "deep meaning . . . streamed forth" from the scarlet letter. In both cases attention is deflected from "ideas" and "objects" to a symbolic medium; and in both cases the perception of a meaningful symbol is opposed to another kind of perception, which Hawthorne calls "analysis." Hawthorne would like to reduce the meaning to the rational terms of logical construct or empirical fact; he is plainly uncomfortable at the disturbance of his "sensibilities." In practice, he not only translates symbolism into allegory but also affects a rational style which ties his language down to the common-sense world. Whitman's awareness of words in themselves is stronger, and he is militantly hostile to reason. He proposes "new law-forces of spoken and written language—not merely the pedagogue-forms, correct, regular, familiar with precedents, made for matters of outside propriety, fine words, thoughts definitely told out." He is indifferent to dictionary words and textbook grammar, which he associates with a barren formalism and externality. Fully accepting the intuition at which Hawthorne boggled, he takes his departure from a denial of conventional distinctions: "Strange and hard that paradox true I give, / Objects gross and the unseen soul are one." Since Whitman regards meaning as an activity of words rather than an external significance attached to them, language, together with the self and the material world, turns out to be a process, the pouring of the flood. "A perfect user of words uses things," while at the same time he *is* both the words and the things:

> Latent, in a great user of words, must actually be all passions, crimes, trades, animals, stars, God, sex, the past, might, space, metals, and the like—because these are the words, and he who is not these, plays with a foreign tongue, turning helplessly to dictionaries and authorities.

This kind of speech "seldomer tells a thing than suggests or necessitates it," because to "tell" something would be to suppose something outside the language. The reader is not given statements but is set in action, "on the assumption that the process of reading is not a half-sleep, but, in highest sense, an exercise, a gymnast's struggle." The poem necessarily works "by curious removes, indirections," rather than direct imitation of nature, since "the image-making faculty" runs counter to the habit of mind which views the material world as separable from ideas and speech. Whitman's running battle with the rational assumptions of conventional thought reaches its peak in the hyperbolical "Song of the Rolling Earth," where he identifies all "audible words" with the marks on the printed page and glorifies, by way of contrast, "the unspoken meanings of the earth." In deliberate paradox he asserts that true poems will somehow be made from these inaudible words. The poem expresses the bravado of his conscious attempt to create a wholly symbolic language in the face of intellectual convention. For that is his purpose: the "tallying" of things and man, to which he often alludes mysteriously, is simply the presence of language in each and the presence of each in language. The "language experiment" of *Leaves of Grass*—its promise of "new potentialities of speech"—depends on the symbolic status claimed by the book as a whole and in every part. "From the eyesight proceeds another eyesight and from the hearing proceeds another hearing and from the voice proceeds another voice eternally curious of the harmony of things with man."

The patent symbols of Whitman's best poem, "When Lilacs Last in the Dooryard Bloom'd," are conditioned by the thoroughgoing symbolism of his poetic attitude. As in most elegies, the person mourned is hardly more than the occasion of the work; but this poem, unlike *Lycidas* or *Adonais,* does not transmute the central figure merely by generalizing him out of all recognition. Lincoln is seldom mentioned either as a person or as a type. Instead, the focus of the poem is a presentation of the poet's mind at work in the context of Lincoln's death. If the true subject of *Lycidas* and *Adonais* is not Edward King or John Keats but the Poet, the true subject of Whitman's "Lilacs" is not the Poet but the poetic process. And even this subject is not treated simply by generalizing a particular situation. The act of poetizing and the context in which it takes place have continuity in time and space but no particular existence. Both are "ever-returning"; the tenses shift; the poet is in different places at once; and at the end this whole phase of creation is moving inexorably forward.

Within this framework the symbols behave like characters in a drama, the plot of which is the achievement of a poetic utterance. The spring, the constant process of rebirth, is threaded by the journey of the coffin, the constant process of death, and in the first section it presents the poet with twin symbols: the perennially blooming lilac and the drooping star. The spring also brings to the poet the "thought of him I love," in which the duality of life and death is repeated. The thought of the dead merges with the fallen star in Section 2; the thought of love merges with the life of the lilac, from which the poet breaks a sprig in Section 3. Thus the lilac and the star enter the poem not as objects to which the poet assigns a meaning but as elements in the undifferentiated stream of thoughts and things; and the spring, the real process of becoming, which involves the real process of dissolution, is also the genesis of poetic vision. The complete pattern of the poem is established with the advent of the bird in the fourth section. For here, in the song of the thrush, the lilac and star are united (the bird sings "death's outlet song of life"), and the potentiality of the poet's "thought" is intimated. The song of the bird and the thought of the poet, which also unites life and death, both lay claim to the third place in the "trinity" brought by spring; they are, as it were, the actuality and the possibility of poetic utterance, which reconciles opposite appearances.

The drama of the poem will be a movement from possible to actual poetic speech, as represented by the "tallying" of the songs of the poet and the thrush. Although it is a movement without steps, the whole being implicit in every moment, there is a graduation of emphasis. Ostensibly, the visions of the coffin and the star (Sections 5 through 8) delay the unison of poet and bird, so that full actualization is reserved for the end of the poem. On the other hand, the verse that renders the apparition of the coffin *is* "death's outlet song of life." The poetic act of evoking the dark journey is treated as the showering of death with lilac:

> Here, coffin that slowly passes,
> I give you my sprig of lilac. . . .
> Blossoms and branches green to coffins all I bring,
> For fresh as the morning, thus would I chant a song for you,
> O sane and sacred death.

Even as the poet lingers, he has attained his end. And the star of Section 8, the counterpart of the coffin, functions in much the same way. The episode that occurred "a month since"—when "my soul in its trouble dissatisfied sank, as where you sad orb, / Concluded, dropt in the night, and was gone"—was a failure of the poetic spring. The soul was united with the star but not with the lilac. Yet the passage is preceded by the triumphant statement, "Now I know what you must have meant," and knowledge issues in the ability to render the episode in verse. The perception of meaning gives life to the fact of death; the star meant the death of Lincoln, but the evolution of the meaning is poetry.

The recurrence of the song of the thrush in the following section and in Section 13 is a reminder of the poetic principle which underlies the entire poem. In a sense, the words, "I hear your notes, I hear your call," apply to all that precedes and all that is to come, for the whole poem, existing in an eternal present, is the "loud human song" of the poet's "brother." But again Whitman delays the consummation. He is "detained" from his rendezvous with the bird—although he really "hears" and "understands" all the time—by the sight of the "lustrous star" and by the "mastering odor" of the lilac. Since both the star and the lilac are inherent in the song of the bird, he actually lingers only in order to proceed. While the song rings in the background, the poet puts the questions presupposed by his own poetizing. How can the life of song be one with the fact of death?—"O how shall I warble myself for the dead one there I loved?" And what will be the content of the song of death?—"O what shall I hang on the chamber walls . . . / To adorn the burial-house of him I love?" The questions answer themselves. The breath by which the grave becomes part of his chant is the breath of life; within the poem the image of the "burial-house" will be overlaid with "pictures of growing spring." The delay has served only to renew the initial theme: the poet's chant, like the song of the thrush, is itself the genesis of life and therefore contains both life and death.

The final achievement of poetic utterance comes in Section 14, when the poet, looking forth on the rapid motion of life, experiences death. More exactly, he walks between the "thought" and the "knowledge" of death, which move beside him like companions. Just as his poem exists between the "thought" of the dead, which is paradoxically an act of life, and the actual knowledge of the bird's song, which embodies both dying star and living lilac, the poet himself is in motion from the potential to the actual. From this point to the end of the poem, the sense of movement never flags. The poet's flight into the darkness is a fusion with the stream of music from the bird:

> And the charm of the carol rapt me,
> As I held as if by their hands my comrades in the night,
> And the voice of my spirit tallied the song of the bird.

As the motion of the poet is lost in the motion of the song, the latter is identified with the "dark mother always gliding near," and in the "floating" carol death itself becomes the movement of waves that "undulate round the world." In effect, poet and bird, poem and song, life and death, are now the sheer process of the carol; as in "Out of the Cradle Endlessly Rocking," reality is the unfolding Word. The presented song merges into the "long panoramas of visions" in Section 15, and then the inexorable process begins to leave this moment behind:

> Passing the visions, passing the night,
> Passing, unloosing the hold of my comrades' hands,
> Passing the song of the hermit bird and the tallying song
> of my soul. . . .
> Passing, I leave thee lilac with heart-shaped leaves, . . .
> I cease from my song for thee, . . .
> O comrade lustrous with silver face in the night.

But the poetic activity is continuous; the passing-onward is not a rejection of the old symbols. "Lilac and star and bird twined with the chant of . . . [the] soul" also pass onward because they are activities and not finite things. The conclusion of this poem dramatizes what Whitman once stated of *Leaves of Grass* as a whole—that the book exists as "a passage way to something rather than a thing in itself concluded." Taken seriously, in the sense in which there *can* be no "thing in itself concluded," this notion is not, as Whitman sometimes pretended, a mere excuse for haphazard technique but the rationale of a symbolistic method.

Yet "When Lilacs Last in the Dooryard Bloom'd" is a successful poem only because it does not fully live up to the theory which it both states and illustrates. The poem really presupposes a static situation, which Whitman undertakes to treat as though it were dynamic; in the course of the poem the death of Lincoln, of which we always remain aware, is translated into Whitman's terms of undifferentiated flow. His other long poems generally lack this stabilizing factor. Whatever the nominal subject, it is soon lost in sheer "process"; all roads lead into the "Song of Myself," in which the bare Ego interacts with a miscellaneous world. The result is Whitman's characteristic disorder and turgidity. When the subject is endless, any form becomes arbitrary. While the antirational conception of a poem as the realization of language gives a new freedom and a new dignity to poetry, it apparently leads to an aimlessness from which the poem can be rescued only by returning to rational categories. Otherwise, the best that can be expected from Whitman's poetic principle is the "long varied train of an emblem, dabs of music,/Fingers of the organist skipping staccato over the keys of the great organ."

And much worse can be expected. In the last section of "Passage to India," Whitman's most deliberate statement of the process theory, the tone is frenetic even for him:

> Sail forth—steer for the deep waters only,
> Reckless O soul, exploring, I with thee, and thou with me,
> For we are bound where mariner has not yet dared to go,
> And we will risk the ship, ourselves and all.

What begins in Emerson as a mild contravention of reason—a peaceful journey "to some frontier as yet unvisited by the elder voyagers"—becomes in Whitman a freedom from all "limits and imaginary lines,"

> . . . from all formules!
> From your formules, O bat-eyed and materialistic priests.

Thus the looseness of form in Whitman's verse is not merely a technical defect; it is the counterpart of an intellectual anarchism designed to overthrow conventional reality by dissolving all rational order. Moreover, like Hawthorne in the malarial gardens of Rome, Whitman has his *frisson* at this inversion of established values—and without Hawthorne's reservations: "I know my words are weapons full of danger, full of death, / For I confront peace, security, and all the settled laws, to unsettle them." Mixed with the obtrusive health of the "Calamus" poems is a daredevil flouting of convention:

> The way is suspicious, the result uncertain, perhaps destructive, . . .
> The whole past theory of your life and all conformity to the lives
>   around you would have to be abandon'd, . . .
> Nor will my poems do good only, they will do just as much evil,
>   perhaps more. . . .

Nowadays we are too much in the habit of blaming "romanticism" for any irrationality in literature. Certainly the romantic spirit was enamored of a fluid reality, which could not be contained in the old channels, and the romantic often opened the dikes deliberately, just to see what would happen. The Voyager is a romantic figure, the ocean a romantic realm. Yet a distinction is in order. The antirationalism of the romantic voyage is a wilful projection of feeling; the romantic sea is the image of a world subservient to emotion. But the symbolistic voyage is a process of becoming: Whitman is less concerned with exploration of emotion than with exploration as a mode of existence. Similarly, his poems not only are *about* voyaging but also enact the voyage, so that their content (the image of the metaphysical journey) is primarily a reflection of their literary method, in which the writer and his subject become part of the stream of language. It follows that Whitman's hostility to reason has another, more complicated source than the romantic vision of a world suffused with feeling. Like Emerson, he finds the antonym of reason not in emotion but in the "symbolical"; like Hawthorne and Melville, he contrasts "analysis" with "meaning," arithmetic with "significance." For his object is not so much to impose a new form on the world as to adopt a new stance in which the world takes on new shapes. His difficulty is that his method works too well: the shapes proliferate endlessly, and, having deprived himself of an external standpoint, he has no means of controlling them. On the other hand, the occasional violence of his antirationalism is the result of an opposite difficulty: while he would like to be sublimely indifferent to established distinctions, reason fights back as he seeks to transcend it, and he is forced into the position of the iconoclast.

Whitman's Style: From Mysticism to Art

by Roger Asselineau

Emerson one day confided to a friend that *Leaves of Grass* reminded him at one time of the *Bhagavad-Gita* and the *New York Herald.*[1] Its style is indeed most incongruous. Lyrical flights are to be found side by side with prosaic banalities, mystical effusions with the most familiar expressions from the spoken language. Sometimes Whitman transcribes an everyday scene with extreme simplicity and the greatest transparence:

> The little one sleeps in its cradle,
> I lift the gauze and look a long time, and silently brush away flies with my hand.[2*]

Sometimes he heaps up abstract words interminably with an enthusiasm which the reader does not always share:

> Great is Liberty! great is Equality! . . .
> Great is Youth—equally great is Old Age . . .
> Great is Wealth—great is Poverty—great is Expression—great is Silence. . . .[3]

"Whitman's Style: From Mysticism to Art." From *L'Evolution de Walt Whitman* (Paris, 1954), pp. 478-492. Translated by Roger Asselineau and Burton L. Cooper.

[1] See Bliss Perry, *Walt Whitman* (1906), p. 276, n. 1.

[2] *LG 1855*, p. 17; *Inc. Ed.*, p. 30; "Song of Myself," §8, ll. 1-2.

* ABBREVIATIONS USED IN THE NOTES: *AL* = *American Literature; CW* = *The Complete Writings of Walt Whitman* (New York, 1902), 10 vols.; *CP* = *The Complete Prose of Walt Whitman*, ed. M. Cowley (New York, 1948); *FC* = *Faint Clews and Indirections*, ed. C. Gohdes and R. Silver (Durham, N. C., 1949); *Inc. Ed.* = *Leaves of Grass, Inclusive Edition*, ed. E. Holloway (New York, 1927); *LG* = *Leaves of Grass; N & F* = *Notes and Fragments*, ed. R. M. Bucke (London, Ontario, 1899); *SD* = *Specimen Days; SPL* = Walt Whitman, *Complete Verse, Selected Prose and Letters*, ed. E. Holloway (London, 1921), 2 vols.; *Uncoll. PP* = *The Uncollected Poetry and Prose of Walt Whitman*, coll. and ed. E. Holloway (New York, 1921), 2 vols.; *With WW in C* = Horace Traubel, *With Walt Whitman in Camden*, 4 vols.; *WWW* = *Walt Whitman's Workshop*, ed. C. J. Furness (Cambridge, 1928).

[3] *LG 1855*, p. 93; *Inc. Ed.*, p. 465; "Great Are the Myths," §1, ll. 4, 7-8.

Even more, the same verse sometimes brings these two clashing elements together:

> I concentrate toward them that are nigh, I wait on the door-slab.[4]

Too often one passes without transition from the loose, woolly, pretentious language of the journalist who pads his text with big words to the rapid and precise evocation of a concrete detail. It even happens that his best passages are spoiled by the brusque intrusion of a learned word in a very simple context:

> The field-sprouts of Fourth-month and Fifth-month became
> part of him.
> Winter-grain sprouts and those of the light-yellow corn and the *esculent roots* of the garden. . . .[5] [Italics mine.]

The same jarring note is sometimes produced by the unexpected use of a slang term:

> The spotted hawk swoops by and accuses me, he complains of my *gab* and my loitering.[6] [Italics mine.]

Thus, most often, the different stylistic elements, instead of being used separately and kept free from all admixture, enter into complex combinations. The concrete passages, in particular, are not always the realistic and perfectly objective little pictures of the sort which we have quoted above. Habitually, the mind of the poet diffuses its own divinity over the void of the external world;[7] grass is not that inert substance which a child carries to him in his fist, but "the flag of [his] disposition, out of hopeful green stuff woven." [8] His sensibility and, all the more, his sensuality often modify the image of things which he gives to us.

> Smile O voluptuous cool-breath'd earth!
> Earth of slumbering and liquid trees . . .

[4] *LG 1855*, p. 55; *Inc. Ed.*, p. 75; "Song of Myself," §51, l. 9.

[5] *LG 1855*, p. 90; *Inc. Ed.*, p. 306; "There was a child went forth," l. 12.

[6] *LG 1855*, p. 55; *Inc. Ed.*, p. 75; "Song of Myself," §52, l. 1. An earlier draft of the passage (p. 583) shows that originally Whitman used a perfectly normal and homogeneous vocabulary and that the introduction of a slang word was therefore conscious and deliberate. When, on the contrary, he introduces a pretentious word into a simple context, he does so inadvertently.

[7] "The mountains, rivers, forests and the elements that gird them round about would be only blank conditions of matter if the mind did not fling its own divinity around them." A sentence in an article entitled "Imagination and Fact" which had appeared in *Graham's Magazine*. Whitman wrote in the margin: "This I think is one of the most indicative sentences I ever read." *CW*, VI, p. 53.

[8] *LG 1855*, p. 16; *Inc. Ed.*, p. 28; "Song of Myself," §6, ll. 3.

> Earth of the vitreous pour of the full moon just tinged with blue. . . .[9]

Matter then is dissolved; trees become liquid and contours fluid (these two adjectives *liquid* and *fluid* recur frequently in his verse). One is witness to a mysterious transmutation of the real in which his imagination also intervenes.[10] For Whitman is not content with what he has before his eyes; he wants to evoke, to imply as it were, all the rest of the world, the infinity of space and the "amplitude of time."[11] He soon abandons the stallion whose beauty and dash so much impressed him:

> I but use a moment and then I resign you stallion—and do not need your paces, and outgallop them,
> And myself as I stand or sit pass faster than you.[12]

Hence cosmic visions of this sort:

> My ties and ballasts leave me, I travel—I sail—my elbows rest in sea-gaps,
> I skirt sierras, my palms cover continents . . .
> I fly those flights of a fluid and swallowing soul,
> My course runs below the soundings of plummets. . . .[13]

He is transformed into a comet and travels round the universe with the speed of light:

> I depart as air, I shake my white locks at the runaway sun,
> I effuse my flesh in eddies, drift it in lacy jags.[14]

This dissolution of himself and this fluidity of the world permit the boldest and most unexpected images:

> My foothold is tenon'd and mortis'd in granite . . .[15]
> . . . a leaf of grass is no less than the jouney-work of the stars . . .
> . . . [I] am stucco'd with quadrupeds and birds all over . . .[16]
> . . . the sobbing liquid of life. . . .[17]

[9] *LG 1855*, p. 27; *Inc. Ed.*, p. 41; "Song of Myself," §21, ll. 17, 18, 20.

[10] See *The Evolution of Walt Whitman* (Paris, 1954), Volume II, Part II, Chapter IV.

[11] *LG 1855*, p. 27; *Inc. Ed.*, p. 41; "Song of Myself," §20, l. 33.

[12] *LG 1855*, p. 35; *Inc. Ed.*, p. 571; "Song of Myself," §32, variant reading of ll. 24-26.

[13] *LG 1855*, p. 35; *Inc. Ed.*, p. 51; "Song of Myself," §33, ll. 5-6 and p. 55, ll. 91-92.

[14] *LG 1855*, p. 56; *Inc. Ed.*, p. 76; "Song of Myself," §52, ll. 7-8.

[15] *LG 1855*, p. 26; *Inc. Ed.*, p. 41; "Song of Myself," §20, l. 31.

[16] *LG 1855*, p. 34; *Inc. Ed.*, p. 50; "Song of Myself," §31, ll. 1, 9.

[17] *LG 1855*, p. 47; *Inc. Ed.*, p. 65; "Song of Myself," §42, l. 15.

The complexity and the discords of his style are not due solely to his lack of education and to his habits as a journalist, they derive also from the duality of his point of view on the world. Sometimes he places himself on the plane of the senses and describes the visible in simple and direct terms; sometimes, as a mystic, he transcends physical appearances and tries to suggest the invisible. As he himself says:

> I help myself to material and immaterial. . . .[18]

Thus is explained the co-existence in his work of descriptive passages and of somewhat obscure lines where he tried to express the inexpressible and translate those mysterious hieroglyphics which all material objects were in his eyes.[19] The problem of the inexpressible haunted him:

> There is something that comes to one now and perpetually,
> It is not what is printed, preach'd, discussed, it eludes discussion and print . . .
> It is for you whoever you are, it is no farther from you than your hearing and sight are from you,
> It is hinted by nearest, commonest, readiest, it is ever provoked by them . . .[20]
> I do not know it—it is without name—it is a word unsaid,
> It is not in any dictionary, utterance, symbol. . . .[21]

How can one resolve this insoluble problem? A frontal attack is impossible. One can only approach it indirectly. And that is precisely what Whitman does. As early as 1855 he understood that in order to evoke "transcendent" reality he had to be "indirect and not direct or descriptive or epic"[22] (what Paul Claudel calls "la divine loi de l'expression détournée"):

> I swear, he said the following year, I see what is better than to tell the best,
> It is always to leave the best untold.[23]

And, in 1860, defining the "laws for creation," he formulated this precept:

[18] *LG 1855*, p. 38; *Inc. Ed.*, p. 55; "Song of Myself," §33, l. 93.

[19] *LG 1855*, p. 16; *Inc. Ed.*, p. 28; "Song of Myself," §6, l. 8.

[20] *LG 1855*, p. 59; *Inc. Ed.*, pp. 180-181; "A Song for Occupations," §2, ll. 17-18, 20-21.

[21] *LG 1855*, p. 55; *Inc. Ed.*, p. 74; "Song of Myself," §50, ll. 4-5.

[22] Preface to 1855 Edition, *Inc. Ed.*, p. 491.

[23] *LG 1856*, "Poem of the Sayers of the Words of the Earth," p. 329; *Inc. Ed.*, p. 190; "A Song of the Rolling Earth," §3, ll. 13-14. See *American Primer*, p. 21: ". . . in manners, poems, orations, music, friendship, authorship, what is not said is just as important as what is said, and holds just as much meaning."

> There shall be no subject too pronounced—all works shall illustrate the divine law of indirections.[24]

So, instead of saying, he must suggest[25]—not by means of the music of his verse, as the symbolists tried to do later—it never for a moment occurred to him—but by means of images since "the unseen is proved by the seen." [26] This may lead to a certain obscurity, but a poem must be a beginning and not an end and it belongs to the reader to take up the poet's suggestions and to finish it.[27] In short, Whitman defined here beforehand the fundamental principles of symbolism; and he was still more explicit in *Specimen Days:* "The play of imagination with the sensuous objects of Nature for symbols, and Faith . . . make up the curious chess-game of a poem. . . ." [28] These ideas were not altogether new; they had already broken through in the subjective theories of the romantics and the transcendentalists,[29] but no one had yet applied them

[24] *LG 1860,* "Chants Democratic" no. 13, p. 185 (2); *Inc. Ed.,* p. 324; "Laws for Creation," l. 5.

[25] "The words I myself put primarily for the description of them (*Leaves of Grass*) as they stand at last, is the word Suggestiveness. I round and finish little if anything; and could not, consistently with my scheme. The reader will always have his or her part to do, just as much as I have mine." "A Backward Glance O'er Travel'd Roads," *Inc. Ed.*, p. 531.

[26] *LG 1855,* p. 14; *Inc. Ed.*, p. 26; "Song of Myself," §3, l. 16.

[27] "A great poem is no finish to a man or woman but rather a beginning." Preface to 1855 Edition, *Inc. Ed.*, p. 505.

[28] "After Trying a Certain Book," *SD,* p. 198; *CP,* p. 196.

[29] Emerson had already used the word *indirection.* See F. O. Matthiessen, *American Renaissance,* p. 57. But Whitman may have borrowed it from Shakespeare: see *Hamlet,* II, 1, l. 66: "By indirections find directions out." As to the romantics, Whitman was quite aware of what he owed to them. In "Poetry To-Day in America" (*SD,* p. 249; *CP,* p. 301), he founds his principle of indirect expression in a quotation from Sainte-Beuve. On the other hand, he had underlined the following passages in an article on *The Princess* by Tennyson bearing the date 1848: ". . . the highest art, which is chiefly dependent for its effect upon suggestion, is by no means universally appreciated, as mere skillful imitation is. . . ." "A poet, by becoming openly didactic, would deprive his work of that essential quality of suggestiveness by which activity on the part of the reader is absolutely demanded. . . ."

In an article entitled "Thoughts on Reading," he had underlined the following passages which seem to have exerted a certain influence on his thought: ". . . it is not the idleness with which we read, but the very intensity of labor which our reading calls forth, that does us good. . . . *To think* ourselves into error, is far better than *to sleep* ourselves into truth. . . ." (Cf. this passage in *Democratic Vistas, SD,* p. 257; *CP,* p. 258: "Books are to be call'd for, and supplied, on the assumption that the process of reading is not half-asleep, but, in highest sense, an exercise, a gymnast's struggle. . . .") "An author enriches us not so much by giving us his ideas as by unfolding in us the same powers that originated in them. Reading, in short, if it be truly such, and not a mere imparted drowsiness, involves a development of the same activities, and voluntary reproduction of the same states of mind, of which the author was subject in writing." Articles listed in the *Catalogue of the Walt Whitman Collection in the Duke University Library* (1945), p. 78. The very fact that Whitman always kept these articles with him shows how deeply attached he was to the ideas

with as much audacity as Whitman and no poet before him had dared to express his joie de vivre by means of an image as "indirect" as this:

> As God comes a loving bed-fellow and sleeps at my side all night and
> close on the peep of the day,
> And leaves for me baskets covered with white towels, swelling the
> house with their plenty.[30]

We have here, it is true, an extreme case where the oneiric character of the evocation and the gratuitousness of the associations almost announce surrealism. Whitman, in general, was reluctant to go in that direction. Comparing himself to Blake about 1868-1870 in an essay which he never had occasion to publish, he wrote:

> Blake's visions grow to be the rule, displace the normal condition, fill the field, spurn this visible, objective life, & seat the subjective spirit on an absolute throne, wilful & uncontrolled. But Whitman, though he occasionally prances off . . . always holds the mastery over himself, &, even in his most intoxicated lunges or pirouettes, never once loses control, or even equilibrium." [31]

The passing from the objective to the subjective plane is thus deliberate and conscious with him, and conscious, too, is his care never to lose contact with objective reality. One is reminded of Wordsworth's skylark which, unlike Shelley's, never forgets in the midst of her wild flight that she has left her nest on the earth; however much Whitman launched his "yawp" over the rooftops of the world, his feet remained firmly planted on the ground.[32]

---

which were developed in them and which he undeniably adopted. He had also underlined in an article from the *American Whig Review* for Jan. 1846 and entitled "A Socratic Dialogue on Phrenology" the following sentence: "We agreed, O Phidias, that it is impossible to speak otherwise than mystically and symbolically concerning the spirit of man." (*Catalogue* . . . p. 75.) The dates of two of these articles show that his thought had already taken this course nearly ten years before the first edition of *Leaves of Grass*. Even while he was writing conventional poems, he was already thinking of another form of art.

[30] *LG 1855*, p. 15; *Inc. Ed.*, p. 554; "Song of Myself," §3, variant reading of ll. 23-24. The passage was later made even more indirect by the suppression of the word *God*.

[31] *FC*, p. 53.

[32] The study of the evolution of Whitman's imagery would reveal nothing special. The drafts which preceded the 1855 text show the chaotic profusion of the original images, but, as early as the first edition, Whitman had to some extent succeeded in simplifying and controlling them. They were never again to be as luxuriant and confused (except in "Calamus" and "Children of Adam" where he purposely took refuge in obscurity in order to tone down the boldness of his subject). This process of clarification and simplification went on during all his career. As a result, at the end of his life, Whitman wrote only very short poems built round a single image. To the last therefore images persisted in his poetry, but they lost in power what they gained in clarity.

The most felicitous passages of *Leaves of Grass* are thus those in which Whitman has succeeded in fusing the diverse elements of his style, those in which he suggests rather than describes and soars rather than trudges through interminable objective catalogues, those, too, in which he takes flight but does not get lost in the clouds. His expression is effective whenever he manages to interweave abstractions and familiar terms as in:

> I believe in those wing'd purposes. . . .[33]

or in:

> Agonies are one of my changes of garments.[34]

These unexpected combinations give a new vigor to his style. But he fails every time he lets one of these elements prevail over the others, notably when he falls into didacticism and preaches in abstract terms his democratic gospel or his personal religion:

> There can be any number of supremes—one does not countervail another any more than one eyesight countervails another, or one life countervails another.
> All is eligible to all . . .[35]
> How plenteous! how spiritual! how résumé! [36]

he went so far as to say in 1860.

Such are the characteristics of Whitman's style in the first two editions of *Leaves of Grass;* but we might have drawn our examples from later editions as well, for until the end his qualities and his faults remained the same. "Grand Is the Seen" written at the end of his career is the exact counterpart of "Great Are the Myths" published in 1855.[37] Is that to say that he made no progress in the interval? Not at all. From 1856 to 1881 he gave himself up to a patient labour of revision of his work which was not in vain and which reveals an increasingly fine artistic sense.[38] Matthiessen claims that these corrections are disconcerting and

[33] *LG 1855,* p. 20; *Inc. Ed.,* p. 34; "Song of Myself," §13, l. 15.

[34] *LG 1855,* p. 39; *Inc. Ed.,* p. 56; "Song of Myself," §33, l. 136.

[35] "Poem of Many in One," *LG 1856,* p. 181; *Inc. Ed.,* p. 287; "By Blue Ontario's Shore," §3, ll. 2-3.

[36] "Leaves of Grass" no. 15, *LG 1860,* p. 234; *Inc. Ed.,* p. 377; "Night on the Prairies," l. 7.

[37] "Great Are the Myths" (1855), *Inc. Ed.,* pp. 465-467; "Grand Is the Seen" (1891), *ibid.,* p. 457.

[38] Killis Campbell is of the same opinion; see his article on "The Evolution of Whitman as an Artist," *AL* VI (Nov. 1934), 254-263. See also Rebecca Coy, "A study of Whitman's Diction," *University of Texas Studies in English,* XVI (Jul. 1936), 115-124.

cannot always be justified,[39] but we do not share his opinion on this point. If some of them appear useless, most of them serve a purpose and can be vindicated.

First of all, as we have pointed out,[40] Whitman in growing old understood that it had been maladroit and tasteless to shock his readers by introducing crude details in contexts where one would not expect to find them. So, without really renouncing his poems which had a sexual inspiration, he gradually eliminated from the others such verses as:

> Have you sucked the nipples of the breasts of the mother of many children? [41]

and:

> And have an unseen something to be in contact with them also.[42]

The first of these lines was suppressed in 1860, that is to say the very year when he added "Calamus" and "Children of Adam" to *Leaves of Grass*.

He very soon also tried to avoid the monotony of certain repetitions and notably coordinating conjunctions which he had over-used in the first edition. Numerous are the *and*'s and the *or*'s which disappeared in 1856.[43] Later he got rid of the *O*'s, realizing that that was a little too facile a method for a lyric take-off. As early as 1867 he suppressed "Apostroph," where they swarmed,[44] and eliminated many others in 1881, in particular in "Out of the Cradle Endlessly Rocking," where one critic in 1860 had counted thirty-five of them.[45] It had taken Whitman twenty

[39] *American Renaissance,* p. 531.

[40] See *The Evolution of Walt Whitman, op. cit.,* Volume I, Chapter VII, pp. 196-198 and Chapter IX, pp. 239-240.

[41] "By Blue Ontario's Shore," *Inc. Ed.,* p. 662, §12, the line which originally followed line 17.

[42] "The Sleepers," *Inc. Ed.,* p. 684, §7, the line which originally followed line 3. The suppression was made in 1881.

[43] Here is a list of some of these suppressions:
"Song of Myself," *Inc. Ed.,* p. 562, §20, ll. 11-12; p. 572, §33, ll. 43, 46-47, 126; p. 573, §34, l. 11; p. 576, §39, ll. 7, 9; p. 578, §42, ll. 19-20; "I Sing the Body Electric," p. 586, l. 24. All these suppressions date back to 1856.

[44] The dispersion in 1867 of "Chants Democratic" to which "Apostroph" served as an introduction in 1860 may have been another reason for suppressing this poem.

[45] See for instance *Inc. Ed.,* p. 638, l. 128. The poem was violently criticized in the *Cincinnati Commercial* when it appeared: "The poem goes on in the same maudlin manner, for a hundred lines or more, in which the interjection 'O' is employed about five and thirty times." The critic then quoted the line: "O I fear it is henceforth chaos!" and treacherously added: "There is no doubt of it, we do assure you." Whitman printed this article in his *Leaves of Grass Imprints,* 1860, p. 59. He also suppressed numerous *O's* in "A Song of Joys"; see *Inc. Ed.,* pp. 610-611 the lines which originally owed ll. 6, 31, etc.

years to come round to his view. Generally speaking, he attempted to remove all the repetitions which had no expressive value and whose monotony weighted his verse, particularly all the useless *I*'s which came after coordinating conjunctions,[46] as well as the numerous *I swear*'s which in fact added nothing.[47] He also cut out a number of awkward lines of this sort:

> A breed whose testimony is behaviour.[48]

or:

> If you would be better than all that has ever been before, come listen to me and I will tell you,

which in 1867 became:

> If you would be freer than all that has been before come listen to me.[49]

He also suppressed a number of colloquial phrases the incongruity of which in certain passages he now perceived. Thus it was that in 1867 he no longer retained "plenty of them" at the end of the following line:

> If you remember your foolish and outlaw'd deeds, do you think I cannot remember my own foolish and outlaw'd deeds? [50]

"You mean devil" similarly disappeared from "Myself and Mine."[51] The Prince of Wales who had been democratically hailed as "sweet boy" in 1860, became "young prince" in 1881.[52] In "The Centenarian's Story" he avoided the colloquial usage of *good* as an adverb,[53] and in 1871 he eliminated from "Crossing Brooklyn Ferry" "Bully for you!" and *Blab, blush, lie, steal* which were undoubtedly very expressive, but which he now considered too slangy.[54] In 1881 he redoubled his severity with himself and suppressed not only these youthful lines from "Song of Myself":

[46] See for instance "Starting from Paumanok," *Inc. Ed.*, p. 551, §11, ll. 17, 19; p. 549, §5.

[47] See for instance "A Song of the Rolling Earth," *Inc. Ed.*, p. 613, §3, l. 10 and §4, second stanza.

[48] "By Blue Ontario's Shore," *Inc. Ed.*, p. 657, §2, l. 4.

[49] *Ibid.*, p. 658, §4, l. 11. For similar changes, see "Passage to India," *ibid.*, p. 653, §15, l. 6 and §16, l. 1.

[50] "A Song for Occupations," *Inc. Ed.*, p. 622, §1, l. 17.

[51] *Ibid.*, p. 633, l. 14; a correction made in 1867.

[52] "Years of Meteors," p. 634, l. 11.

[53] *Ibid.*, p. 607, §9, the line which preceded line 7 of "Terminus."

[54] *Ibid.*, p. 607, §9, the line which followed lines 5 and 7.

> That life is a suck and a sell, and nothing remains in the end but threadbare crape and tears.
> Washes and razors for foofoos—for me freckles and a bristling beard.[55]

but also these playful lines which he had composed in 1871 to amuse his audience at the American Institute Exhibition:

> She comes! this famous Female [the Muse]—as was indeed to be expected;
> (For who, so ever youthful, 'cute and handsome would wish to stay in mansions such as those . . .
> With all the fun that's going—and all the best society?).[56]

But all his corrections did not have such a negative character. He profited from this minute labour of revision to render his text more expressive and to choose his words with more care. In particular he ridded himself of a number of catch-all adjectives like *wondrous* or *mystic*,[57] either suppressing them completely, or replacing them by less vague and more appropriate epithets. Thus, "the mystic midnight" became "the vacant midnight"[58] and "my insolent poems" was changed in 1881 into "my arrogant poems," which is certainly more appropriate.[59] In "To Think of Time," speaking in the name of the dead, he had at first written:

> To think of all these wonders of city and country and . . . we taking small interest in them. . . .

but even *small* was exaggerated and he replaced it later with *no*. He had in the same way rather imprudently qualified the trot of the horses of a hearse as *rapid*; after 1860 he contented himself with *steady*.[60]

Sometimes he introduced colour adjectives to enhance the descriptive passages. For example, he added the entire line:

> Scarlet and blue and snowy white,

[55] *Ibid.*, p. 561, §20, the line which followed line 7 and p. 563, the line which followed line 16.

[56] "Song of the Exposition," *Ibid.*, p. 619, §3, the line which followed line 3.

[57] See for instance "As I Ebb'd with the Ocean of Life," *Inc. Ed.*, p. 639, §3, l. 16 ("the wondrous murmuring" became "the murmuring" in 1871) and "When Lilacs Last in the Dooryard Bloom'd," p. 654, the line which followed line 2 and contained the adjective *mystic* was suppressed in 1881. See also "Out of the Cradle Endlessly Rocking," *ibid.*, p. 637, l. 132.

[58] "The Artilleryman's Vision," *Inc. Ed.*, p. 651, l. 2.

[59] "As I Ebb'd with the Ocean of Life," *ibid.*, p. 639, §2, l. 11.

[60] *Inc. Ed.*, p. 685, §3, l. 2 and §4, l. 7.

to "Cavalry Crossing a Ford,"[61] and appended the complementary indication "yellow-flower'd" to the rather uninteresting mention of a cotton wood in a Southern landscape.[62] Almost everywhere dull and banal expressions gave place to more expressive words. Whereas in 1867 he merely "sang" on the shores of Lake Ontario, in 1881 he "thrill'd."[63] "The English pluck" of John Paul Jones's adversaries later became "the surly English pluck," which is indeed a very apt phrase.[64]

Certain lines were thus completely transformed, like:

> Alone, held by the eternal self of me that threatens to get the better of me, and stifle me,

which was, in 1881, changed to:

> Held by this electric self out of the pride of which I utter poems.[65]

The poetic charge of the second version is singularly higher; it is magnetized, as it were, by the introduction of the adjective *electric*. "I hear American mouthsongs" was flat and awkward; it became "I hear America singing" in 1867 and the line now really sings.[66]

He also added some images here and there, for example the line "Thou but the apples, long, long, a-growing" to "Thou Mother with Thy Equal Brood,"[67] and realizing the evocative power of the historical present he substituted it for the preterite in some stories like that of the seafight between Bonhomme Richard and an English frigate.[68] All these corrections liberated the latent energy of many passages.

But he turned his attention more particularly to titles and first lines and it was there that he obtained the most spectacular results. While in 1856 all his titles were of a depressing monotony and an annoying clumsiness—"Poem of Walt Whitman, an American," "Poem of the Daily Work of the Workmen and the Workwomen of These States," "Poem of the Heart of the Son of Manhattan Island," "Poem of the Last Explanation of Prudence," "Poem of the Propositions of Nakedness"—and in 1860 were not much better since most of the poems were simply numbered, in 1867 he did his best to find picturesque titles. Thus,

[61] "Cavalry Crossing a Ford," *Inc. Ed.*, p. 649, l. 6. See also "Thou Mother with Thy Equal Brood," *ibid.*, pp. 379 and 691, §2, l. 10.

[62] "Song of Myself," *Inc. Ed.*, p. 571, §33, l. 17.

[63] "By Blue Ontario's Shore," *Inc. Ed.*, p. 666, §19, l. 3.

[64] "Song of Myself," *Inc. Ed.*, p. 574, §35, l. 5.

[65] "As I Ebb'd with the Ocean of Life," *Inc. Ed.*, pp. 216, 638-639, §1, ll. 7 and 17.

[66] *Inc. Ed.*, p. 545.

[67] *Ibid.*, pp. 380, 691, §3, l. 12. See also "Out of the Cradle Endlessly Rocking," *ibid.*, pp. 215, 638, l. 182.

[68] "Song of Myself," *Inc. Ed.*, p. 574, §35, *passim*. See also "Camps of Green," *ibid.*, p. 701, l. 21.

"Proto-Leaf," a barbarous expression, was replaced by "Starting from Paumanok" which is concrete and dynamic, and the former "Poem of Walt Whitman, an American" became in 1881, after many metamorphoses, "Song of Myself," a title which admirably sums up its central theme. The "Poem of the Body" which originally began with:

> The bodies of men and women engirth me and I engirth them . . .[69]

started in 1867 with:

> I sing the body electric . . .

which is singularly more promising. It was that year that he found the title of "One Hour of Madness and Joy,"[70] of "Trickle-Drops,"[71] of "On the Beach at Night Alone."[72] But it was only later and after much searching that he arrived at "As I ebb'd with the ocean of life,"[73] "By Blue Ontario's Shore,"[74] "Aboard at a Ship's Helm,"[75] "Out of the Cradle Endlessly Rocking,"[76] "A Song of the Rolling Earth,"[77] etc.

He also took great care in rounding off certain lines whose ends seemed too abrupt—especially, it appears, while preparing the 1881 edition. Thus,

> You shall sit in the middle well-poised thousands of years,

became:

> You shall sit in the middle well-pois'd thousands and thousands of years. . . .[78]

and in the poem entitled "I was looking a long while" the last line:

> All for the average man of to-day,

[69] *LG 1855*, p. 77; "I Sing the Body Electric," *Inc. Ed.*, p. 584.
[70] *Ibid.*, p. 589.
[71] *Ibid.*, p. 594.
[72] *Ibid.*, p. 641. This title was merely the first line in 1867.
[73] *Ibid.*, p. 638. Title added in 1881.
[74] *Ibid.*, p. 656. Title added in 1881.
[75] *Ibid.*, p. 640. Title added in 1871. In 1881 he made an interesting change in line 3. He had originally written in 1867: "A bell through fog on a sea-coast dolefully ringing, An ocean-bell . . ." In 1881, he cut out "A bell," so that we now deal with a raw sensation gradually worked into a perception.
[76] *Inc. Ed.*, p. 636. In 1860 the first line was: "Out of the rocked cradle," but the rhythm was not smooth enough and it was only in 1871 that the line received its present shape.
[77] *Inc. Ed.*, p. 630. Title added in 1881.
[78] "A Broadway Pageant," *Inc. Ed.*, pp. 208, 636, §3, l. 2.

which lacked force and vividness, was changed to:

> All for the modern—all for the average man of to-day,[79]

which is at once more rhythmical and more vehement. Whitman, moreover, took pains not only with his titles and with the ends of lines but also with the ends of his poems. In particular, he added to "A Farm Picture" a last line which has a most happy effect and enlarges to infinity what was originally only a rather banal vignette.[80] And, what was an even more characteristic correction, he introduced into his longer poems, like "Song of Myself," either at the beginning or at the end of the different sections, lines destined to be used, according to the individual instance, as an introduction or a conclusion, in order to prepare the transitions and reinforce the cohesiveness of the whole.[81] In other words, he became increasingly mindful of form.[82]

At the same time, in proportion as his inspiration lost its force, he tended more and more to be content with very short poems for which no problem of composition existed. He had already used this formula as early as 1865 in *Drum-Taps* where he had included a number of short descriptive poems like "A Farm Picture," "Cavalry Crossing a Ford," "By the Bivouac's Fitful Flame," "The Torch," "The Ship," "The Runner," [83] etc . . . or very brief philosophical poems like "A Child's Amaze." From 1881 on, he wrote only poems of this sort, but, refusing to admit the decline of his inspiration, he claimed that in so doing he was deliberately limiting himself in order to conform to a principle posed by Poe, namely "that (at any rate for our occasions, our day) there can be no such thing as a long poem. The same thought," he added, "had been haunting my mind before, but Poe's argument, though short, work'd the sum and proved it to me." [84] He merely omitted to say that, to Poe's mind, the short poem adapted to the capabilities of the modern reader might reach a length of about a hundred lines, as in the

[79] *Inc. Ed.*, pp. 325, 678, l. 10. The addition of "and ready" to "A Song of the Rolling Earth," *ibid.*, pp. 191, 631, §4, l. 10, had a similar effect.

[80] *Inc. Ed.*, pp. 233, 645.

[81] See for instance *Inc. Ed.*, p. 533, §1, l. 1; p. 599, §15, l. 66; p. 570, §32, l. 1; p. 571, §33, l. 1; p. 575, §38, l. 1; p. 581, §45, l. 31; p. 583, §50, l. 10.

[82] One could even go further back, to the time when *Leaves of Grass* was gradually taking shape in Whitman's mind. *Pictures* (published by Emory Holloway in 1927) essentially consists of a series of vignettes similar to the ones which are to be found in *Drum-Taps*. The same remark applies to the catalogues. One of the reasons why the later editions do not contain any is that Whitman cut them up, so to speak, and published them in the form of short poems.

[83] This particular poem did not appear in *Drum-Taps*, but in the 1867 edition of *LG*, p. 214.

[84] "A Backward Glance O'er Travel'd Roads," *Inc. Ed.*, p. 530.

case of "The Raven," [85] which was rather far from the few lines with which the author of *November Boughs* now contented himself.

Whitman thus attached more and more importance to form as his poetic material became thinner. Whereas in the Preface to the 1855 edition of *Leaves of Grass* he affected a sovereign scorn for polish and ornaments,[86] and made everything depend on the power of inspiration, ten years later he rejoiced that *Drum-Taps* was "certainly more perfect as a work of art, being adjusted in all its proportions, and its passion having the indispensable merit that . . . the true artist can see it is . . . under control." [87] And it is probably towards this period that he gave himself this advice:

> In future *Leaves of Grass. Be more severe* with the final revision of the poem, nothing will do, not one word or sentence, that is not *perfectly clear*—with positive purpose—harmony with the name, nature, drift of the poem. Also *no ornaments,* especially *no ornamental adjectives,* unless they have come molten hot, and imperiously prove themselves. *No ornamental similes at all—not one: perfect transparent clearness* sanity and health are wanted—that is the *divine style*— O if it can be attained—[88]

It is obvious that he was then very far from the superb assurance he had shown in 1855 and this text proves that all his later revisions were perfectly conscious. As early as 1860 he had begun to understand his error:

> Now I reverse what I said, and affirm that all depends on the aesthetic
> or intellectual,
> And that criticism is great—and that refinement is greatest of
> all . . .[89]

Unfortunately it was too late. He could still revise his early poems, but he could not recast them, and, in spite of the progress he achieved, his art remained fundamentally the same. So, at the end of his life, he realized himself the inferiority of his work from the point of view of form. Casting a backward glance over the roads he had traveled he

[85] See "The Philosophy of Composition": "Holding in view these considerations, as well as the degree of excitement which I deemed not above the popular, while not below the critical taste, I reached at once what I conceived the proper *length* for my intended poem—a length of about one hundred lines."

[86] "Preface to 1855 Edition," *Inc. Ed.*, p. 530.

[87] Letter to O'Connor, Jan. 6, 1865, *SPL.*, p. 949. But that very year he wrote in "Shut not your doors to me proud libraries" (*Inc. Ed.*, p. 545): "The words of my book nothing, the life of it everything."—which proves that even then he considered his message more important than his art.

[88] *CW*, VI, pp. 32-33. Unfortunately this fragment bears no date. The passages in italics are underlined on the original.

[89] "Says," *LG 1860*, p. 420; *Inc. Ed.*, p. 481, §7, ll. 2-3.

readily acknowledged in 1888 that as far as descriptive talent, dramatic situations and especially verbal melody and all the conventional techniques of poetry were concerned *Leaves of Grass* was eclipsed by many masterpieces of the past.[90] And beating his breast three years later he added: "I have probably not been enough afraid of careless touches, from the first . . . nor of parrot-like repetitions—nor platitudes and the commonplace." [91]

Thus the mystic who, in 1855, had wished to communicate the revelation which he had received and announce to the world a new gospel, by slow degrees became an artist more and more conscious of his imperfections, but, to a large extent, incapable of remedying them. How could he have done it? In spite of his growing respect for art, all discipline seemed to him a useless constraint and all convention a dangerous artifice which risked raising a barrier between his thought and the reader. To art he opposed what he called simplicity,[92] that is to say strict adherence to nature. As a mystic, he was thus able to write: "In these *Leaves* everything is literally photographed. Nothing is poetized, no divergence, not a step, not an inch, nothing for beauty's sake, no euphemism, no rhyme." [93] And, in the same year, as an artist, he on the contrary affirmed the necessity of a transposition: "No useless attempt to repeat the material creation, by daguerreotyping the exact likeness by mortal mental means." [94] This contradiction gives the measure of his predicament. In fact, of course, he had to transpose, but he was not any less convinced that he had remained completely faithful to nature. When in 1879 he traveled in the Rocky Mountains he thought that he saw in their chaotic mass the symbol of his own poems. "I have found the law of my own poems," he exclaimed at the sight of "this plenitude of material, complete absence of art." [95] To art, for him a synonym for artifice, he thus preferred Nature, "the only complete, actual poem," [96] with its disorder, its immensity, its indescribably secret life.[97]

[90] "A Backward Glance O'er Travel'd Roads," *Inc. Ed.*, p. 527.

[91] "Preface Note to 2nd Annex" (1891), *Inc. Ed.*, p. 537.

[92] "Preface to 1855 Edition," *Inc. Ed.*, pp. 495-496.

[93] *CW*, VI, p. 21. This fragment bears the date of 1871.

[94] *Democratic Vistas, SD,* p. 252, *CP*, p. 253.

[95] "An Egotistical Find," *SD,* p. 143, *CP,* p. 142. The same idea is expressed in "Spirit that Form'd This Scene" (1881), *Inc. Ed.*, p. 403.

[96] *Democratic Vistas, SD,* p. 253, *CP,* p. 254. That is why during all his life he meant to write poems capable of producing the same impression on the reader as natural sights. See "On Journeys through the States" (1860), *Inc. Ed.*, p. 8, ll. 6, 13-14, "As I Ebb'd with the Ocean the Crowd," (1860), p. 638, variant reading of the beginning of §1, "A Song of Joys" (1860), p. 149, ll. 4-6 and in 1885, taking up the image of the wave again: "Had I the Choice," p. 425, ll. 5-9. In 1856, he distinguished "real poems," i.e., objects, from the poems written by poets which he called "pictures"; see "Spontaneous Me," *Inc. Ed.,* p. 88, l. 8 and also "A Song of the Rolling Earth" (1856), p. 186, §1, l. 1-14.

[97] He returned repeatedly to this principle of the superiority of nature over art; see in particular· "New Senses—New Joys," *SD*, p. 143, *CP*, p. 142; "Art Features," *SD*,

To this instinctive preference his belief in the unlimited power of inspiration was obscurely related, as well as his faith in the efficacy of the slow germination which precedes the birth of a poem:

> The rhyme and uniformity of perfect poems show the free growth of metrical laws and bud from them as unerringly and loosely as lilacs or roses on a bush, and take shapes as compact as the shapes of chestnuts and oranges and melons and pears and shed the perfume impalpable to form.[98]

In other words, thought and inspiration determine expression, so that what counts in the last analysis is thought and not form which is only its reflection. Whatever its apparent disorder may be, the poem, simply because it grew and matured in the soul of the poet, has the same profound unity and the same beauty as Nature, which was created by God, the supreme poet. The theory was not new. We recognize here the principle of organic unity which Coleridge had borrowed from Schlegel and had discussed many times in his critical writings, in particular in the *Biographia Literaria,* where Whitman may have discovered it. This doctrine suited him perfectly since it authorized him to reject every rule of composition or of prosody.[99]

If it permits one to break free from rules, the theory of organic unity, however, does not exempt the poet from work. It requires much groping to release what is gestating within him. The impression of ease or "abandon," as he said, which Whitman's work gives, was, in fact, the result of careful planning. His simplicity is laboured, and that is why he approved the famous line of Ben Jonson: "A good poet's made as well as born."[100] The first version of *Leaves of Grass,* far from having been written at one sitting, evolved slowly from a considerable number of drafts of the kind which Emory Holloway has published and which represent the work of several years.[101] The short poems of his old age required as much trouble. There exist at the Library of Congress ten different drafts of "Supplement Hours."

An examination of the papers left by Whitman permits a reconstruction of his method. Contrary to poets like Valéry for whom the starting-point is a rhythm or a musical motif, Whitman seems always to have taken off from a word or an idea expressed in prose. His manu-

---

p. 145, *CP,* pp. 144-145: "Capes Eternity and Trinity," *SD,* p. 164, *CP,* pp. 164-165; "Final Confessions—Literary Tests," *SD,* p. 199, *CP,* pp. 196-197.

[98] "Preface to 1885 Edition," *Inc. Ed.,* p. 493.

[99] See *Coleridge's Shakesperian Criticism,* ed. by T. M. Raysor, 1930, I, p. 224 and *Biographia Literaria,* ed. by Shawcross, 1907, II, p. 109. Whitman had reviewed the *Biographia Literaria* in the *Brooklyn Eagle* on Dec. 4, 1847 (*G of the F,* II, pp. 298-299). On the theory of organic unity, see James Benziger, "Organic Unity: Leibniz to Coleridge," *PMLA,* LXVI (March 1951), 24-28 and Gay W. Allen, *Walt Whitman Handbook,* pp. 218-219, 292-302, 409-422, 428-437.

[100] *CW,* VI, p. 189.

[101] See *Uncoll. PP,* and *FC,* pp. 3-7.

scripts show it. This initial material was later elaborated and expressed rhythmically. That is what happened for instance to this list of words which R. M. Bucke published in *Notes and Fragments:* "Perfect Sanity—Divine Instinct—Breadth of Vision—Healthy Rudeness of Body. Withdrawnness. Gayety. Sun-tan and air-sweetness." Out of this material Whitman later made two lines of the poem which eventually became "Song of the Answerer":

> Divine instinct, breadth of vision, the law of reason, health, rudeness
> of body, withdrawnness,
> Gayety, sun-tan, air-sweetness, such are some of the words of poems.[102]

The germ of "Night on the Prairies" which has been found in his papers also appears in the form of a brief sketch in prose entitled "Idea of a poem." [103] And on another rough draft one can read this revealing injunction: "Make this more rhythmic." [104] Sometimes the first line provoked a rich germination within him and in that case, as the ideas appeared, he noted them down on the first scrap of paper he could find: old envelopes, the backs of proof-sheets, etc., all of which gradually accumulated and soon formed a bundle which he pinned together so as not to lose them. (He often proceeded in the same way when he wrote in prose. . . .) Then he would sort his scraps, add, cut out, change the order of the various fragments, re-arrange them endlessly. When he felt that the process of germination was complete, he placed his pieces of paper end to end and recopied them, or pasted them on large sheets, as he did for "Eidolons," the definitive manuscript of which may be seen at the Boston Public Library.[105] Thus, his method was essentially agglutinative. His poems were composed like mosaics and, as in mosaics, a number of lines or passages are interchangeable.[106] Whitman himself, in the course of the successive editions, did not hesitate to change the order of certain paragraphs. This method of composition explains the looseness and desultoriness of so many of his poems, but it enabled him to gather all the insights that a poetic idea gave birth to in his mind

[102] See *N&F*, p. 93 (40) and "Poem of the Singers of the Words of Poems," *LG 1856*, p. 263; "A Song of the Answerer," *Inc. Ed.*, p. 143, §2, ll. 19-20.

[103] See Oscar L. Triggs, "The Growth of Leaves of Grass," *CW*, VII, p. 125.

[104] *N&F*, p. 38 (118). He differed from Bryant in this respect and noted the fact in one of his common-place books: "William Cullen Bryant surprised me once, relates a writer in a New York paper, by saying that prose was the natural language of composition, and he wonder'd how anybody came to write poetry." *SD*, p. 184, n.; *CP*, p. 204, n. 17.

[105] On his methods of composition, see W. S. Kennedy, *Reminiscences of Walt Whitman* (London: Alexander Gardner, 1896), p. 24—quoted by Furness, *WWW*, p. 118, n. ll. See also Sculley Bradley and John A. Stevenson, *Walt Whitman's Backward Glances* (University of Pennsylvania Press, 1947), pp. 4, 12, 13.

[106] Whitman used the image himself: "Life Mosaic of Native Moments." He had at first thought of using it as a title for *Specimen Days*.

and to respect the slow organic growth of his work. So he used it all his life. It was his way of reconciling his mysticism with his art, of preserving the spontaneity of his inspiration while imposing upon it a certain form.

This loose method was thus one of the constants of Whitman's art. For him the spirit always took precedence of the letter. He said one day to Horace Traubel: "I have never given any study merely to expression."[107] He was right, but he might well have added: "I have thought increasingly of form."

[107] *With WW in C,* III, p. 84.

The New Adam: Whitman

by R. W. B. Lewis

Whitman appears as the Adamic man reborn here in the 19th century. [JOHN BURROUGHS (1896)]

In his old age, Dr. [Oliver Wendell] Holmes derived a certain amount of polite amusement from the poetry of Walt Whitman. Whitman, Holmes remarked, "carried the principle of republicanism through the whole world of created objects"; he smuggled into his "hospitable vocabulary words which no English dictionary recognizes as belonging to the language—words which will be looked for in vain outside of his own pages." Holmes found it hard to be sympathetic toward *Leaves of Grass*; it seemed to him windy, diffuse, and humorless; but his perceptions were as lively as ever. In these two observations he points to the important elements in Whitman which are central here: the spirit of equality which animated the surging catalogues of persons and things (on its more earthy level, not unlike Emerson's lists of poets and philosophers, with their equalizing and almost leveling tendency); the groping after novel words to identify novel experiences; the lust for inventiveness which motivated what was for Whitman the great act, the creative act.

Holmes's tone of voice, of course, added that for him Whitman had gone too far; Whitman was too original, too republican, too entire an Adam. Whitman had indeed gone further than Holmes: a crucial and dimensional step further, as Holmes had gone further than Channing or Norton. In an age when the phrase "forward-looking" was a commonplace, individuals rarely nerved themselves to withstand the shock of others looking and moving even further forward than they. Emerson himself, who had gone so far that the liberal Harvard Divinity School forbade his presence there for more than thirty years, shared some of Holmes's feeling about Whitman. When his cordial letter welcoming

"The New Adam: Whitman." Reprinted from *The American Adam*, pp. 41-53, by R. W. B. Lewis by permission of The University of Chicago Press.

Leaves of Grass in 1855 was published in the *New York Tribune*, Emerson muttered in some dismay that had he intended it for publication, he "should have enlarged the *but* very much—enlarged the *but*." *Leaves of Grass* "was pitched in the very highest key of self-reliance," as a friend of its author maintained; but Emerson, who had given that phrase its contemporary resonance, believed that any attitude raised to its highest pitch tended to encroach dangerously on the truth of its opposite.

It would be no less accurate to say that Walt Whitman, instead of going too far forward, had gone too far backward: for he did go back, all the way back, to a primitive Adamic condition, to the beginning of time.

In the poetry of Walt Whitman, the hopes which had until now expressed themselves in terms of progress crystallized all at once in a complete recovery of the primal perfection. In the early poems Whitman accomplished the epochal return by huge and almost unconscious leaps. In later poems he worked his way more painstakingly up the river of history to its source: as, for example, in "Passage to India," where the poet moves back from the recently constructed Suez Canal, back past Christopher Columbus, past Alexander the Great and the most ancient of heroes and peoples, to the very "secret of the earth and sky." "In the beginning," John Locke once wrote, "all the world was America." Whitman manages to make us feel what it might have been like; and he succeeds at last in presenting the dream of the new Adam —along with his sorrows.

A measure of Whitman's achievement is the special difficulty which that dream had provided for others who tried to recount it. Its character was such that it was more readily described by those who did not wholly share in it. How can absolute novelty be communicated? All the history of the philosophy of language is involved with that question, from *The Cratylus* of Plato to the latest essay on semantics; and one could bring to bear on it the variety of anecdotes about Adam's naming the animals by the disturbingly simple device of calling a toad a toad.

Hawthorne conveyed the idea of novelty by setting it in an ancient pattern: allowing it thereby exactly to be *recognized;* and reaching a sharpness of meaning also to be found in Tocqueville's running dialectic of democracies and aristocracies. Whitman employed the same tactic when he said of Coleridge that he was "like Adam in Paradise, and just as free from artificiality." This was a more apt description of himself, as he knew:

I, chanter of Adamic songs,
Through the new garden the West, the great cities calling.

It is, in fact, in the poems gathered under the title "Children of Adam" (1860) that we have the most explicit evidence of his ambition to reach behind tradition to find and assert nature untroubled by art, to re-establish the natural unfallen man in the living hour. Unfallen man is, properly enough, unclothed as well; the convention of cover came in with the Fall; and Whitman adds his own unnostalgic sincerity to the Romantic affection for nakedness:

> As Adam, early in the morning,
> Walking forth from the bower refresh'd with sleep,
> Behold me where I pass, hear my voice, approach,
> Touch me, touch the palm of your hand to my body as I pass,
> Be not afraid of my body.

For Whitman, as for Holmes and Thoreau, the quickest way of framing his novel outlook was by lowering, and secularizing, the familiar spiritual phrases: less impudently than Thoreau but more earnestly, and indeed more monotonously, but with the same intention of salvaging the human from the religious vocabulary to which (he felt) it had given rise. Many of Whitman's poetic statements are conversions of religious allusion: the new miracles were acts of the senses (an odd foreshortening, incidentally, of Edwards' Calvinist elaboration of the Lockian psychology); the aroma of the body was "finer than prayer"; his head was "more than churches, bibles and all creeds." "If I worship one thing more than another," Whitman declaimed, in a moment of Adamic narcissism, "it shall be the spread of my own body." These assertions gave a peculiar stress to Whitman's seconding of the hopeful belief in men like gods: "Divine am I, inside and out, and I make holy whatever I touch." Whitman's poetry is at every moment an act of turbulent incarnation.

But although there is, as there was meant to be, a kind of shock-value in such lines, they are not the most authentic index to his pervasive Adamism, because in them the symbols have become too explicit and so fail to work symbolically. Whitman in these instances is stating his position and contemplating it; he is betraying his own principle of indirect statement; he is telling us too much, and the more he tells us, the more we seem to detect the anxious, inflated utterance of a charlatan. We cling to our own integrity and will not be thundered at. We respond far less willingly to Whitman's frontal assaults than we do to his dramatizations; when he is enacting his role rather than insisting on it, we are open to persuasion. And he had been enacting it from the outset of *Leaves of Grass*.

This is the true nature of his achievement and the source of his claim to be the representative poet of the party of Hope. For the "self" in the very earliest of Whitman's poems is an individual who is always moving forward. To say so is not merely to repeat that Whitman believed in progress; indeed, it is in some sense to deny it. The young Whitman, at least, was not an apostle of progress in its customary meaning of a motion from worse to better to best, an improvement over a previous historic condition, a "rise of man." For Whitman, there was no past or "worse" to progress from; he moved forward because it was the only direction (he makes us think) in which he could move; because there was nothing behind him—or if there were, he had not yet noticed it. There is scarcely a poem of Whitman's before, say, 1867, which does not have the air of being the first poem ever written, the first formulation in language of the nature of persons and of things and of the relations between them; and the urgency of the language suggests that it was formulated in the very nick of time, to give the objects described their first substantial existence.

Nor is there, in *Leaves of Grass*, any complaint about the weight or intrusion of the past; in Whitman's view the past had been so effectively burned away that it had, for every practical purpose, been forgotten altogether. In his own recurring figure, the past was already a corpse; it was on its way out the door to the cemetery; Whitman watched it absent-mindedly, and turned at once to the living reality. He did enjoy, as he reminds us, reciting Homer while walking beside the ocean; but this was just because Homer was exempt from tradition and talking at and about the dawn of time. Homer was the poet you found if you went back far enough; and as for the sea, it had (unlike Melville's) no sharks in it—no ancient, lurking, indestructible evil powers. Whitman's hope was unspoiled by memory. When he became angry, as he did in *Democratic Vistas* (1871), he was not attacking his generation in the Holgrave manner for continuing to accept the old and the foreign, but for fumbling its extraordinary opportunity, for taking a wrong turn on the bright new highway he had mapped for it. Most of the time he was more interested in the map, and we are more interested in him when he was.

It was then that he caught up and set to music the large contemporary conviction that man had been born anew in the new society, that the race was off to a fresh start in America. It was in *Leaves of Grass* that the optative mood, which had endured for over a quarter of a century and had expressed itself so variously and so frequently, seemed to have been transformed at last into the indicative. It was there that the hope that had enlivened spokesmen from Noah Webster in 1825 ("American glory begins at the dawn") to the well-named periodical, *Spirit of the Age* in 1849 ("The accumulated atmosphere of ages, containing stale ideas and opinions . . . will soon be among the things that were")—that all that stored-up abundance of hope found its full poetic realization. *Leaves of Grass* was a climax as well as a beginning, or rather, it was the climax of a long effort to begin.

This was why Emerson, with whatever enlarged "buts" in his mind, made a point of visiting Whitman in New York and Boston; why Thoreau, refusing to be put off "by any brag or egoism in his book," preferred Whitman to Bronson Alcott; and why Whitman, to the steady surprise of his countrymen, has been regarded in Europe for almost a century as unquestionably the greatest poet the New World has produced: an estimate which even Henry James would come round to. European readers were not slow to recognize in Whitman an authentic rendering of their own fondest hopes; for if much of his vision had been originally imported from Germany and France, it had plainly lost its portion of nostalgia en route. While European romanticism continued to resent the effect of time, Whitman was announcing that time had only just begun. He was able to think so because of the facts of immediate history in America during the years when he was maturing: when a world was, in some literal way, being created before his eyes. It was this that Whitman had the opportunity to dramatize; and it was this that gave *Leaves of Grass* its special quality of a Yankee Genesis: a new account of the creation of the world—the creation, that is, of a new world; an account this time with a happy ending for Adam its hero; or better yet, with no ending at all; and with this important emendation, that now the creature has taken on the role of creator.

It was a twofold achievement, and the second half of it was demanded by the first. We see the sequence, for example, in the development from section 4 to section 5 of "Song of Myself." The first phase was the identification of self, an act which proceeded by distinction and differentiation, separating the self from every element that in a traditional view might be supposed to be part of it: Whitman's identity card had no space on it for the names of his ancestry. The exalted mind which carried with it a conviction of absolute novelty has been described by Whitman's friend, the Canadian psychologist, Dr. R. M. Bucke, who relates it to what he calls Whitman's "cosmic consciousness." "Along with the consciousness of the cosmos [Dr. Bucke wrote], there occurs an intellectual enlightenment which alone would place the individual on a new plane of existence—would make him almost a member of a new species." *Almost a member of a new species:* that could pass as the slogan of each individual in the party of Hope. It was a robust American effort to make real and operative the condition which John Donne once had merely feared:

> Prince, Subject, Father, Son are things forgot,
> For every man alone thinks he has got
> To be a Phoenix and that then can be
> None of that kind, of which he is, but he.

Whitman achieves the freedom of the new condition by scrupulously peeling off every possible source of, or influence upon, the "Me myself," the "what I am." As in section 4 of "Song of Myself":

> Trippers and askers surround me
> People I meet, the effect upon me of my early life, or the ward and
>   the city I live in or the nation. . . .
> The sickness of one of my folks, or of myself, or the ill-doing or loss
>   or lack of money, or depressions or exaltations,
> Battles, the horror of fratricidal wars, the fever of doubtful news, the
>   fitful events,
> These come to me days and nights and go from me again,
> But they are not the Me myself.
> Apart from the pulling and hauling stands what I am;
> Stands amused, complacent, compassionating, idle, unitary;
> Looks down, is erect, or bends an arm on an impalpable certain rest,
> Looking with side-curved head curious what will come next,
> Both in and out of the game, and watching and wondering at it.

There is Emerson's individual, the "infinitely repellent orb." There is also the heroic product of romanticism, exposing behind the mass of what were regarded as inherited or external or imposed and hence superficial and accidental qualities the true indestructible secret core of personality. There is the man who contends that "nothing, not God, is greater to one than one's self."

There, in fact, is the new Adam. If we want a profile of him, we could start with the adjectives Whitman supplies: amused, complacent, compassionating, idle, unitary; especially unitary, and certainly very easily amused; too complacent, we frequently feel, but always compassionate—expressing the old divine compassion for every sparrow that falls, every criminal and prostitute and hopeless invalid, every victim of violence or misfortune. With Whitman's help we could pile up further attributes, and the exhaustive portrait of Adam would be composed of a careful gloss on each one of them: hankering, gross, mystical, nude; turbulent, fleshy, sensual, eating, drinking, and breeding; no sentimentalist, no stander above men and women; no more modest than immodest; wearing his hat as he pleases indoors and out; never skulking or ducking or deprecating; adoring himself and adoring his comrades; afoot with his vision,

> Moving forward then and now and forever,
> Gathering and showing more always and with velocity,
> Infinite and omnigenous.

And announcing himself in language like that. For an actual illustration, we could not find anything better than the stylized daguerreotype of himself which Whitman placed as the Frontispiece of the first edition. We recognize him at once: looking with side-curved head, bending an arm on the certain rest of his hip, evidently amused, complacent, and curious; bearded, rough, probably sensual; with his hat on.

Whitman did resemble this Adamic archetype, according to his friend John Burroughs. "There was a look about him," Burroughs remembered, "hard to describe, and which I have seen in no other face, —a gray, brooding, elemental look, like the granite rock, something primitive and Adamic that might have belonged to the first man." The two new adjectives there are "gray" and "brooding"; and they belong to the profile, too, both of Whitman and of the character he dramatized. There was bound to be some measure of speculative sadness inherent in the situation. Not all the leaves Whitman uttered were joyous ones, though he wanted them all to be and was never clear why they were not. His ideal image of himself—and it is his best single trope for the new Adam—was that of a live oak he saw growing in Louisiana:

> All alone stood it and the mosses hung down from the branches,
> Without any companion it grew there uttering joyous leaves of dark green,
> And its look, rude, unbending, lusty, made me think of myself.

But at his most honest, he admitted, as he does here, that the condition was somehow unbearable:

> I wondered how it could utter joyous leaves standing alone there without a friend near, for I knew I could not. . . .
> And though the live-oak glistens there in Louisiana solitary in a wide flat space,
> Uttering joyous leaves all its life without a friend a lover near,
> I knew very well I could not.

Adam had his moments of sorrow also. But the emotion had nothing to do with the tragic insight; it did not spring from any perception of a genuine hostility in nature or lead to the drama of colliding forces. Whitman was wistful, not tragic. We might almost say that he was wistful because he was not tragic. He was innocence personified. It is not difficult to marshal a vast array of references to the ugly, the gory, and the sordid in his verses; brought together in one horrid lump, they appear as the expression of one who was well informed about the shabby side of the world; but though he offered himself as "the poet of wickedness" and claimed to be "he who knew what it was to be evil," every item he introduced as vile turns out, after all, to be merely a particular beauty of a different original coloration. "Evil propels me and reform of evil propels me, I stand indifferent." A sentiment like that can make sense only if the term "evil" has been filtered through a transfiguring moral imagination, changing in essence as it passes.

That sentiment, of course, is not less an expression of poetic than of moral motivation. As a statement of the poetic sensibility, it could have been uttered as easily by Shakespeare or Dante as by Whitman. Many of the very greatest writers suggest, as Whitman does, a peculiar artistic innocence, a preadolescent wonder which permits such a poet to take in and reproject whatever there is, shrinking from none of it. But in Whitman, artistic innocence merged with moral innocence: a preadolescent ignorance of the convulsive undertow of human behavior—something not at all shared by Dante or Shakespeare. Both modes of innocence are present in the poetry of Walt Whitman, and they are not at any time to be really distinguished. One can talk about his image of moral innocence only in terms of his poetic creation.

"I reject none, accept all, then reproduce all in my own forms." The whole spirit of Whitman is in the line: there is his strategy for overcoming his sadness, and the second large phase of his achievement, following the act of differentiation and self-identification. It is the creative phase, in that sense of creativity which beguiles the artist most perilously into stretching his analogy with God—when he brings a world into being. Every great poet composes a world for us, and what James called the "figure in the carpet" is the poet's private chart of that world; but when we speak of the poet's world—of Dostoevski's or Balzac's—we knowingly skip a phrase, since what we mean is Dostoevski's (or Balzac's) selective embodiment of an already existing world. In the case of Whitman, the type of extreme Adamic romantic, the metaphor gains its power from a proximity to the literal, as though Whitman really were engaged in the stupendous task of building a world that had not been there before the first words of his poem.

The task was self-imposed, for Whitman's dominant emotion, when it was not unmodified joy, was simple, elemental loneliness; it was a testimony to his success and contributed to his peculiar glow. For if the hero of *Leaves of Grass* radiates a kind of primal innocence in an innocent world, it was not only because he had made that world, it was also because he had begun by making himself. Whitman is an early example, and perhaps the most striking one we have, of the self-made man, with an undeniable grandeur which is the product of his manifest sense of having been responsible for his own being—something far more compelling than the more vulgar version of the rugged individual who claims responsibility only for his own bank account.

And of course he was lonely, incomparably lonely; no anchorite was ever so lonely, since no anchorite was ever so alone. Whitman's image of the evergreen, "solitary in a wide, flat space . . . without a friend a lover near," introduced what more and more appears to be the central theme of American literature, in so far as a unique theme may be claimed for it: the theme of loneliness, dramatized in what I shall later describe as the story of *the hero in space.* The only recourse for a poet like Whitman was to fill the space by erecting a home and populating it with companions and lovers.

Whitman began in an Adamic condition which was only too effectively realized: the isolated individual, standing flush with the empty universe, a primitive moral and intellectual entity. In the behavior of a "noiseless, patient spider," Whitman found a revealing analogy:

> A noiseless, patient spider
> I mark'd, where, on a little promontory, it stood out, isolated,
> Mark'd how, to explore the vacant, vast surrounding,
> It launched forth filament, filament, filament, out of itself,
> Ever unreeling them—ever tirelessly speeding them.

"Out of itself." This is the reverse of the traditionalist attitude that, in Eliot's phrase, "home is where one starts from." Whitman acted on the hopeful conviction that the new Adam started from himself; having created himself, he must next create a home. The given in individual experience was no longer a complex of human, racial, and familial relationships; it was a self in a vacant, vast surrounding. Each simple separate person must forge his own framework anew. This was the bold, enormous venture inevitably confronted by the Adamic personality. He had to become the maker of his own conditions—if he were to have any conditions or any achieved personality at all.

There were, in any case, no conditions to *go back to*—to take upon one's self or to embody. There is in fact almost no indication at all in *Leaves of Grass* of a return or reversion, even of that recovery of childhood detected in *Walden.* Whitman begins after that recovery, as a child, seemingly self-propagated, and he is always going *forth;* one of his pleasantest poems was constructed around that figure. There is only the open road, and Whitman moves forward from the start of it. Homecoming is for the exile, the prodigal son, Adam after the expulsion, not for the new unfallen Adam in the western garden. Not even in "Passage to India" is there a note of exile, because there is no sense of sin ("Let others weep for sin"). Whitman was entirely remote from the view of man as an orphan which motivated many of the stories of

Hawthorne and Melville and which underlay the characteristic adventure they narrated of the search for a father. Hawthorne, an orphan himself and the author of a book about England called *Our Old Home*, sometimes sent his heroes to Europe to look for their families; Melville dispatched his heroes to the bottom of the sea on the same mission. This was the old way of posing the problem: the way of mastering life by the recovery of home, though it might require descent to the land of the dead; but Whitman knew the secret of his paternity.

Whitman was creating a world, even though he often sounds as though he were saluting a world that had been lying in wait for him: "Salut au monde." In one sense, he is doing just that, welcoming it, acknowledging it, reveling in its splendor and variety. His typical condition is one of acceptance and absorption; the word which almost everyone who knew him applied to his distinguishing capacity was "absorptive." He absorbed life for years; and when he contained enough, he let it go out from him again. "I . . . accept all, then reproduce all in my own forms." He takes unflagging delight in the reproductions: "Me pleased," he says in "Our Old Feuillage"; it is the "what I am." But the pleasure of seeing becomes actual only in the process of naming. It is hard to recall any particular of life and work, of men and women and animals and plants and things, of body and mind, that Whitman has not somewhere named in caressing detail. And the process of naming is for Whitman nothing less than the process of creation. This new Adam is both maker and namer; his innocent pleasure, untouched by humility, is colored by the pride of one who looks on his work and finds it good. The things that are named seem to spring into being at the sound of the word. It was through the poetic act that Whitman articulated the dominant metaphysical illusion of his day and became the creator of his own world.

We have become familiar, a century after the first edition of *Leaves of Grass*, with the notion of the poet as the magician who "orders reality" by his use of language. That notion derived originally from the epochal change—wrought chiefly by Kant and Hegel—in the relation between the human mind and the external world; a change whereby the mind "thought order into" the sensuous mass outside it instead of detecting an order externally existing. Whitman (who read Hegel and who wrote a singularly flatulent poetic reflection after doing so) adapted that principle to artistic creativity with a vigor and enthusiasm unknown before James Joyce and his associates in the twentieth century. What is implicit in every line of Whitman is the belief that the poet *projects* a world of order and meaning and identity into either a chaos or a sheer vacuum; he does not *discover* it. The poet may salute the chaos; but he creates the world.

Such a conviction contributed greatly to Whitman's ever enlarging idea of the poet as the vicar of God, as the son of God—as God himself. Those were not new labels for the artist, but they had been given fresh currency in Whitman's generation; and Whitman held to all of them more ingenuously than any other poet who ever lived. He supervised the departure of "the priests" and the arrival of the new vicar, "the divine litteratus"; he erected what he called his novel "trinitas" on the base of "the true son of God, the poet"; he offered himself as a cheerful, divine scapegoat and stage-managed "my own crucifixion." And to the extent that he fulfilled his own demands for *the* poet—as laid down in the Preface to *Leaves of Grass* and in *Democratic Vistas*—Whitman became God the Creator.

This was the mystical side of him, the side which announced itself in the fifth section of "Song of Myself," and which led to the mystical vision of a newly created totality. The vision emerges from those lyrical sweeps through the universe in the later sections of the poem: the sections in which Whitman populated and gave richness and shape to the universe by the gift of a million names. We can round out our picture of Whitman as Adam—both Adam as innocent and Adam as namer—if we distinguish his own brand of mysticism from the traditional variety. Traditional mysticism proceeds by denial and negation and culminates in the imagery of deserts and silence, where the voice and the being of God are the whole of reality. Whitman's mysticism proceeds by expansive affirmation and culminates in plenitude and huge volumes of noise. Traditional mysticism is the surrender of the ego to its creator, in an eventual escape from the limits of names; Whitman's is the expansion of the ego in the act of creation itself, naming every conceivable object as it comes from the womb.

The latter figure is justified by the very numerous references, both by Whitman and by his friends, to his "great mother-nature." We must cope with the remarkable blend in the man, whereby this Adam, who had already grown to the stature of his own maker, was not less and at the same time his own Eve, breeding the human race out of his love affair with himself. If section 5 of "Song of Myself" means anything, it means this: a miraculous intercourse between "you my soul" and "the other I am," with a world as its offspring. How the process worked in his poems can be seen by examining any one of the best of them. There Whitman skilfully brings into being the small world of the particular poem by introducing a few items one by one, linking them together by a variety of devices, running back over them time and again to reinsure their solidity and durability, adding further items and quickly forging the relations between them and the cluster already present, announcing at the end the accomplished whole and breathing over all of it the magical command *to be*.

Take, for example, "Crossing Brooklyn Ferry":

> Flood-tide below me! I see you face to face!
> Clouds of the west—sun there half an hour high—I see you also face to face.
> Crowds of men and women attired in the usual costumes, how curious you are to me!
> On the ferry-boats the hundreds and hundreds that cross, returning home, are more curious to me than you suppose,
> And you that shall cross from shore to shore years hence are more to me, and more in my meditations, than you might suppose.

This is not the song of a *trovatore,* a finder, exposing bit by bit the substance of a spectacle which is there before a spectator looks at it. It is the song of a poet who creates his spectacle by "projecting" it as he goes along. The flood tides, the clouds, the sun, the crowds of men and women in the usual costumes: these exist in the instant they are named and as they are pulled in toward one another, bound together by a single unifying eye through the phrases which apply to them severally ("face to face," "curious to me"). The growth of the world is exactly indicated in the increasing length of the lines; until, in the following stanza, Whitman can observe a "simple, compact, well-join'd scheme." Stabilized in space, the scheme must now be given stabilizing relations in time; Whitman goes on to announce that "fifty years hence, others will see them as they cross, the sun half an hour high" (the phrase had to be repeated) "a hundred years hence, or ever so many hundred years hence, others will see them." With the world, so to speak, a going concern, Whitman is able now to summon new elements into existence: sea gulls, the sunlight in the water, the haze on the hills, the schooners and sloops and ships at anchor, the large and small steamers, and the flags of all nations. A few of the conspicuous elements are blessed and praised, in an announcement (stanza 8) not only of their existence but now rather of the value they impart to one another; and then, in the uninterrupted prayer of the final stanza (stanza 9—the process covers nine stanzas, as though it were nine months) each separate entity is named again as receiving everlasting life through its participation in the whole:

> Flow on river! flow with the flood-tide, and ebb with the ebb-tide!
> Frolic on, crested and scallop-edg'd waves!

And so on: until the mystery of incarnation has been completed.

Whitman's Poetic Ensembles

by Walter Sutton

I will not make poems with reference to parts
But I will make poems, songs, thoughts, with reference to
ensemble. . . .

When Whitman wrote of his concern for poetic "ensemble" rather than "parts," he was thinking more of his theme of natural and cosmic unity than of questions of prosody. Yet his words, taken either in or out of their context in "Starting from Paumanok," are also in accord with his poetics. If the "ensemble" is identified with the poem, the statement reveals an interest in the organic unity of the whole rather than in such "parts" as rime or meter, which Whitman, like Coleridge, regarded as superficial aspects of form. In their specific context, the lines express Whitman's insistence that he was singing not just of a day "but with reference to all days"—that he was interested not simply in particulars as such but in particulars as manifestations of the unity of man and nature in a larger scheme. The word *reference* reminds us of Whitman's conviction that the value of his poems lay not so much in their words as in the world of shared experience evoked by their language. It was his custom to identify his poems with their human and natural subjects and to prize the referents of his words more highly than the words themselves. In "So Long" he says of his poetry, "Camerado, this is no book,/ Who touches this touches a man," and in "A Song of the Rolling Earth" he sees "little or nothing in audible words" in the face of "the unspoken meanings of the earth." We find in Whitman a repeated emphasis upon the organic nature of poetic form, but his organicism—unlike much recent contextualist theory—assumes the openness of the poem and the identification of its formal elements with the shared experiences of its readers. . .

"Whitman's Poetic Ensembles" (Original title: "The Analysis of Free Verse Form, Illustrated by a Reading of Whitman"). From the *Journal of Aesthetics and Art Criticism,* XVIII (1959), 241-257.

Romantic organic theory stimulated the development of the modern free verse movement, but it provides little help to the practical critic of free verse form. The comparisons made by Emerson and Whitman of poetic form and the growth of plants or the movements of the sea testify to their regard for nature and their commitment to the idea that form follows function, but they do not help us order our responses to poems such as Whitman wrote. Even Coleridge's description of the poetic power as manifesting itself in "the balance or reconciliation of opposite or discordant qualities" has proved to be of limited usefulness, since it has been appropriated by critics concerned with a narrow range of structural principles, or "strategies," such as irony, paradox, and tension.

As we confront the problem of ordering the often bewildering complexity of the interrelated formal elements of Whitman's free verse poems (or of any literary work), we are aware of the inadequacy of the conception of any single structural device such as irony or of "parts" such as rime or meter. The poem is, rather, an "ensemble" or complex presenting interrelated patterns of organization that together constitute a "form" only partially apprehended by any one reader.

Although the patterns of organization are necessarily interrelated, they can be identified with one or more of four formal dimensions: sound, syntax, image or event, and meaning. Sound patterns include such devices as rime and meter (often over-emphasized as formal elements of traditional verse), alliteration, assonance, euphony, dissonance, cadence, or onomatopoeia, depending upon the nature of the given work. Syntax has to do with the grammatical relationship of the elements of the poem. It may be involved with the dimension of sound, as when parallel constructions provide riming effects, and it is necessarily involved with questions of meaning. The dimension of image and event includes the imagined events represented by the words of the poem—actions, thoughts, feelings, dreams, as well as sensory experiences—all of which contribute to the integrity of the imagined world of the work. Meaning, which is both conceptual and emotive, exists on two distinguishable levels. On the plain-sense level the events have meaning in terms of the world of the work. On the level of metaphor, the events are value-charged in the consciousness of the reader and invested with meanings and values commensurate with the reader's experience, social and aesthetic. The metaphorical level includes both the argument and theme of the work, however defined, and the individual images and events that support it.

Some such idea of interrelated formal dimensions is necessary for the analysis of the form of Whitman's distinctive free verse poems in *Leaves of Grass*. Of these, the longest and best known—untitled in the first edition of 1855, entitled "A Poem of Walt Whitman, an American," in 1856, and known to us now, since the edition of 1881, as "Song of

Myself"—contains many but not all of the techniques employed by Whitman in such later and more complex poems as "Out of the Cradle Endlessly Rocking," "When Lilacs Last in the Dooryard Bloom'd," and "Passage to India."

As we read "Song of Myself" in its final version, we are aware of certain recurrent organizing devices, the most conspicuous of which are syntactical. Of these, the use of grammatical parallelism and of the sentence, or paragraph, as a containing unit comparable to the stanza in conventional verse, is consistent throughout the poem and contributes to its metrical unity. Both devices may be seen in the first verse sentence-stanza of section 31:

> I believe a leaf of grass is no less than the journey-work of the stars,
> And the pismire is equally perfect, and a grain of sand, and the egg
> of the wren,
> And the tree-toad is a chef-d'oeuvre for the highest,
> And the running blackberry would adorn the parlors of heaven,
> And the narrowest hinge in my hand puts to scorn all machinery,
> And the cow crunching with depress'd head surpasses any statue,
> And a mouse is miracle enough to stagger sextillions of infidels.

There are other types of parallelism employed in "Song of Myself," but this example illustrates a number of its effects. In the relation of syntax to meaning, it has been observed that grammatical parallelism is an appropriate form for a poet like Whitman with a democratic equalitarian point of view. Yet his equalitarianism is pantheistic as well as political, and the consonance of syntax and meaning is apparent in these lines. The relation of syntax to sound is also apparent, since the repeated initial "And the's" rime. They also echo the parallelism of the King James *Bible* and thus point to a traditional model for Whitman's metrical form, one that is especially important because of his conception of the poet as a seer and prophet who would proclaim the gospel of the truly democratic society of the future.

As for the sound pattern, both alliteration and assonance are important integrating devices. Sound also involves rhythm and stress. Although "Song of Myself" begins with a perfectly regular iambic pentameter line—"I celebrate myself, and sing myself"—and although certain lines and passages approach metrical regularity, most of the verses are irregular in their stress pattern, and conventional scansion is not applicable. Other sound devices, such as onomatopoeia, assonance, and alliteration, are present in "Song of Myself," but they are not as effectively exploited here as in some of the later poems.

In identifying himself with the manifold aspects of American life, Whitman presents a great variety of particular images (the contralto, the carpenter, the farmer, the lunatic, the printer, the quadroon girl, the machinist, the squaw, etc., of section 15, for example). In addition to such apparently unrelated particular images, there are several dominant images basic to Whitman's controlling point of view and to his work as a whole. One is the grass itself (section 6), identified with the principle of life manifested by the persistent life nature cycle and with the impulse to creative expression manifested in the poems themselves as individual "leaves of grass." Another is water, or the sea (sections 17, 22), like the grass a symbol of the life force, containing as a womb-tomb image (both "cradle" and "unshovelled graves") the terminal experiences of the life cycle. Then, too, there is the thematic image of the journey, introduced in section 32 and continued in 44 and following sections. The journey represents the progress, not only of man, but of the physical universe as well. It encompasses the process of evolution, optimistically regarded as directed toward a goal of perfectibility in which man's divine potential is to be realized in the meeting with the "great Camerado," who waits at the end of the journey. It is also the progress of a free nation along the "open road" toward the ideal of democratic community and brotherhood. For the individual, as for the boy disciple who accompanies the poet, it is the journey of life and the quest for truth.

These dominant images are not explicitly interrelated within the poem as events except as we recognize that they are all a part of the experience of the poet, who at the beginning of the poem assumes an identification with all mankind ("And what I assume you shall assume") and who introduces himself in section 24 as

> Walt Whitman, a kosmos, of Manhattan the son,
> Turbulent, fleshy, sensual, eating, drinking and breeding,
> No sentimentalist, no stander above men and women or apart
>   from them
> No more modest than immodest.

This characterization tallies with the portrait of Whitman in workman's clothes that faces the poem in the later editions. The *persona* of the poet as the common man *and* seer who also identifies with all aspects of life helps to explain the apparently fragmented and discontinuous sequence of images and events in "Song of Myself." The device is not entirely satisfactory, however, because it does not require any integration of the particular events or aspects of experience presented. There *is*, of course, a selection of details, as there is in all art, but the rationale of the selection is not apparent. For all the wealth of imagery, the reader is left with a sense of diffuseness and of the lack of an adequate control of form.

This weakness in "Song of Myself" is emphasized by contrast as we turn to "Crossing Brooklyn Ferry," first published in 1856 as "Sun-Down

Poem." Its images and events all relate to a single experience and a single setting: the crossing of the East River by ferryboat, with a view of the river and harbor and of Brooklyn and Manhattan. Within these limits, or within this frame, the sensuous images presented in the opening sections of the poem (1-3) contribute to the sense of verisimilitude. The details of the scene—the soaring gulls, the ships with the flags of all nations, the hills of Brooklyn, the light on the water—reflect the close observation of a coherent experience. Moreover, these complementary images contribute to a sense of the unity of the experience, both for the individual crossing and for crossings separated in time. Image becomes metaphor as the crossing, or transit, is seen to relate both to the life of the individual and to the lives of separate generations. For the many visual images representing the experience of the voyaging poet are all subordinated to the image of the ship, or ferryboat, which crosses the river (of time) from gate to gate (birth and death) and which supplies the poet his perspective as he recognizes the "universality" of his particular experience.

By appealing through sensory images to a sense of shared experience, the poet asserts a sense of unity, or *community,* that provides a bond between individuals of the same generation and between the poet and later generations:

> It avails not, time nor place—distance avails not,
> I am with you, you men and women of a generation, or ever so many
>   generations hence,
> Just as you feel when you look on the river and sky, so I felt,
> Just as any of you is one of a living crowd, I was one of a crowd. . . .

Beyond the identity of experience, there is, for the romantic poet, the recognition of an identity of soul, as well, among all men:

> I too had been struck from the float forever held in solution,
> I too had receiv'd identity by my body. . . .

The images of the harbor scene are again invoked in the conclusion, but in a more exalted mood, as the poet's feeling of alienation, or individuation, is resolved by the assurance of the identity of soul as well as the community of experience. This confidence is also supported by an assertion of the unity of body and soul, for Whitman, unlike the Transcendentalist, regards physical nature as a "necessary film" which "envelops" the soul and without which the soul cannot be known.

The introduction of a set of images relating to a single experience, the speculation upon their meaning, and the re-evocation which resolves the dualism of body and soul represent a new development in Whitman's technique, one that suggests the influence of music upon the poet's conception of form. This device serves to interrelate effects within the dimensions of sound, syntax, and meaning as well as that of the image. The principle involved is comparable to that of rime, if we recognize that in a broad sense rime involves the repetition and resolution not only of sounds, but of grammatical units, sense impressions, and ideas. In this way we see that the repetition of the harbor images involves auditory rime through the repetition of words, visual rime through the images which the repeated words evoke, and conceptual and emotive rime through the associations of the words and images. All contribute to the central theme which they sustain and develop. William Carlos Williams' observation, in "The Orchestra," that "it is a principle of music to repeat the theme" applies to the poem as well.

"Out of the Cradle Endlessly Rocking"—first published in 1860 as "A Word Out of the Sea" and in approximately final form by 1871—is Whitman's most complex and successfully-integrated poem. Several effective new techniques are apparent. One is the use of a triad of images (boy, bird, and sea) through which the poet develops his theme by means of a dramatic colloquy. (A comparable triadic pattern, but without the same dramatic quality, is employed in such later poems as "When Lilacs Last in the Dooryard Bloom'd" and "Passage to India.") There is also a recurrence and resolution in the ordering of images comparable to that in "Crossing Brooklyn Ferry." The influence of music is seen here too in the device, inspired by the model of the opera, of the arias or bird songs, of fulfillment and frustration, which provide interludes of lyric expression of the feelings and emotions aroused by the events presented and analyzed in the narrative and dramatic framework of the poem.

The arias are operative in all formal dimensions: sound (as their lyric intensity enhances the emotive quality of the language of these verses); syntax (as they are set off in relatively self-contained italicized units which provide a complementing of the mood and a counterpointing of the events of the remainder of the poem); image (as they present images from nature—the heavy moon, the sea pushing upon the land—to express the subjective feelings of love and frustration); and meaning (primarily emotive but also metaphorically expressive as the bird's songs of "lonesome love" of the "throbbing heart") brings a realization to the boy, the "outsetting bard," of the relation between suffering and art, of the fact that, for him, poetry is to be a sublimated expression of frustrated love.

The opening section reveals the interrelationship of the four formal dimensions of the poem. It presents a reminiscence of a childhood experience in which the poet, as a boy, saw a pair of mocking birds nesting on the beach. (The impression of love fulfilled which they convey is heightened by the brief "two-together" aria.) The disappearance of the female and the grief of the remaining mate (expressed in the longer aria) introduce the boy to the experience of loss and frustration, which the maturing poet comes to recognize as the basic motive for his poetic expression.

The first verse stanza of the poem brings together images relating to the childhood experience, now interwoven into a symbolic poetic fabric which involves meaning, as metaphor, beyond the context of the events of the remembered experience:

> Out of the cradle endlessly rocking,
> Out of the mocking-bird's throat, the musical shuttle,
> Out of the Ninth-month midnight,
> Over the sterile sands and the fields beyond, where the child leaving
> his bed wander'd alone, bareheaded, barefoot,
> Down from the shower'd halo,
> Up from the mystic play of shadows twining and twisting as if they
> were alive,
> Out from the patches of briers and blackberries,
> From the memories of the bird that chanted to me,
> From your memories sad brother, from the fitful risings and fallings
> I heard,
> From under that yellow half-moon late-risen and swollen as if with
> tears,
> From those beginning notes of yearning and love there in the mist,
> From the thousand responses of my heart never to cease,
> From the myriad thence-aroused words,
> From the word stronger and more delicious than any,
> From such as now they start the scene revisiting,
> As a flock, twittering, rising, or overhead passing,
> Borne hither, ere all eludes me, hurriedly,
> A man, yet by these tears a little boy again,
> Throwing myself on the sand, confronting the waves,
> I, chanter of pains and joys, uniter of here and hereafter,
> Taking all hints to use them, but swiftly leaping beyond them,
> A reminiscence sing.

The images from remembered experience are interwoven into a poetic context. The weaving process, in which the voice of the bird is a "musical shuttle," is suggested by syntactical and sound devices particularly. The repeated introductory prepositions—*out of, over, down from, up from*—serve to indicate the converging movements of an interweaving. The sound pattern of the lines is particularly rich in devices which interrelate the verbal elements of this section. Assonance, alliteration, and internal rime are combined in such sequences as *rocking-mocking, beyond-wander'd, bareheaded-barefoot.* The same qualities, with onomatopoeia as well, are seen in such a phrase as "the mystic play of shadows twining and twisting as if they were alive."

The argument of the poem is also foreshadowed in this section as the poet identifies with the bird, his "sad brother," and sees in the experience of frustration the awakening of his own sense of vocation, the "thousand responses" of his heart and the "myriad thence-aroused words." There is finally the suggestion that the ultimate release from the tension of individual existence (partially resolved through art) is death, "the word stronger and more delicious than any," whispered to the poet by the old crone, the sea. The poet is here identified as the "uniter of here and hereafter," in accordance with Emerson's definition of the poet as the "integrating seer." Whitman's poet is conceived as "taking all hints to use them, but swiftly leaping beyond them," as the images from remembered experience are value charged in the poetic, or metaphoric process.

A reading of the complete poem sustains the reader's impression of an interrelationship of formal elements that can be only briefly suggested here. The sound devices already mentioned are supported by the rhythm of the verses, beginning with the irregularly-stressed but strongly rhythmic opening lines with their intermingled trochees and dactyls, appropriate to both the movement of the sea and the weaving process:

ˈ ˘ ˘ ˈ ˘ ˈ ˘ ˘ ˈ ˘
ˈ ˘ ˘ ˈ ˘ ˘ ˈ ˘ ˈ ˘ ˘ ˈ
ˈ ˘ ˘ ˈ ˘ ˈ ˘

As for syntax, besides parallelism, which contributes also to the effect of rime, the sentence stanzas provide a periodic control for the rhythm of the individual lines as well as a pattern for the expression of meaning. The events of the childhood experience, ordered by the reminiscing poet, support the theme of the awakening sense of poetic vocation. Meaning is found both on the plain sense level, in the recountal of the child's experience, and on the level of metaphor which rises from this and in which both thought and feeling are involved. Metaphorically, the remembered events relate to the meaning of art and the function of the poet. The theme of the poem embraces not only the maturation process, as the boy is introduced to the experiences of love and death, but also a strongly regressive motive, as the experience of frustration turns the poet's thoughts first to the idea of art as sublimation, then to the welcome recognition of death as a release from tension. Emotive values are most strongly evident in the boy's empathic responses to the bird's songs of love and grief and in the exaltation that accompanies his sense of vocation.

"Out of the Cradle Endlessly Rocking" is one of the most successfully-integrated complex poems in our literature. Its organization easily refutes the blanket indictment of formlessness sometimes levelled against Whitman's poetry because of his tendency to identify and merge with his subjects and to be indiscriminate in the selection of detail. This poem reveals the detachment of the poet and a distancing of subject through the device of the three related central figures who as dramatic characters contribute to the development of the theme. The poem's dramatic quality is heightened by the lyric interludes already discussed. The figures of the boy, the bird, and the sea (as earth-mother) are introduced, the significance of their roles is revealed, and the conclusion of the poem resolves the colloquy as the bird's cries of unsatisfied love and the message of death whispered by the sea are fused with the poet's "own songs awakened from that hour."

Other successful poems in *Leaves of Grass* are more simply organized. Some of Whitman's most effective short poems are the vignettes of Civil War experiences in *Drum-Taps,* first published separately in 1865 and later incorporated into *Leaves of Grass.*

"Cavalry Crossing a Ford" presents a picture of observed war experience:

> A line in long array where they wind betwixt green islands,
> They take a serpentine course, their arms flash in the sun—hark to
> the musical clank,
> Behold the silvery river, in it the splashing horses loitering stop
> to drink,
> Behold the brown-faced men, each group, each person a picture, the
> negligent rest on the saddles,
> Some emerge on the opposite bank, others are just entering the
> ford—while,
> Scarlet and blue and snowy white,
> The guidon flags flutter gayly in the wind.

Imagistic in quality, the poem is of interest primarily as a visual composition conveying the color and other sensuous details of a military action. The pictorial effect is comparable, in its detachment and objectivity, to that of a camp sketch by Winslow Homer. Although there is movement and sound, the pause at the ford provides a relative stasis that enables the observer to focus the scene and compose its details. Although the most conspicuous formal element is visual imagery, the poem is not purely imagistic. The serpent-like column and the brown faces relate the men to primitive nature, and the scene in general conveys a sense of fitness, grace, and competence. The flashing of arms and the clanking of equipment suggest the efficiency of the war machine. This brief glimpse of cavalry campaigning effectively communicates the impression of adjustment to nature, of excitement, and color. This metaphorical meaning is not developed, however; it rises spontaneously from a treatment which seems concerned primarily with the level of physical, primarily visual, experience.

Another poem of the same order is "An Army Corps on the March":

> With its cloud of skirmishers in advance,
> With now the sound of a single shot snapping like a whip, and now
>   an irregular volley,
> The swarming ranks press on and on, the dense brigades press on,
> Glittering dimly, toiling under the sun—the dust cover'd men,
> In columns rise and fall to the undulations of the ground,
> With artillery interspers'd—the wheels rumble, the horses sweat,
> As the army corps advances.

The poem reveals the same concern for sensory detail, the same association of human and physical nature. There is a difference in the quality of the impressions, however, in keeping with the nature of the subject. Here is no stasis but rather confusion and movement. The individual forms do not stand out but rather are absorbed in the masses: "clouds of skirmishers," "swarming ranks," "dense brigades." Of course, in both of these brief poems, other kinds of organization are involved besides that of image and event. The sound pattern is particularly important. In the third verse, the regular iambic rhythm and the incremental repetition of the parallel clauses ("The swarming ranks press on and on, the dense brigades press on") contribute to the sense of the remorseless forward motion of a mass within which human identity is lost.

Another brief poem from *Drum-Taps,* "A Sight in Camp in the Daybreak Gray and Dim," also presents a limited and sharp experience but one which is metaphorically developed as well:

> A sight in camp in the daybreak gray and dim,
> As from my tent I emerge so early sleepless,
> As slow I walk in the cool fresh air the path near by the hospital
>   tent,
> Three forms I see on stretchers lying, brought out there untended
>   lying,
> Over each the blanket spread, ample brownish woolen blanket,
> Gray and heavy blanket, folding, covering all.
>
> Curious I halt and silent stand,
> Then with light fingers I from the face of the nearest the first just
>   lift the blanket;

Who are you elderly man so gaunt and grim, with well-gray'd hair, and flesh all sunken about the eyes?
Who are you my dear comrade?

Then to the second I step—and who are you my child and darling?
Who are you sweet boy with cheeks yet blooming?

Then to the third—a face nor child nor old, very calm, as of beautiful yellow-white ivory;
Young man I think I know you—I think this face is the face of the Christ himself,
Dead and divine and brother of all, and here again he lies.

The three figures are associated with the ages of man; but, as the third is identified with Christ, we are also reminded of the Savior and his two companions in death and, by extension, of the Christian Trinity, which Whitman typically supplants with a secular triadic image of three soldiers who have died in the common struggle of existence. The "brownish woolen blanket, / Gray and heavy blanket," is the earth, the physical nature into which the three forms are merging. The poet, who lifts the blanket, penetrates the veil of the flesh, of nature, and recognizes the divine potential of the human individual. The syntactical arrangement of the lines (the recurrent pattern of "I . . . stand, / Then . . . ," "Then . . . I step . . . ," "Then to the third . . . ," followed respectively by "Who are you . . . ?" "and who are you . . . ?" and "I think I know you . . .") serves to integrate the verses, to suggest a symbolic progression, and to develop a suspense which is resolved by the recognition of the third encounter.

This brief poem is more complex than the two preceding because of the interrelationship of the levels of image and meaning. The metaphor of the human victim of war as a Christ figure is clearly suggested, although it is not developed to an extent comparable to the treatment of Lincoln in the long elegy, "When Lilacs Last in the Dooryard Bloom'd."

The intimate relation of image and meaning can be seen in a short poem, "The Dismantled Ship," composed late in Whitman's life and first published in 1888:

In some unused lagoon, some nameless bay,
On sluggish, lonesome waters, anchor'd near the shore,
An old, dismasted, gray and batter'd ship, disabled, done,
After free voyages to all the seas of earth, haul'd up at last and hawser'd tight,
Lies rusting, mouldering.

Here, as in "Cavalry Crossing a Ford," there is a concentration upon visual imagery and an avoidance of any direct statement of meaning. Yet the imagery of this poem, in contrast with that of the other, is immediately recognizable as metaphoric, suggesting the pathos of old age, its sense of futility and desolation. The reason is that the images used—ship, voyage, harbor—while they undoubtedly reflect the poet's observed experience, are also traditional as metaphors of human experience and thus immediately convey the burden of associated concepts and feelings which they have accumulated through centuries of use. Furthermore, the image of the ship had been used by Whitman to suggest a life-quest in both "Crossing Brooklyn Ferry" and "Passage to India," and the reader is struck by the contrast in tone in the treatment of this central image between the confident out-setting of the latter poem ("Sail forth —steer for the deep waters only, / Reckless O soul, exploring, I with thee, and thou with me . . .") and the terminus of the voyage in "The Dismantled Ship."

The interrelated formal dimensions of Whitman's free verse poems can be distinguished in any poem or literary work. While a high degree of differentiation and integration of the formal patterns enhances the interest of a work, complexity cannot be regarded as an arbitrary requirement or criterion. A brief and comparatively simple poem, which may seem disproportionately developed in any one formal dimension may be extremely effective.

Also, even relatively simple poems, if successful, will be found to have a fuller development than is apparent from a casual reading. Thus in the poem "The Dismantled Ship"—which is syntactically organized as one sentence—the devices of sound, as well as the visual imagery, contribute to the effect. The long vowels and the interrupting consonants retard the tempo and support the sense of the sluggishness of age. The long deep vowels of "unused lagoon," "lonesome," "shore," contribute to the tone of melancholy. These are the "dark" vowels in terms of mood as well as of the sound spectrum. The alliteration of *g*'s and *d*'s, the onomatopoeia of *batter'd,* and the harshness of the *a* sounds all reinforce the sense of the line, "An old, dismasted, gray and batter'd ship, disabled, done." As image rises into meaning the relationship of "dismasted" to the impotence of age and of "nameless bay" to the problem of identity as life draws close to its source in nature, becomes apparent.

Whitman's poems demonstrate that poetic form is an open rather than a closed system. It is susceptible always to re-definition and further development in the shifting perspective of the reader. The form of the work is a potential of its verbal structure, and, while we may discuss it from one viewpoint or another, we can never complete an analysis which is commensurate with the "complexity" of the work, however "simple" it may appear upon casual reading. Any analysis which presents itself as systematic and completely definitive is to that extent false to the nature of the work and a belittling of it, perhaps to the temporary advantage of the critic.

Whitman is a useful figure to consider in relation to this idea of open and relative form (which applies to prose as well as to verse) because he himself never regarded his poems as "complete" but instead revised them from edition to edition of *Leaves of Grass.* Also, although he wished his poems to tally with the world of nature, he recognized their limitations as verbal abstractions. Yet he also recognized their peculiar power—that as poetic ensembles they related to the larger scheme in ever-changing ways and that they were inexhaustible to interpretation. Consequently the act of reading, or the perception of form, was for him a dynamic never-to-be-completed process. In the 1855 preface to *Leaves of Grass* he spoke of the poet as one who brings his readers to no terminus but who leads them on a continuing quest for the meaning of the forms of art and the common life expressed through them: "Whom he takes he takes with firm sure grasp into live regions previously unattained . . . thenceforward is no rest. . . ."

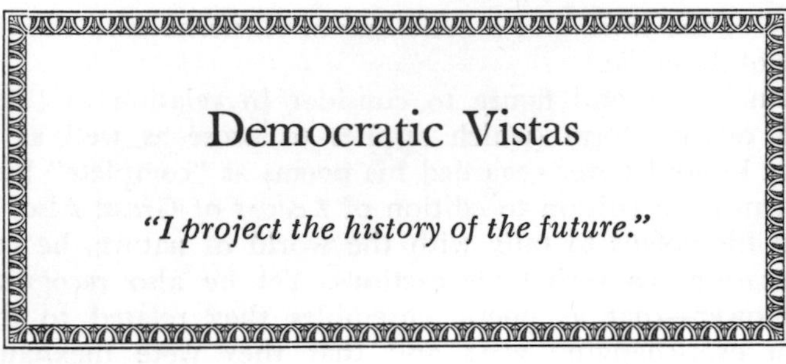

Democratic Vistas

"I project the history of the future."

The Shaping of the American Character

by Perry Miller

In 1867 Walt Whitman brought out a revision of *Leaves of Grass.* He was constantly revising; this was the fourth version. The first had been in 1855, the second in 1856, the third in 1860. Virtually all approved and respectable critics of the time who even bothered to consider Whitman were hostile; they believed a "poetry" that could be so recklessly revised to be obviously no poetry at all. Nowadays there are many who regard him as our greatest poet; when Lucien Price asked Alfred North Whitehead what, if anything, original and distinctively American this country has produced, the philosopher answered without hesitation, "Whitman." I suspect that Whitman, at this moment, is not so popular as he was thirty years ago; if I am right, then this is a sign of the times, one which I must consider ominous. But be that as it may, Whitman's successive revisions, Whitman being what he was, are apt to come not from a heightened sense of form or from a quest for more precise language, but simply out of his constantly changing sense of the American destiny. He could never make up his mind, though at each point he had to pretend that he did and so declaim with a finality whose very flamboyance betrays the uncertainty.

In 1856 he printed one of his most interesting songs, the one called in the collected works, "As I Sat Alone by Blue Ontario's Shore." In this

"The Shaping of the American Character." From *The New England Quarterly*, XXVIII (1955), 435-454.

version, and again in 1860, the poem is an exaltation of the rôle he assigned himself, the poet-prophet of democracy. But by 1867 he had lived through the central ordeal of this Republic, the war we call variously "Civil" or "Between the States." Something profoundly disturbing had happened to Walt Whitman; it is expressed not only in poems written directly out of his experience, like "Drum-Taps" and "When Lilacs Last in the Dooryard Bloom'd," but in the revisions of previous utterances. In 1856 and 1860, for instance, one line of "By Blue Ontario's Shore" had gone, "Give me to speak beautiful words! take all the rest." In 1867 this became "Give me to sing the song of the great Idea! take all the rest." After the war, he would celebrate the democracy itself, not merely the poet. These changes, commentators theorize, record a chastening of Whitman's egotism; they indicate his belated realization that this country is bigger than any man, even a Whitman, and from the realization he learned humility.

However, the sort of humility one acquires only from discovering that his nation is large and he himself small is by definition suspect. In Whitman, there are some curious additions to the postwar announcement of self-abnegation. This couplet for example:

> We stand self-pois'd in the middle, branching thence over the world;
> From Missouri, Nebraska, or Kansas, laughing attack to scorn.

Or, still more striking, this verse:

> America isolated I sing;
> I say that works made here in the spirit of other lands, are so much poison in The States.
> (How dare such insects as we assume to write poems for America?
> For our victorious armies, and the offspring following the armies?)

Recently a French critic, commenting on this passage, has called it the tirade of a narrow and contemptuous isolationism. Perhaps a Frenchman at this point in history has a reaction different from ours to a boast about the offspring following our victorious armies!

In the light of M. Asselineau's opinion, it is of some significance that Whitman himself, in the 1881 revision of *Leaves of Grass,* suppressed these pieces of strident isolationism. By then he had received further lessons in humility, not from victorious armies but from the stroke that paralyzed him; the last poems, as has often been remarked, show an aspiration toward universality with which the mood of 1867 was in open opposition. However, of one fact there can be no doubt: Walt Whitman, self-appointed spokesman for America, found himself responding in a fashion which may, indeed, be characteristic of the patriot in any country, but has been most conspicuously characteristic of the American: exulting in military victory, he proclaimed that an isolated America has nothing and should have nothing to do with the rest of the world.

This episode in the history of the text is only one out of a thousand which underscore that quality in *Leaves of Grass* that does make it so peculiarly an American book: its extreme self-consciousness. Not only does Whitman appoint himself the poet-prophet of the nation, and advertise to the point of tedium that he sings America, but in the incessant effort to find out what he is singing, what America is, he must always be revising his poems to suit a fluctuating conception. As Archibald MacLeish wrote in 1929 (he as much as Whitman shows how acutely self-conscious about nationality our artists must be), "It is a strange thing—to be an American":

> This, this is our land, this is our people
> This that is neither a land nor a race.

Whether the American public dislikes Whitman or is indifferent to him, still, in this respect he is indeed the national poet Mr. Whitehead called him. So, if we then examine closely this quality of Whitman's awareness, even though we do not pretend to be professional psychologists, we are bound to recognize that it emanates not from a mood of serene self-possession and self-assurance, as Whitman blatantly orated, but rather from a pervasive self-distrust. There is a nervous instability at the bottom of his histrionic ostentation—an anxiety which foreign critics understandably call neurotic. In fact these critics, even our friends, tell us that this is precisely what Americans are: insecure, gangling, secret worriers behind a façade of braggadocio, unable to live and to let live.

Some of the articles in the massive supplement on *American Writing To-Day* which the *Times* of London brought out in September, 1954, are by Americans, but one called "A Search for the Conscience of a People" sounds as though of English authorship; either way, it declares an opinion I have frequently heard in England and on the Continent. Americans, particularly from the early nineteenth century on, have been in search of an identity. "The Englishman," says the writer, "takes his Englishness for granted; the Frenchman does not constantly have to be looking over his shoulder to see if his Frenchiness is still there." The reason for this national anxiety is that being an American is not something to be inherited so much as something to be achieved. This, our observer concludes, is "a complex fate."

Surely it is, as complex for a nation as for a person. Yet what compounds complexity is that all the time we are searching for ourselves we keep insisting that we are a simple, uncomplicated people. We have no social classes, our regional variations are not great compared with those of France or Germany, no weight of tradition compels us to travel in well-worn ruts. From coast to coast we all buy the same standard brands in chain stores built to a standard pattern, we see the same television shows, laugh at the same jokes, adore the same movie stars, and hear the same singing commercials. How, then, can we be complex? Europe is complex—it is civilized, old, tormented with ancient memories; but we are as natural as children. Then, why are we so nervous? Why do we so worry about our identity? One can imagine an English college setting up a conference on the constitutional principles of the Cromwellian Protectorate, or on the issues of the Reform Bill of 1832, but never, I am sure, one entitled, "On Values in the British Tradition." At Oxford and Cambridge those would be so much taken for granted that even to mention them aloud would be bad form, and to insinuate that they needed discussion would become indecent exposure.

As far as I read the history of the West, I find only one other great civilization that faced an analogous predicament, and that was the Roman Empire. Not the Republic: the original Rome emerged gradually, as have the modern nations of Europe, out of the mists of legend, mythology, vaguely remembered migrations of prehistoric peoples. The Republic had traditions that nobody created, which had been there beyond the memory of mankind, atavistic attachments to the soil. But after the murderous Civil Wars and wars of conquest, the old Roman stock was either wiped out or so mixed with the races of the Mediterranean that the Empire had become as conglomerate a population as ours, the social cohesion as artificial. As with us, there was not time to let the people fuse by natural and organic growth over several centuries: Rome was no longer a country but a continent, no longer a people but an institution. The aggregation would have fallen apart in the first century B.C. had not somebody, by main force, by deliberate, conscious exertion, imposed unity upon it. Julius Caesar attempted this, but his nephew and ultimately his successor, Augustus Caesar, did it.

This analogy, as I say, has often struck me, but I should be hesitant to construct so seemingly far-fetched a parallel did I not have at least the authority of Alfred North Whitehead for entertaining it. Actually, it was a favorite speculation with Mr. Whitehead, and I may well have got it from him in some now forgotten conversation. However, it comes back to us, as though Whitehead were still speaking, in Lucien Price's *Dialogues.* Augustus Caesar's foundation of an empire would not, Whitehead agrees, satisfy our ideal of liberty, yet it saved civilization. It is, in the very deliberateness of the deed, a complete contrast to the unconscious evolution of the English constitution. Nobody here, Whitehead remarks, can say at exactly what point the idea of a limited monarchy came in; the conception originated with no one person nor at any specific time, and even today no scientifically precise definition is possible. Though the Roman Empire was not the result of any long-range plan, once it existed, it was recognized as being what it had become, and systematically organized; the British acquired their empire, as the saying goes, in a fit of absence of mind, and have never quite found a way to administer the whole of it. So they surrender to nature and let irresistible forces guide it into forms that are not at all "imperial."

Now Whitehead's point is that the only other creation of a nation and an administration by conscious effort, the only other time statesmen assumed control of historic destinies and, refusing to let nature take its course, erected by main force a society, was the American Revolution and the Constitutional Convention. To read the history of the first sessions of the Congress under President Washington in 1789 and 1790 is to be driven either to laughter or to tears, or to both. Even more than in the first years of Augustus' principate, I suspect, it presents the spectacle of men trying to live from a blueprint. The document prescribed two houses of legislators, a court, and an executive; as men of cultivation they had some knowledge of parliamentary procedure, but beyond such elementary rules of order they knew not how to behave. They did not know how to address the President, and nobody could figure in what manner a cabinet officer was related to the Congress. That is why, although certain customs have been agreed upon, such as "Senatorial courtesy," we do not have the immemorial traditions that govern, let us say, conduct in the House of Commons. Hence, when one of our customs appears to be violated, we behold a Select Committee of Senators trying to find out what the Senate is. We can do nothing by instinct.

As a matter of historical fact, Professor Whitehead might have pushed that moment of conscious decision further back than the Constitutional Convention. Settlers came to the colonies for a number of reasons that were, so to speak, in the situation rather than in their minds, yet none came without making an anterior decision in his mind. They may have been forced by famine, economic distress, a lust for gold or land, by religious persecutions, but somewhere in their lives there had to be the specific moment when they said to themselves or to each other, "Let's get out, let's go to America." The only exception to this rule is, of course, the Negroes; they came not because they wanted to but because they were captured and brought by force. Maybe that is why they, of all our varied people, seem to be the only sort that can do things by instinct. Maybe that is why Willie Mays is the greatest of contemporary outfielders.

Also, the Indians did not come by *malice prépensé*. They are the only Americans whose historical memory goes back to the origin of the land itself; they do not have to look over their shoulders to see if their Indianness is still there. So, they astonished the first Americans by acting upon instinct. One of the most charming demonstrations of this native spontaneity was Pocahontas' rush to the block to save Captain John

Smith from having his brains beaten out. Later on, Indian rushes were not so charming, but even in warfare they exhibited a headlong impetuosity that bespoke an incapacity to make deliberate plans. They could never construct an assembly line or work out a split-second television schedule.

As for Captain John Smith himself, we may doubt that this impetuous adventurer came at first to America out of the sort of conscious decision Whitehead had in mind. To begin with, America meant no more to him than Turkey, and Pocahontas no more than the Lady Tragabigzanda, who inspired his escape from slavery in Constantinople—at least, so he says. But even he, who became a temporary American by accident, after a brief two-years' experience of the land, realized that here lay a special destiny. The initial disorders at Jamestown—which were considerable—convinced him that God, being angry with the company, plagued them with famine and sickness. By the time he was summoned home, the dream of an empire in the wilderness was upon him, and he reviewed these afflictions not as merely the customary and universal rebukes of Providence upon sinners, but as ones specially dispensed for the guidance of Americans. He spent twenty-two years selflessly propagandizing for settlement. By 1624, after he had digested the lesson of his intense initiation, he had thoroughly comprehended that migrating to America was serious business, much too strenuous for those he called the "Tuftaffaty" gentlemen who had come along, as we might say, only for the ride, in the expectation of picking up easy gold from the ground. No: mere tourists, traveling nobles, would not build an empire; it needed people who, having decided to remove, would as a consequence of decision put their backs into the labor. In 1624 he reprinted and emphasized a cry he had written to the company back in 1608, when the lesson was just beginning to dawn upon him:

> When you send againe I entreat you rather send but thirty Carpenters, husbandmen, gardiners, fisher men, blacksmiths, masons, and diggers up of trees, roots, well provided; then a thousand of such as we haue: for except wee be able to lodge them, and feed them, the most will consume with want of necessaries before they can be made good for any thing.

Smith was more prophetic than even he comprehended: America has not time to make people good for anything; they have to be good for something to start with.

The outstanding case of the conscious act of decision was, we all know, the Puritan migration to New England. Whenever we find the religious incentive strong among immigrating groups, something of the same history can be found, but the New Englanders were so articulate, produced so voluminous a literature in explanation of their conduct, and through the spreading of the stock across the continent have left so deep an impress on the country, that the Puritan definition of purpose has been in effect appropriated by immigrants of other faiths, by those who in the nineteenth century left lands of a culture utterly different from the English. The act was formally committed to paper by the "Agreement" signed and ratified at Cambridge in the summer of 1629. The great John Winthrop, the Moses of this exodus, was able to give full expression to the idea even before he set foot ashore; he did it by preaching a lay sermon aboard the flagship of the fleet, on the deck of the *Arabella,* when still in mid-ocean. It was published under the title "A Modell of Christian Charity," in 1630. Chronologically speaking, Smith and a few others in Virginia, two or three at Plymouth, published works on America before the "Modell," but in relation to the principal theme of the American mind, the necessity laid upon it for decision, Winthrop stands at the beginning of our consciousness.

We wonder whether, once Southampton and Land's End had sunk beneath the eastern horizon, once he had turned his face irrevocably westward, Winthrop suddenly realized that he was sailing not toward another island but a continent, and that once there the problem would be to keep the people fixed in the mold of the Cambridge Agreement, to prevent them from following the lure of real estate into a dispersion that would quickly alter their character. At any rate, the announced doctrine of his sermon is that God distinguishes persons in this world by rank, some high, some low, some rich, some poor. Ostensibly, then, he is propounding a European class structure; but when he comes to the exhortation, he does not so much demand that inferiors remain in pious subjection to superiors, but rather he calls upon all, gentlemen and commoners, to be knit together in this work as one man. He seems apprehensive that old sanctions will not work; he wants all the company to swear an oath, to confirm their act of will. This band have entered into a Covenant with God to perform the specific work: "We have taken out a Commission, the Lord hath giuen vs leaue to drawe our owne Articles, we haue professed to enterprise these Accions vpon these and these ends." Because this community is not merely to reproduce an English social hierarchy, because over and above that, more important even than an ordered way of life, it has a responsibility to live up to certain enumerated purposes. Therefore this society, unlike any in Europe, will be rewarded by Divine Providence to the extent that it fulfills the Covenant. Likewise it will be afflicted with plagues, fires, disasters, to the extent that it fails. Profound though he was, Winthrop probably did not entirely realize how novel, how radical, was his sermon; he assumed he was merely theorizing about this projected community in relation to the Calvinist divinity, absolute sovereign of the universe. What in reality he was telling the proto-Americans was that they could not just blunder along like ordinary people, seeking wealth and opportunity for their children. Every citizen of this new society would have to know, completely understand, reckon every day with, the enunciated terms on which it was brought into being, according to which it would survive or perish. This duty of conscious realization lay as heavy upon the humblest, the least educated, the most stupid, as upon the highest, the most learned, the cleverest.

There is, I think all will acknowledge, a grandeur in Winthrop's formulation of the rationale for a society newly entered into a bond with Almighty God to accomplish "these and these ends." However, enemies of the Puritans even at the time did more than suggest that the conception also bespeaks an astounding arrogance. Who was Winthrop, critics asked, and who were these Puritans, that they could take unto themselves the notion that the Infinite God would bind himself to particular terms only with them, while He was leaving France and Germany and even England to shift for themselves? One can argue that coming down from this Puritan conception of America's unique destiny—"Wee must consider," said Winthrop, "that wee shall be as a Citty vpon a Hill, the eies of all people vppon us"—has descended that glib American phrase, "God's country," which so amuses when it does not exasperate our allies. But the important thing to note is that after a century or more of experience on this continent, the communities, especially the Puritan colonies, found the Covenant theory no longer adequate. It broke down because it tried, in disregard of experience, in disregard of the frontier and a thriving commerce, to stereotype the image of America, to confine it to the Procrustean bed of a priori conception. Not that the theology failed to account for empirical phenomena; only, the effort to keep these aligned within the original rubrics became too exhausting. The American mind discarded this notion of its personality because the ingenuity required to maintain it was more than men had time or energy to devise.

The little states suffered many adversities—plagues, wars, crop failures, floods, internal dissension. According to Winthrop's reasoning, the communities could not accept these as the normal hazards of settling a wilderness or augmenting the wealth; they had to see in every reverse an intentional punishment for their sins. By the time they had undergone several Indian wars and frequent hurricanes, a tabulation of their sins would obviously become so long as to be crushing. We can imagine, for instance, what Cotton Mather would have made in his Sabbath sermons, morning and afternoon, each over two hours in duration, of the fact that New England was struck by not one but *two* hurricanes, and that the first, proceeding according to divine appointment, carried away the steeple of his own church, the Old North. He would perfectly understand why, since the population did not immediately reform their criminal habits, even upon such a dramatic admonition, another storm must come close upon the other. Were we still livingly persuaded that we actually are God's country, we would not now be arguing with insurance companies or complaining about the Weather Bureau, but would be down on our knees, bewailing the transgressions of New England, searching our memories to recall, and to repent of, a thousand things we have contrived to forget. We would be reaffirming our Americanism by promising with all our hearts to mend the evil ways that brought upon us the avenging fury of Carol and Edna.

In pious sections of America at the time of the Revolution some vestiges of the Covenant doctrine remained. Historians point out how effective was the propaganda device employed by the Continental Congresses, their calling for national days of fasting and humiliations. Historians regard these appeals as cynical because most of the leaders, men of the Enlightenment, were emancipated from so crude a theology as Winthrop's. Certainly you find no trace of it in the Declaration of Independence. Yet I often wonder whether historians fully comprehend that the old-fashioned religious sanction could be dispensed with only because the Revolutionary theorists had found a substitute which seemed to them adequate to account for a more complex situation. Being classicists, they read Latin; while nurtured on authors of Republican Rome, they were as much if not more trained in the concepts of the empire, not only in writers like Tacitus and Marcus Aurelius, but in the Roman law. Which is to say, that the imperial idea, as Augustus made it manifest, was second nature to them. Whether Madison appreciated as keenly as Whitehead the highly conscious nature of Augustus' statesmanship, he had no qualms about going at the business of constitution making in a legal, imperial spirit. The problem was to bring order out of chaos, to set up a government, to do it efficiently and quickly. There was no time to let Nature, gradually, by her mysterious alchemy, bring us eventually to some such fruition as the British Constitution; even so, had time not been so pressing, Madison and the framers saw nothing incongruous in taking time by the forelock, drawing up the blueprint, and so bringing into working operation a government by fiat. Analysts may argue that separation of powers, for instance, had in practice if not in theory come about by historical degrees within the colonial governments, but the framers did not much appeal to that sort of wisdom. They had a universal rule: power must not be concentrated, it must be divided into competing balances; wherefore America decrees its individuality through a three-fold sovereign, executive, legislative, and judicial, and then still further checks that authority by an enumerated Bill of Rights.

The Revolutionary chiefs were patriots, but on the whole they were less worried by the problem of working out an exceptional character for America than the spokesmen of any other period. Patriotism was a virtue, in the Roman sense, but one could be an ardent American without, in the Age of Reason, having to insist that there were special reasons in America, reasons not present in other lands, why citizens must inordinately love this nation. Franklin, Jefferson, Madison were as near to true cosmopolitans as the United States has ever produced. But on the other hand, in order to win the war, pamphleteers for the patriot side did have to assert that the Revolution carried the hopes not only of America but of the world. The immense effectiveness of Thomas Paine's *Common Sense,* for example, consisted not so much in its contention that independence of England made common sense but that only America was close enough to Nature, only these simple people were so uncorrupted by the vices of decrepit civilizations, that only here could common sense operate at all.

It is a fanciful speculation, but suppose that the intellectual world of the late eighteenth century had persisted unchanged from 1776 to the present. In that case, through one and three-quarters centuries we should have had a steady and undisturbing task: merely refining on and perfecting the image of ourselves we first beheld in the mirror of the Declaration of Independence. Had there been no Romantic poetry, no novels by Scott, no railroads and steam engines, no Darwin, no machine gun, no dynamo, no automobile, no airplane, no atomic bomb, we would have had no reason to suppose ourselves other than what we were at Concord and Yorktown. We would remain forever formerly embattled farmers listening complacently from our cornfields to the echoes rolling round the world of the shot we fired, without working ourselves into a swivet worrying about whether we should again shoot. However, even before Jefferson and Adams were dead in 1826, the mind of America was already infected from abroad with concepts of man and nature which rendered those of the patriarchs as inadequate as the Covenant theology, while at the same time the nation itself was being transformed by an increase of population and of machines, and so had to rethink entirely anew the question of its identity.

The French Revolution and the Napoleonic Wars, it is a truism to say, aroused all over Europe a spirit of nationalism which the eighteenth century had supposed forever extinct. One manifestation of the new era was an assiduous search in each country for primitive, tribal, barbaric orgins. Germans went back to medieval legends, to the Niebelungenlied, to fairy tales. Sir Walter Scott gave the English a new sense of their history, so that the ideal British hero was no longer Marlborough or Pitt, but Ivanhoe, Rob Roy, and Quentin Durward, while the yeomen suddenly gloried in having come down from Gurth the Swineherd. Realizing that the evolution of English society as well as of the constitution had been organic, natural, spontaneous, illogical, the English renounced reason; they challenged America to show what more profound excuse for being it had than a dull and rationalistic convention. All at once, instead of being the hope of the enlightened world,

America found itself naked of legends, primitive virtues, archaic origins. It might be full of bustle and progress, but romantically speaking, it was uninteresting, had no personality.

Americans tried to answer by bragging about the future, but that would not serve. In the first half of the nineteenth century many of our best minds went hard to work to prove that we too are a nation in some deeper sense than mere wilfulness. At this time Europeans began that accusation which some of them still launch, which drives us to a frenzy: "You are not a country, you are a continent." Not at all, said James Fenimore Cooper; we too have our legends, our misty past, our epic figures, our symbolic heroes. To prove this, he created Natty Bumppo—Leatherstocking the Deerslayer, the Pathfinder, the embodiment of an America as rooted in the soil, as primordial as the Germany that gave birth to Siegfried.

Professor Allan Nevins recently brought out a selection from the five Leatherstocking volumes of the portions that tell the biography of Natty Bumppo, arranged them in chronological order instead of the sequence in which Cooper composed them, and thus reminded us that Cooper did create a folk-hero, achieving in his way a success comparable to Homer's. Modern readers have difficulty with Cooper's romances because they do seem cluttered with pompous courtships and tiresome disquisitions; these were not annoyances to readers in his day (though I must say that even then some critics found his women rather wooden), so that they had no trouble in appreciating the magnificence of his Scout and of Chingachgook. Mr. Nevins says that when he was a boy, he and his companions played at being Natty and Chingachgook; children nowadays do not read Cooper—I am told that if they can so much as read at all, they peruse nothing but comic books—and they play at being Superman and space cadets. But for years Cooper more than any single figure held up the mirror in which several generations of Americans saw the image of themselves they most wished to see—a free-ranging individualist, very different from Winthrop's covenanted saint or from Paine's common-sensical Revolutionary.

Cooper persuaded not only thousands of Americans that he was delineating their archetype but also Europeans. One does not readily associate the name of Balzac with Cooper, but Balzac was an enthusiastic reader of Leatherstocking and in 1841 wrote a resounding review, praising the mighty figures but explaining what was an even more important element in Cooper's achievement:

> The magical prose of Cooper not only embodies the spirit of the river, its shores, the forest and its trees; but it exhibits the minutest details, combined with the grandest outline. The vast solitudes, in which we penetrate, become in a moment deeply interesting. . . . When the spirit of solitude communes with us, when the first calm of these eternal shades pervades us, when we hover over this virgin vegetation, our hearts are filled with emotion.

Here was indeed the answer to the problem of American self-recognition! We may have come to the land by an act of will, but despite ourselves, we have become parts of the landscape. The vastness of the continent, its very emptiness, instead of meaning that we are blank and formless, makes us deeply interesting amid our solitudes. Our history is not mechanical, calculated; it is as vibrant with emotion as the history of Scott's Britain.

On every side spokesmen for the period between Jackson and Lincoln developed this thesis; by the time of the Civil War it had become the major articulate premise of American self-consciousness. Let us take one example. George Bancroft's *History of the United States* had a success with the populace at large which no academic historian today dares even dream of. When he came to the Revolution, he recast it into the imagery of nature and instinct, so that even Jefferson became as spontaneous (and as authentic a voice of the landscape) as Natty Bumppo:

> There is an analogy between early American politics and the earliest heroic poems. Both were spontaneous, and both had the vitality of truth. Long as natural affection endures, the poems of Homer will be read with delight; long as freedom lives on earth, the early models of popular legislation and action in America will be admired.

So, for Bancroft and his myriad readers, the lesson of the Revolution and the Constitution was precisely opposite to what Whitehead sees in the story. Prudent statesmanship, Bancroft says, would have asked time to ponder, "would have dismissed the moment for decision by delay." Conscious effort "would have compared the systems of government, and would have lost from hesitation the glory of opening a new era on mankind." But the common people—the race of Natty Bumppo—did not deliberate: "The humble train-bands at Concord acted, and God was with them."

We can easily laugh at such language. We may agree that Cooper and Bancroft were noble men, patriotic Americans, but to our ears something rings terribly false in their hymns to the natural nation. Perhaps the deepest flaw is their unawareness of, or their wilful blindness to, the fact that they are constructing in a most highly conscious manner an image of America as the creation of unconscious instinct. They apply themselves to supplying the country with an archaic past as purposefully as General Motors supplies it with locomotion. They recast the conception of America into terms actually as a priori as Winthrop's Covenant, and then do just what he did: they say that these spontaneous and heroic terms are objectively true, fixed and eternal. Within them and only them America shall always make decisions, shall always, like the train-bands at Concord, act in reference to their unalterable exactions. We are what we have always been, and so we are predictable. He who acts otherwise is not American.

Behind the Puritan, the Revolutionary and the Romantic conception of social identity lies still another premise; in all these formulations it is *not* articulated. I might put it roughly like this: they all take for granted that a personality, a national one as well as an individual, is something pre-existing, within which an invariable and foreseeable pattern of decision reigns. If, let us say, a man is brave, he will always act bravely. If a nation is proud, chivalric, religious, it will be Spanish; if it is frivolous, amatory, cynical, it will be French. I need hardly remind you that a powerful movement in modern thought has, in a hundred ways, called in question this "deterministic" method. There may be, and indeed there are, physical conditions, such as sex or size, such as climate or mineral resources; but these are not what make the personality we deal with, the nation we must understand. What constitutes the present being is a series of past decisions; in that sense, no act is spontaneous, no decision is imposed, either by the Covenant, by common sense, or by Nature.

In the later nineteenth century, as Romantic conceptions of the universe died out, another determined effort was made to recast the image of America in the language of Darwinian evolution. In this century, as the faith weakened that evolution would automatically carry us forward, we have, in general, reformulated our personality into a creature preternaturally adept in production—the jeep and the know-how. Each successive remodeling retains something of the previous form: we echo the Covenant not only in the phrase "God's country," but when we pray for the blessing of Heaven upon our arms and our industries, we invoke Revolutionary language in our belief that we, of all the world, are preeminently endowed with common sense; we also imagine ourselves possessed of the pioneer virtues of Natty Bumppo, by calling ourselves "nature's noblemen," yet simultaneously suppose ourselves evolving into an industrial paradise, complete with television and the deep freeze. When we try to bundle up these highly disparate notions into a single definition, we are apt to come up with some such blurb as "The American Way of Life."

I am attempting to tell a long story in too short a compass, but I hope my small point is moderately clear. As a nation, we have had a strenuous experience, as violent as that Walt Whitman records; he spent a lifetime trying to put America into his book, to discover himself bedevilled by changing insights, buffeted by unpredicted emotions, rapid shifts, bewildered by new elements demanding incorporation in the synthesis. He who endeavors to fix the personality of America in one eternal, unchangeable pattern not only understands nothing of how a personality is created, but comprehends little of how this nation has come along thus far. He who seeks repose in a unitary conception in effect abandons personality. His motives may be of the best: he wants to preserve, just as he at the moment understands it, the distinctive American essence—the

Covenant, common sense, the natural grandeur, the American Way of Life. But he fools himself if he supposes that the explanation for America is to be found in the conditions of America's existence rather than in the existence itself. A man *is* his decisions, and the great uniqueness of this nation is simply that here the record of conscious decision is more precise, more open and explicit than in most countries. This gives us no warrant to claim that we are higher in any conceivable scale of values; it merely permits us to realize that to which the English observer calls attention, that being an American is not something inherited but something to be achieved.

He says this condemns us to a "complex fate." Complexity is worrisome, imparts no serenity, only anxiety. It keeps us wondering whether we might now be something other, and probably better, than we are had we in the past decided otherwise, and this in turn makes decision in the present even more nerve-wracking. Trying to escape from such anxiety by affixing our individuality to a scheme of unchanging verities is a natural response. Yet our national history promises no success to the frantic gesture. Generalizations about the American character can amount to no more than a statistical survey of the decisions so far made, and these warrant in the way of hypotheses about those yet to be made only the most tentative estimates. However, if my analysis has any truth in it, a backhanded sort of generalization does emerge: he who would fix the pattern of decision by confining the American choice to one and only one mode of response—whether this be in politics, diplomacy, economics, literary form, or morality itself—such a one, in the light of our history, is the truly "Un-American."

An Essay on *Leaves of Grass*

by William Carlos Williams

Leaves of Grass! It was a good title for a book of poems, especially for a new book of American poems. It was a challenge to the entire concept of the poetic idea, and from a new viewpoint, a rebel viewpoint, an American viewpoint. In a word and at the beginning it enunciated a shocking truth, that the common ground is of itself a poetic source. There had been inklings before this that such was the case in the works of Robert Burns and the poet Wordsworth, but in this instance the very forms of the writing had been altered: it had gone over to the style of the words as they appeared on the page. Whitman's so-called "free verse" was an assault on the very citadel of the poem itself; it constituted a direct challenge to all living poets to show cause why they should not do likewise. It is a challenge that still holds good after a century of vigorous life during which it has been practically continuously under fire but never defeated.

From the beginning Whitman realized that the matter was largely technical. It had to be free verse or nothing with him and he seldom varied from that practice—and never for more than the writing of an occasional poem. It was a sharp break, and if he was to go astray he had no one but himself to blame for it. It was a technical matter, true enough, and he would stick it out to the end, but to do any more with it than simply to write the poems was beyond him.

He had seen a great light but forgot almost at once after the first revelation everything but his "message," the idea which originally set him in motion, the idea on which he had been nurtured, the idea of democracy—and took his eye off the words themselves which should have held him.

The point is purely academic—the man had his hands full with the conduct of his life and couldn't, if they had come up, be bothered with

"An Essay on *Leaves of Grass*." From *Leaves of Grass One Hundred Years After*, edited by Milton Hindus (Stanford, Calif., 1955), pp. 22-31.

other matters. As a result, he made no further progress as an artist but, in spite of various topical achievements, continued to write with diminishing effectiveness for the remainder of his life.

He didn't know any better. He didn't have the training to construct his verses after a conscious mold which would have given him power over them to turn them this way, then that, at will. He only knew how to give them birth and to release them to go their own way. He was preoccupied with the great ideas of the time, to which he was devoted, but, after all, poems are made out of words not ideas. He never showed any evidence of knowing this and the unresolved forms consequent upon his beginnings remained in the end just as he left them.

Verses, in English, are frequently spoken of as measures. It is a fortunate designation as it gives us, in looking at them, the idea of elapsed time. We are reminded that the origin of our verse was the dance—and even if it had not been the dance, the heart when it is stirred has its multiple beats, and verse at its most impassioned sets the heart violently beating. But as the heart picks up we also begin to count. Finally, the measure for each language and environment is accepted. In English it is predominantly the iambic pentameter, but whether that is so for the language Whitman spoke is something else again. It is a point worth considering, but apart from the briefest of notices a point not to be considered here. It may be that the essential pace of the English and the American languages is diametrically opposed each to the other and that that is an important factor in the writing of their poetry, but that is for the coming generations to discover. Certainly not only the words but the meter, the measure that governed Whitman's verses, was not English. But there were more pressing things than abstract discussions of meter to be dealt with at that time and the poet soon found himself involved in them.

Very likely the talk and the passionate talk about freedom had affected him as it had infected the French and many others earlier. It is said that, when as a young man he lived in New Orleans, he had fallen in love with a beautiful octoroon but had allowed his friends and relatives to break up the match. It is possible that the disappointment determined the pattern of his later rebellion in verse. Free verse was his great idea! *Versos sueltos* the Spanish call them. It is not an entirely new idea, but it was entirely new to the New York Yankee who was, so to speak, waiting for it with open arms and an overcharged soul and the example of Thomas Jefferson to drive him on.

But verse had always been, for Englishmen and the colonials that imitated them, a disciplined maneuver of the intelligence, as it is today, in which measure was predominant. They resented this American with his new idea, and attacked him in a characteristic way—*on moral grounds*. And he fell for it. He had no recourse but to defend himself and the fat was in the fire. How could verse be free without being immoral? There is something to it. It is the same attack, with a more modern tilt to it, that undoubtedly bothers T. S. Eliot. He is one of the best informed of our writers and would do us a great service, if free verse—mold it as he will—is not his choice, to find us an alternative. From the evidence, he has tried to come up with just that, but up to the present writing he has not brought the thing off.

The case of Mr. Eliot is in this respect interesting. He began writing at Harvard from a thoroughly well-schooled background and produced a body of verse that was immediately so successful that when his poem *The Waste Land* was published, it drove practically everyone else from the field. Ezra Pound, who had helped him arrange the poem on the page, was confessedly jealous. Other American poets had to take second place. A new era, under domination of a return to a study of the classics, was gratefully acknowledged by the universities, and Mr. Eliot, not Mr. Pound, was ultimately given the Nobel Prize. The drift was plainly away from all that was native to America, Whitman among the rest, and toward the study of the past and England.

Though no one realized it, a violent revolution had taken place in American scholarship and the interests from which it stemmed. Eliot had completely lost interest in all things American, in the very ideology of all that America stood for, including the idea of freedom itself in any of its phases. Whitman as a symbol of indiscriminate freedom was completely antipathetic to Mr. Eliot, who now won the country away from him again. The tendency toward freedom in the verse forms, which seemed to be thriving among American poets, was definitely checked and the stage was taken over for other things. I shall never forget the impression created by *The Waste Land;* it was as if the bottom had dropped out of everything. I had not known how much the spirit of Whitman animated us until it was withdrawn from us. Free verse became overnight a thing of the past. Men went about congratulating themselves as upon the disappearance of something that had disturbed their dreams; and indeed it was so—the dreams of right-thinking students of English verse had long been disturbed by the appearance among them of the horrid specter of Whitman's free verse. Now it was as if a liberator, a Saint George, had come just in the nick of time to save them. The instructors in all the secondary schools were grateful.

Meanwhile, Mr. Eliot had become a British subject and removed himself to England where he took up residence. He became a member of the Church of England. He was determined to make the break with America complete, as his fellow artist Henry James had done before him, and began to publish such poems as *Ash Wednesday* and the play *Murder in the Cathedral,* and the *Four Quartets.* Something had happened to him, something drastic, something to do, doubtless, with man's duty and his freedom in the world. It is a far cry from this to Whitman's thought of man as a free agent. The pendulum had gone the full swing.

It is inevitable for us to connect the happenings in the world generally with what takes place in the poem. When Mr. Eliot quit writing, when he quit writing poems, it looked as if he had got to a point where he had nowhere else to turn, and as if in his despair he had given up not only the poem but the world. A man as clever and well informed as he was had the whole world at his feet, but the only conclusion that he reached was that he wanted none of it. Especially did he want none of the newer freedom.

Not that he didn't in his verse try it on, for size, let us say, in his later experiments, particularly in *Four Quartets,* but even there he soon came to the end of his rope. The accented strophe he had definitely given up, as Wagner in the prelude to *Parsifal* had done the same, but to infer from that fact that he had discovered the freedom of a new measure was not true. It looked to me, at least, as if there were some profound depth to his probing beyond which he dared not go without compromising his religious faith. He did not attempt it. It is useful to record the limits of his penetration and the point at which he gave up his attempts to penetrate further. Just how far shall we go in our search for freedom and, more importantly, how shall our efforts toward a greater freedom be conditioned in our verses? All these decisions, which must be reached in deciding what to do, have implications of general value in our lives.

The young men who are students of literature today in our universities do not believe in seeking within the literary forms, the lines, the foot, the way in which to expand their efforts to know the universe, as Whitman did, but are content to follow the theologians and Mr. Eliot. In that, they are children of the times; they risk nothing, for by risking an expanded freedom you are very likely to come a cropper. What, in the words of Hjalmar Ekdahl in *The Wild Duck,* are you going to invent?

Men, offering their heads, have always come up with new proposals, and the world of events waits upon them, and who shall say whether it were better to close one's eyes or go forward like Galileo to the light or wait content in the darkness like the man in the next county? Whitman went forward to what to him seemed desirable, and so if we are to reject him entirely we must at least follow him at the start to find out what his discoveries were intended to signify and what not to signify.

Certainly, we are in our day through with such loose freedom as he employed in his verses in the blind belief that it was all going to come out right in the end. We know now that it is not. But are we, because of that, to give up freedom entirely? Merely to put down the lines as they happen to come into your head will not make a poem, and if, as happened more than once in Whitman's case, a poem result, who is going to tell what he has made? The man knew what he was doing, but he did not know all he was doing. Much still remains to discover, but that freedom in the conduct of the verses is desirable cannot be questioned.

There is a very moving picture of Whitman facing the breakers coming in on the New Jersey shore, when he heard the onomatopoeic waves talk to him direct in a Shakespearean language which might have been Lear himself talking to the storm. But it was not what it seemed; it was a new language, an unnamed language which Whitman could not identify or control.

For as the English had foreseen, this freedom of which there had been so much talk had to have limits somewhere. If not, it would lead you astray. That was the problem. And there was at about that time a whole generation of Englishmen, prominent among whom was Frank Harris, whom it did lead astray in moral grounds, just as there were Frenchmen at the time of the French Revolution who were led astray and are still being led astray under the difficult conditions that exist today. It is the reaction against such patterns of thought that moved Eliot and that part of the present generation which is not swallowed up by its fascination with the scene which draws them to Paris whenever they get the opportunity to go there. For in your search for freedom—which is desirable—you must stop somewhere, but where exactly shall you stop? Whitman could not say.

To propose that the answer to the problem should lie in the verse itself would have been to those times an impertinence—and the same would be the case even now. The Greeks had their Dionysia in the spring of the year, when morals could be forgotten, and then the control of life resumed its normal course. In other words, they departmentalized their lives, being of an orderly cast of mind, but we do not lend ourselves easily to such a solution. With us it is all or nothing, provided we are not caught at it. Either we give ourselves to a course of action or we do not give ourselves. Either we are to be free men or not free men—at least in theory. Whitman, like Tom Paine, recognized no limits and that got him into trouble.

But the waves on the Jersey shore still came tumbling in, quieting him as their secret escaped him, isolating him and leaving him lonesome—but possessed by the great mystery which won the world to his side. For he was unquestionably the child of the years. What was the wave that moved the dawning century also moved him and demanded his recognition, and it was not to be denied. All the discoveries and inventions which were to make the twentieth century exceed all others, for better or worse, were implicit in his work. He surpassed the ritualistic centuries which preceded him, just as Ehrlich and Koch and finally Einstein were to exceed Goethe. It was destined to be so, and the

New World of which he was a part gave him birth. He had invented a new way of assaulting fate. "Make new!" was to him as it was to Pound much later on an imperious command which completely controlled him.

If he was to enlarge his opportunity he needed room, in verse as in everything else. But there were to be no fundamental changes in the concepts that keep our lives going at an accepted pace and within normal limits. The line was still to be the line, quite in accord with the normal contours of our accepted verse forms. It is not so much that which brought Whitman's verse into question but the freedom with which he laid it on the page. There he had abandoned all sequence and all order. It was as if a tornado had struck.

A new order had hit the world, a relative order, a new measure with which no one was familiar. The thing that no one realized, and this includes Whitman himself, is that the native which they were dealing with was no longer English but a new language akin to the New World to which its nature accorded in subtle ways that they did not recognize. That made all the difference. And not only was it new to America—it was new to the world. There was to be a new measure applied to all things, for there was to be a new order operative in the world. But it has to be insisted on that it was not disorder. Whitman's verses seemed disorderly, but ran according to an unfamiliar and a difficult measure. It was an order which was essential to the new world, not only of the poem, but to the world of chemistry and physics. In this way, the man was more of a prophet than he knew. The full significance of his innovations in the verse patterns has not yet been fully disclosed.

The change in the entire aesthetic of American art as it began to differ not only from British but from all the art of the world up to this time was due to this tremendous change in measure, a relative measure, which he was the first to feel and to embody in his works. What he was leaving behind did not seem to oppress him, but it oppressed the others and rightly so.

It is time now to look at English and American verse at the time Whitman began to write, for only by so doing can we be led to discover what he did and the course that lay before him. He had many formidable rivals to face on his way to success. But his chief opponent was, as he well knew, the great and medieval Shakespeare. And if any confirmation of Shakespeare's sacrosanct position in the language is still sought it is easily to be obtained when anything is breathed mentioning some alteration in the verse forms which he distinguished by using them. He may be imitated as Christopher Fry imitates him, but to vary or depart from him is heresy. Taken from this viewpoint, the clinical sheets of Shakespeare as a writer are never much studied. That he was the greatest word-man that ever existed in the language or out of it is taken for granted but there the inquiry ends.

Shakespeare presented Whitman with a nut hard to crack. What to do with the English language? It was all the more of a problem since the elements of it could not be presented at all or even recognized to exist. As far as the English language was concerned, there was only to use it and to use it well according to the great tradition of the masters.

And indeed it was a magnificent tradition. At the beginning of the seventeenth century it had reached an apogee which it had, to a great extent, maintained to the present day and of which it was proud and jealous. But when Shakespeare wrote, the laurels were new and had so recently been attained and had come from such distinguished achievements that the world seemed to pause for breath. It was a sort of noon and called for a halt. The man himself seemed to feel it and during an entire lifetime did no more than develop to the full his talents. It was noon sure enough for him, and he had only to stretch out in the sun and expand his mood.

Unlike Whitman, he was or represented the culmination of a historic as well as literary past whose forms were just coming to a head after the great trials which were to leave their marks on the centuries. There had been Chaucer, but the language had come of age since then as had the country. Now America had been discovered and the world could not grow much larger. Further expansion, except in a limited degree, was unlikely, so that the poet was left free to develop his world of detail but was not called upon to extend it. More was not necessary than to find something to do and develop it for the entire span of a long life. But as always with the artist, selection was an important point in the development.

For instance, as his sonnets show, Shakespeare was an accomplished rhymer, but he gave it up early. The patches of heroic couplet which he wrote for the Players in *Hamlet* are among the best examples of that form. Yet his main reliance was on blank verse—though he did, on occasion, try his hand at a triple accent which he rejected without more than a thought. The demands of the age called for other things and he was, above everything else, a practical man.

Practicing for so long a time upon the iambic pentameter, he had the opportunity to develop himself prodigiously in it. Over the years he shows a technical advance, a certain impatience with restraint in his work which makes it loose and verges more toward the conformation of prose. There is a great difference between Shakespeare's earlier and later work, the latter being freer and more natural in tone.

A feeling for prose began to be felt all through his verse. But at his death the form began to lapse rapidly into the old restrictions. It got worse and worse with the years until all the Elizabethan tenor had been stripped away, or as Milton phrased it speaking of his illustrious predecessor:

> Sweetest Shakespeare, Nature's child,
> Warbled his native woodnotes wild.

With Milton came Cromwell and the English Revolution, and Shakespeare was forgotten, together with the secrets of his versification, just as Whitman today is likely to be forgotten and the example of his verses and all that refers to him.

The interest that drove Whitman on is the same one that drove Shakespeare at the end of his life in an attempt to enlarge the scope of written verse, to find more of expression in the forms of the language employed. But the consequences of such experimentation are always drastic and amount in the end to its suppression, which in the person of a supreme genius is not easy.

From what has been said thus far, you can see why it is impossible to imitate Shakespeare; he was part of a historic process which cannot repeat itself. All imitations of the forms of the past are meaningless, empty shells, which have merely the value of decorations. So that, if anything is now to be created, it must be in a new form. Whitman, if he was to do anything of moment, could not, no matter how much he may have bowed down to the master, imitate him. It would not have had any meaning at all. And his responsibility to the new language was such that he had no alternative but to do as it bade him.

Though he may not have known it, with Whitman the whole spirit of the age itself had been brought under attack. It was a blind stab which he could not identify any more than a child. How could he, no matter how acute his instincts were, have foreseen the discoveries in chemistry, in physics, in abnormal psychology, or even the invention of the telephone or the disclosure of our subterranean wealth in petroleum? He knew only, as did those who were disturbed by his free verse, that something had occurred to the normal structure of conventional aesthetic and that he could not accept it any longer. Therefore, he acted.

We have to acknowledge at once in seeking a meaning involving the complex concerns of the world that the philosophic, the aesthetic, and the mechanical are likely to stem in their development from the same root. One may be much in advance of the other in its discoveries, but in the end a great equalizing process is involved so that the discovery of the advance in the structure of the poetic line is equated by an advance in the conception of physical facts all along the line. Man has no choice in these matters; the only question is, will he recognize the changes that are taking place in time to make the proper use of them? And when time itself is conceived of as relative, no matter how abstruse that may sound, the constructions, the right constructions, cannot be accepted with a similar interpretation. It may take time to bring this about, but when a basic change has occurred in our underlying concern it brooks no interference in the way it will work itself out.

Whitman didn't know anything about this, nor does Mr. Eliot take it into his considerations nor Father Merton either, but if they had to construct a satisfactory poetic line it had and still has to be done according to this precept. For we have learned, if we have learned anything from the past, that the principles of physics are immutable. Best, if you do not approve of what writing has become, to follow in Mr. Eliot's footsteps.

For it is important to man's fate that these matters be—if anything is important to man's fate in this modern world. At least, you cannot retrace steps that have been taken in the past. And you don't know, you simply do not know, what may come of it. No more than Whitman knew what his struggle to free verse may have implied and may still imply for us no matter how, at the moment, the world may have forsaken him. The books are not closed even though the drift in the tide of our interest may at the moment be all the other way. It cannot so soon have reversed itself. Something is still pending, though the final shape of the thing has not yet crystallized. Perhaps that is the reason for the regression. There are too many profitable leads in other associated fields of the intelligence for us to draw back now.

Where have the leads which are *not* aesthetic tended to take us in the present century? By paying attention to detail and our telescopes and microscopes and the reinterpretations of their findings, we realize that man has long since broken from the confinement of the more rigid of his taboos. It is reasonable to suppose that he will in the future, in spite of certain setbacks, continue to follow the same course.

Man finds himself on the earth whether he likes it or not, with nowhere else to go. What then is to become of him? Obviously we can't stand still or we shall be destroyed. Then if there is no room for us on the outside we shall, in spite of ourselves, have to go *in*: into the cell, the atom, the poetic line, for our discoveries. We have to break the old apart to make room for ourselves, whatever may be our tragedy and however we may fear it. By making room within the line itself for his inventions, Whitman revealed himself to be a worthy and courageous man of his age and, to boot, a farseeing one.

Walt Whitman as American Spokesman

by Richard Chase

[The speakers in the following dialogue, so the author informs us, "in order to give a clear idea of themselves . . . speak, a little artificially, as members of different generations. Yet they all illustrate different facets of the 'interim' or cold-war state of mind which has typified the last ten or fifteen years of American life." "Maggie Motive" is "a glamorous amateur and woman of projects, out of a gay past." "Rinaldo Schultz" is an "optimist, engineer, and newly naturalized American." "George Middleby" is a "solid citizen of the new generation." "Ralph Headstrong" is "a professor. middle aging."—R.H.P.]

MAGGIE: I insist that we talk about Whitman. Rinaldo won't mind. I happen to know that he is fond of Whitman.

RINALDO: Certainly I won't mind. I notice, however, that whenever I talk to the pessimistic and world-weary Americans about Whitman, they think I am a mad European full of naïve optimism and an unexamined belief in progress. They say I have not considered the nature of evil.

GEORGE: But Maggie, you cannot be, as it were, serious in saying that Whitman is funny, I mean as a comic poet is funny. I think of him as uttering vague, humorless, rhetorical assertions about Democracy. Then, too, he keeps solemnly assuring us that he has experienced life to the full, but he never gives us any sense of real experience or knowledge of the actual world. Instead he gives us either empty abstractions or lists of things out of the newspaper morgue, the primer of American history, the dictionary, and the atlas. Of course, he is very "American," but I don't really accept him as spokesman of his country, although I know that many people regard him as such.

"Walt Whitman as American Spokesman" (Original title: "Comedians All"). From *The Democratic Vista* by Richard Chase (New York, 1958), pp. 104-115.

MAGGIE: What do you say to that, Rinaldo?

RINALDO: As for Whitman being a comic poet, I believe that he is, although this is certainly not what I would say first about him. First of all he is the celebrant of American material and spiritual progress, of the dynamic, open, productive New World, with all of its brash power. I know that most Americans are ashamed of this side of Whitman, thinking that he is little better than the inspired George Babbitt when he made his passionate speech about the Standardized American to the Boosters Club. But Whitman is not Babbitt, and there is no reason to be ashamed of him, naïve and strident as he occasionally is. It is true that Whitman is very abstract on the one hand and given to making "catalogues" on the other, but I think he makes real aesthetic capital out of this habit of mind. As for being the spokesman of his country, I positively assert that he is—and by no means only as the inspired Rotarian or political prophet but because he reflects many dilemmas and contradictions, many subtle turns of mind and speech that strike me as very American indeed.

MAGGIE: I think George takes him too hard. What is your naïve and unreflecting response to Walt when he says, "I have never read Mill. What did he stand for, teach, saliently promulge?" I wouldn't trade that delicious "saliently promulge" for all the language of *The Golden Bowl.*

GEORGE: It is a delightful oddity, I admit.

MAGGIE: As another test case, what about these lines from "Song of the Exposition" in which Whitman welcomes the muse of poetry as "the illustrious emigre" who has left the fabled haunts of Europe and come to America. She is

> Bluff'd not a bit by drain-pipe, gasometers, artificial fertilizers,
> Smiling and pleas'd with palpable intent to stay,
> She's here, install'd among the kitchen ware!

GEORGE: What do I think of that? Well, that it's a free country and that if Whitman wants to depict the Muse as one of the TV kitchen goddesses of the hard sell, it's all right with me. The lines are amusing. But I should think that you, glamorous amateur, would be the first to object to the rather obvious and deplorable philistinism of taking the erstwhile nymph of the Fountain of Arethuse and plunking her down among the Norges, Hotpoints, and Coldspots.

RINALDO: I think those lines are delightful and witty. I trust my response and leave it to George to worry about philistinism.

MAGGIE: Gaiety and the excellent arrangement of words transmute all, even philistinism. How about the moment in "Song of Myself" when Whitman pauses before embarking on an evolutionary extravaganza and gravely observes: "I find I incorporate gneiss"?

GEORGE: Yes, I remember that. It really is a great comic moment. But the question that bothers me is: When we smile at something Whitman says, are we smiling with him or at him?

MAGGIE: I would stake my soul on its being *with* him in this case, as in most of the Whitman passages I remember best. True, we often laugh at him when he is not laughing at himself—that has unhappily become the standard response to Whitman, though it was not so in my youth. Many of his sillier passages warrant this kind of laughter. Yet at other times, when Whitman is functioning as the great comic poet he is, we laugh *with* him. Sometimes, to be sure, when we laugh with him, we suspect he is not laughing enough—that his comedy is more or less unintentional. But isn't it true that in every great man who has a streak of humor, the humor is partly unconscious?

RINALDO: That is surely true. I can say, too, that Maggie has perfectly expressed the response I have had to Whitman, ever since I had enough English to read him. A good deal of the true quality comes through in German, French, and Italian translation.

GEORGE: Did Whitman ever say he was a comic poet?

RALPH: In effect he did, yes. When one of the Camden friends of his old age called him an incorrigible "comedian" because of something he had said, Whitman replied that "one might end up worse" and declared: "I pride myself on being a real humorist underneath everything else."

MAGGIE: I don't say that Whitman is first and foremost a comic writer. But especially in "Song of Myself" the comic poet is heard—the Dionysian humor of the poet whose room was adorned, as I remember reading, by two pictures, "one of Silenus and one of Bacchus." But aside from any and all argument, Whitman is funny, he makes me laugh, he makes me smile even oftener. So I simply conclude that this reaction is the proper one and that one highroad to an appreciation of Whitman is his humor. Am I right, Ralph? What do you think of Walt?

RALPH: May I turn that question over to Rinaldo?

RINALDO: I think Whitman is not the greatest of your nineteenth-century writers, but that he is the most delightful and valuable. He is an ever-flowing source of inspiration. From what I know of the critics of the last two decades, they have assumed that because in some obvious ways the Whitman influence has been bad, it has been all bad. They have assumed that whatever was good about Whitman has long since been discovered and its influence exhausted. I am bold enough to assert that they were wrong on both counts. We have already, at least for this epoch, assimilated Hawthorne and most of Melville. We have absorbed from them, that is, whatever can do us any good. Whitman is of the future.

RALPH: I agree with that, although in subscribing to what Rinaldo has said, I would not mean to reinstate Whitman as the "focal center" of American culture—the position assigned to him by Van Wyck Brooks and by the 1920's in general. Whitman's occupation of the focal center is too strongly contested by writers very unlike him, notably Melville. Which is one way of saying that our culture is multiform, and has no focal center.

Maggie is playing the sibyl tonight. But her idea that Whitman is a comic poet does not sound sibylline to me. It sounds both obvious and profound. The comic sense, as the theoreticians tell us, is often born of incongruities and contradictions. Any moderately well-disposed reader of Whitman will see that he is very far from stamping out distinctions and inner tensions with his flow of universals and abstractions and his sometimes neurotic desire to "merge" with everyone and everything. Take another test case:

> Do I contradict myself?
> Very well then I contradict myself,
> (I am large, I contain multitudes.)

The tendency used to be to pass this off as mere bravado, or to use it as proof of the self-confessed intellectual and literary incompetence of the poet, or (if one felt favorably toward Whitman) to say that it referred to a Hegelian universe. If one wanted to defend Whitman, in other words, one felt that it was necessary to justify the contradictions of his personality and of his work or to show that he wrote good poetry in spite of them. But nowadays one should be ready to accept his contradictions as integral oppositions and polarities, not of the Hegelian order, but as the elements of a more or less sustained ironic view with which Whitman regarded himself and the world. There is an intermittent but strong comic intent, which not only appears in poems like "Song of Myself" but is carried over into the great elegiac poems—for example "As I Ebb'd with the Ocean of Life," where the poet momentarily faces the ultimate irrationality of the universe while

> the real Me stands yet
> untouch'd, untold, altogether unreach'd,
> Withdrawn far, mocking me with mock-congratulatory signs and bows,
> With peals of distant ironical laughter at every word I have written,
> Pointing in silence to these songs, and then to the sand beneath.

To take Whitman as existing in or through his polarities is the first step toward a fuller acceptance and enjoyment of his work. It is the poet who "knitted the old knot of contrariety" that appeals to the reader who is free of the tiresome old prejudices against our greatest poet.

RINALDO: Most of the professors seem to regard Whitman as some sort of philosopher, don't they? They want to "place" him in relation to Neoplatonism, pan-psychism, and God knows what all. No?

RALPH: Yes. The routine academician likes Whitman the "sublime" poet of time and space, Whitman the mystic, the stoic, the Quaker, the cosmic thinker. He pays little attention to Whitman the poet of the self, and is embarrassed by the poet's boastfulness and vaunting Americanism. He explains away or discounts Whitman's poses. He understands Whitman's contradictions, ambiguities, and ironies, not as native to the man, but as inadvertent results of his intellectual naïveté.

Thus when Whitman's official biographer remarks that "this was the real Walt Whitman, undiscriminating, easily stimulated by noise, color, and movement, happy to lose himself in the ceaseless flux of people going and coming," I want to reply: No, that is the mistake of D. H. Lawrence and Santayana and all those who see in Whitman only his "merging" with experience and do not see the recalcitrance with which Whitman could also meet life. The routine academician does not understand the Whitman who described himself as "furtive" and "artful." He does not perceive the alien, neurotic, divided, covertly musing Whitman, the envious, fearful, power-seeking, sagacious Whitman who could stand aside from life and adopt a series of attitudes toward it.

For after all, however much Whitman might pose as a burly proletarian with flowing beard, open collar, and pants tucked in boots, he was in fact a petty-bourgeois intellectual. His life is a series of such paradoxes and symbolic gestures. His charlatanism is a part of the whole man and a part of his work. And, charlatan or not, one of the most consistently remarkable things about him is his ability to make out of his life a series of indestructible ideals, of exemplary acts which belong to any American's cultural heritage. Whitman is only somewhat less recalcitrant to the miscellaneous circumstance of his life as the enfeebled sage of Camden, in his late years, than he had been as the nursing father and hospital visitor of the middle years, or as the proletarian Pan and Christlike carpenter and common man of the period just before the publication of *Leaves of Grass*.

Well, fair Sibyl, what have you to say to all this? Have you a reprise or a summary?

MAGGIE: It appears that Whitman appeals to anyone who reads him with any fresh excitement as the comic poet, the elegist, the singer of the plight and career of the self, the creator both in his personal life and in his poems of various ideal images which we can regard with affection and respect.

GEORGE: But isn't there a danger of being too sophisticated about Whitman?

RALPH: Yes. One can even over-respond to Whitman's own sophistication (he is always setting traps like that), and thus neglect his simplicity, his plain democratic faith, his undistorted intuition of the natural sources of being. However many ironies and ambiguities his recalcitrance to life may generate, one of the ways in which he appeals to us is not in the tensions of his mind but in his "loafing," his flowing, pleasurable intimacy with the world around him. It is easy to smile (but wasn't Walt smiling too?) at the surprised and delighted poet who calls himself a "caresser of life," the musing Dionysus to whom life cries "Ahoy! from the rocks of the river." But it is not so easy, so hectic in us are the distortions of will and intellect, to honor Whitman's receptivity to experience and to recognize the liberating effect it had on a hitherto squeamish American mentality.

GEORGE: I see I must have another look at the Good Gray. Still, I don't suppose you deny there is a lot of awful fustian in him.

MAGGIE: Oh, an immense amount.

RALPH: It was there from the beginning, even in his greatest poem, "Song of Myself." And it got worse as Whitman grew older. Despite his isolation and his relatively small circle of readers, Whitman gradually succumbed to the peculiar pressure a democracy puts on its great writers to become self-publicists, pundits, prophets, theologians, and political oracles.

RINALDO: I have noticed that. Now Faulkner seems in danger of this democratic fate.

GEORGE: Supposing that as I reread Whitman, I should find that you are right about his peculiar excellence, still I should protest that he knew little of the actualities of institutional life, of the life of society.

RINALDO: George is right about that. Walt is too preoccupied with the self as something apart from history and from social and political reality. He thinks of it merely in its ethical, spiritual, and literary relations. In *Democratic Vistas* he simply assumes that history is benign and maternal. One of the things that amazes a European reader is Whitman's belief that America is exempt from all such historical catastrophes as overtook "feudalism"—by feudalism, meaning everything that happened before 1776. In effect, he assumes that America is exempt not only from historical tragedy but from history itself. His sense of things in *Democratic Vistas* is that history really ended at the inception of the Republic, and that from then on change would never be radical but would be merely a matter of gradual unfolding and realization. This view is not only historically unrealistic, as viewed by us unhappy citizens of the atomic age, but it is oddly conservative too.

GEORGE: Yes, I've noticed that. How do we reconcile this conservatism with the usual view of Whitman as the prophet of the future and the "promulger" of those radical changes which were supposed finally to bring about a truly democratic world?

RALPH: Everything Rinaldo says about Whitman's lack of historical realism is true. As for the contradiction between his conservatism and his radicalism, there are many things to be noted, the most obvious being that this contradiction, as I am sure Rinaldo will agree, is extremely common among Americans. One way of getting at it is to notice what Whitman meant by "prophecy." Do you recall what he says in *Specimen Days*? He says "the word prophecy is much misused; it seems narrow'd to prediction merely. That is not the main sense of the Hebrew word translated 'prophet'; it means one whose mind bubbles up and pours forth as a fountain, from inner divine spontaneities revealing God. Prediction is a very minor part of prophecy." Although he is perhaps not speaking directly of social prophecy, what he says here accords with that sense he gives us in *Democratic Vistas* that the purpose of prophecy is to reveal a perfect dispensation already given, but now debased, distorted, or imperfectly realized. Like many, perhaps most, prophets, Whitman employs radically novel emotions, an apparently disruptive philosophical indeterminism, and a new language in behalf of conservative ideals. And thus in *Democratic Vistas* he commits himself to an implied conservatism strangely at odds with his declared principles.

George: But is there any intellectual substance to his conservatism?

Ralph: No. Whitman's conservatism is real enough as a prophetic attitude and as a form of instinctive prudence. He makes apparent declarations of principle in his later years, such as "I am a conservative of conservatives." But these do not constitute a "position." So that after all, his conservative tendencies as they appeal to us in his poems and dithyrambic prose remain memorable impulses merely, and do not, on the level of ideas, affect in any way the buoyant democratic idealism which also makes itself felt in *Democratic Vistas* or the radical utopian vision of "Song of Myself" or "Song of the Open Road."

So you see, George, the contradictoriness of Whitman's politics is typical of all the "old knots of contrariety" which are found in his personality and his work. In Whitman's mind political radicalism, though dominant, is held in a state of ironic tension with political conservatism. In *Specimen Days,* Whitman noticed a similar conflict in Carlyle, although in Carlyle he found that conservatism dominated; and he spoke eloquently of the "two conflicting agonistic elements" that "seem to have contended" in Carlyle's mind. We will always be wrong about Whitman, the man and his works, if we think of him as in any way monolithic or single-mindedly tendentious, or if we think of him as being merely confused. Whitman too was "agonistic." And it is not out of any love of literary intricacy for its own sake, but in recognition of the facts and because one wants to arrive at a steady and untroubled appreciation of his simplicities, that one tries to conceive of Whitman in his contrarieties.

George: As I recall, it was Santayana who said that Americans do not regard Whitman as the "spokesman of the tendencies of his country," that he appeals only to the "dilettanti" and that only foreigners regard him as a representative American.

MAGGIE: I love that "dilettanti"! It's so—so *Italian.*

RINALDO: Santayana has hit on an unhappy truth. I do not understand why Americans disown their great spokesman.

RALPH: Obviously Whitman has never been read by a large proportion of his countrymen. And in our drab decade, the literary people have not responded to Walt. But Whitman really is an authentic spokesman for the tendencies of his country. In describing Carlyle as "agonistic" Whitman recognized the fact that to exist in one's contrarieties is not an exclusively American fate. Yet Whitman's writings show his perception that although American democracy offers to the world an appearance of unrelieved uniformity, contrariety is in fact more nearly of the essence of life in America than it has ever been in any great civilization. We now begin to see, perhaps for the first time, the extent to which the life and works of Whitman exemplify what this fate may mean to Americans.

The Poetry of Praise

by Josephine Miles

Often we think of the main tradition in American poetry as that of the intense and cryptic metaphors of Emerson, Dickinson, Frost, and Eberhart, and we think of the very opposite style of Whitman, as almost alien, unexplainable. Under the scrutiny of the metaphysical critics for whom irony and paradox are major criteria of value, the loose clusterings of *Leaves of Grass* seem to become almost an historical anomaly.

What I should like to try is to describe briefly the historical nature of the high style which we see not only in Whitman but also in Anne Bradstreet, in Whittier, in Pound and Hart Crane, especially in many Californians from Charles Erskine Scott Wood on to the active present, to suggest its essential differences in structure and vocabulary from other basic American styles, and to suggest what are its powers for our future. While it is a style that many of us cannot write in, it is one we may become increasingly aware of. In the past year, a number of books have been concerned with it: notably Miller, Shapiro, and Slote's *Start with the Sun*, Wayne Shumaker's *Literature and the Irrational*, and Ernest Tuveson's *The Imagination as a Means of Grace*.

The classical rhetoricians distinguished three sorts of style—the low or colloquial, the middle observational and meditational, the high, ceremonial. Critics today have not regarded these distinctions as useful, because they have wanted to treat all poetry as a function of the first or second low or natural styles. For example, T. S. Eliot, though he has made allowances for Milton, and though he defines three different *voices* in poetry, makes these voices all non-Miltonic, all versions of dramatic colloquial poetry. The high style has been ignored, or at best, since Pope's *Peri Bathous*, has had an unfavorable press. Yet if we think of the high style also as *deep*, not only as empyrean but as subterranean and submarine, I believe we may recognize its serious function for the

"The Poetry of Praise." From *The Kenyon Review*, XXIII (Winter, 1961), 104-125.

present day. To clear and polished surfaces, it adds depths, however murky; to the objectivities of thought, action, and the thing in itself, it adds the subjectivity of inward feeling tumultuously expressed. Like the word *altus* in Latin, which means both high and deep, it relates the gods of the solar system to the gods of the solar plexus. Indeed it is one of the three great modes of poetry through time, and we may look to see how, historically, it has come so strongly into practice in America in its special complex of sound-structure, sentence-structure, and sense.

When American poetry began with the American revolutions of the seventeenth and eighteenth centuries, it was a poetry not of revolt but of enthusiasm, not analysis of America's situation but panegyric for the American land. In a century and a half it has not materially changed; despite the fashions of irony, drama, and complex involvement in the present day, still a prevailing tone is praise; and still a prevailing substance, the country's bounty and beauty. "My country 'tis of thee, Sweet land of liberty, I love thy rocks and rills, Thy woods and templed hills. . . ." These words have prospered and endured longer and stronger than the militant political ones for "Columbia the gem of the ocean" or "Oh say can you see by the dawn's early light What so proudly we hailed at the twilight's last gleaming." Our popular care has been not so much for the America of conflict, trouble, and doubt, as for the America of triumphant abundance. "From the mountains, to the prairies, to the oceans white with foam."

Thinking of the satiric models of the late eighteenth century, of Pope, for example, whom American gentlemen idolized; thinking of America's own native skepticism in the later generation of Emerson and Holmes; and thinking of the jazz of the twentieth century, we may well call into doubt any such generalization about our poetic tradition until we look at its sources.

In the first place, consider the nature or natures of English poetry from which America stemmed, the poetry, that is, of the Renaissance of the sixteenth and seventeenth centuries: we can think what it is like if we think of Chaucer and the Chaucerian tradition: a lively, active, humorous, and intensely human poetry, with people in it, and the sense of their relationships, their stations, high and low, with lords, knights, ladies, kings, fathers and sons living, loving, seeking, giving, taking, telling, in a world of interaction. This world of Skelton, Sackville, the pastoralists and the satirists came to a narrower lyrical focus in two ways: in the specific relation of a courtier to his lady, the poetry of courtly love and Donne's mockery of it; and in the specific relation of the poet to his God, as in the metaphysical verse of Herbert, Herrick, and Vaughan. Speaking either to lady or to God, the poet was colloquial, argumentative, dramatic; the lyric could be the scene from a play; and it was usually more figurative than literal in expression, using irony, exaggeration, and transformation of accepted categories to make its intellectual point. As a whole, this has been called the poetry of wit; there have been many admirers of it but few inheritors in America: none, except perhaps Frost, so close as Hardy or Auden in England.

Concurrent with this verse in the sixteenth and seventeenth centuries ran a kind which was consciously more classical, more objective and observational. It tended to use a long smooth line rather than intricate stanzas, and to describe rather than to argue, in the tradition of Virgil's *Georgics* or of Horace's *Satires*. For a while in England, its function was mainly satiric or deliberative: to mark the fall of a prince in history and cause, to analyze and mock something so specific as political factions or something so general as the foolishness and corruption of mankind; this was social poetry, and its greatest successful exponents were Dryden and Pope, whom the American colonists read avidly in order to keep track of what was wrong in London and the world, as they would read Arnold in the nineteenth century and T. S. Eliot in the twentieth. The more positive and cheerful descriptions of the land and its products, in the Virgilian tradition, grew up more slowly in England and for some reason less richly, but as they grew, served to support and strengthen a third kind of poetry which was just beginning to emerge, and which did not reach full force until the revolutionary and democratic eighteenth century, the poetry of rhapsody, the ode, hymn, dithyramb of praise. Familiar in the Homeric Hymns and in the Odes of Pindar, and powerfully joined by the Hebraic tradition of the Psalms, this was the form which grew in force from Spenser and Sylvester to More and Milton and which provided the whole basis of the vast odes of the eighteenth century, Thomson's pioneering book of *The Seasons*, the work of the Wartons, and Blake's Prophetic Books.

This third kind of English poetry, along with its more classical Virgilian counterpart, was what America brought across the ocean in full force. Not the earlier humanistic verse prevailed here, nor the satiric, nor even the religious and metaphysical work of the seventeenth century, traces of which we see in such early poets as Edward Taylor; but rather the newest, most revolutionary verse which England had to offer, the work of the Whig democrats, of the Protestants, and of the philosophers of benevolence like Shaftesbury and Locke, the work of men not more than a generation older than the first solid poetic group in America; the writers of the new nation, John Trumbull, Timothy Dwight, Philip Freneau, Joel Barlow, and their successors Sigourney, Percival, Drake, and Halleck. These took on wholeheartedly the new vocabulary of English rhapsody, and carried it into the present, while England itself in the nineteenth century nearly abandoned this tradition, returning to it in the twentieth under the leadership of American augmentation and innovation.

This is not the pattern of relationship and development we are usually given by scholars, yet it is a believable one, if we remember some clear distinctions. First, both the religious verse and the social verse of the seventeenth century, which the Puritans might have brought with them directly, with their love of moral criticism and their sense of a personal god, was after all not *their* sort of verse, but indeed the verse they were fleeing, as it was aristocratic and intellectual rather than democratic and enthusiastic. The good Puritan book was the Bible itself, and works most reliant on Biblical language and concept, like Sylvester's translation of Du Bartas' *Divine Week,* for example, meant most to the first tentative and isolated poets of America like Anne Bradstreet. This "tenth muse lately sprung up in America" was more Hebraic than the other nine muses; and sought sometimes the high style of ceremony, not always the low style of colloquy, because she held strongly to Biblical and Pindaric tradition.

Also, the high style seemed suited to the high adventure of America. Remembering that a translation of Ovid's *Metamorphoses* was the first English poetry written on this continent, by George Sandys in Virginia, as early as 1616, we may realize that men's minds were attuned to the idea of marvels and transformations here, of richness and abundance and of a suitably rich diction. Not Horace's mellow humor, not Catullus' sophisticated individuality, but something rarer, if we must be classical, like Ovid or like Virgil, would do better; and nothing was too good.

Thirdly, the political mentor of the constitution makers was John Locke, and it is not unnatural that our poetical mentors should have been his friends and followers, successors to the revolution of 1688, not old-regime roundheads but new parliamentarians, libertarians, latitudinarians, believers in progress and the pursuit of happiness. Here was the psychology of sense and common sense, of the marvels of wonder and imagination; here was the philosophy of men born equal and much alike; here was the cosmic science which followed Newton and Boyle, seeing the universe in wider and wider terms; here was the belief in physical laws and universal truths.

These all fitted together, the alliance of Protestant with Whig in political enthusiasm, the sense of the high style, the philosophy of universals, in encouraging a general ceremonious American style, stressing not what was peculiar or individual, or singular in America, but what it shared with the universe at large, namely, nature itself, in its abundance and splendor. Eighteenth century philosophers and critics had noted that the materials of satire were particularities, the oddities of men, the specific details which stood for trivia; by an inversion of logic, then, the poets in America felt that when they wrote about their country's own singularities they were in a sense mocking her—thus the many satiric poems, half-hearted in their specific characterizations which seemed to lead away from praise, yet eager to record the qualities and characteristics of the American scene.

Here was a dilemma for the poets: how to write a great and noble poem about a special place and situation, America, when universality not specialness was great and noble. The answer came gradually, in the stressing of those traits in which the country was not singular but was, rather, superlative, the traits of natural divine endowment. Once this pattern of emphasis was established, it was not broken even by those later nineteenth century poets who cried for the romantic richness of distinguishing detail: they got no further complexity of human American character nor even more complexity of nature. There was a lot of talk about more bobolinks and grasshoppers for the realism of the scene, but poetry persisted in lofty generality, in the sublime and universal mode which crossed the Atlantic from England and established itself strongly on these shores in philosophic democracy and Protestant theology of praise of the works of God. We are often confused when we look back upon this transit, because we expect a low, modest, and sober plain style from Puritans and democrats. But the eighteenth century democracy of man was based in the universality of sense impressions, the common accessibility of beauty, and the development from sense to soul; the eighteenth century religion of Protestant dissent, while it opposed the artifice of stained glass windows in churches, hailed with joy the art of nature as the most direct revelation of God's handiwork. So the high style of beauty and praise was considered natural.

Just how did this high style sound? We have heard it in the lofty passages of the Bible, possibly in Homer, Pindar, and Lucretius, and in English in Spenser, Sylvester, and Milton. But most precisely we may hear it in that work of their own day, which eighteenth century American poets admired so profoundly and perpetuated so vigorously, James Thomson's poem *The Seasons*. Here are the introductory lines to his "Hymn on the Seasons." Notice the long rolling blank-verse invocation, the progressive round of scene and time, the sense of illimitable and almost inexpressible power, all characteristics of the sublime style.

> These, as they change, Almighty Father! these
> Are but the varied God. The rolling year
> Is full of thee. Forth in the pleasing Spring
> Thy beauty walks, thy tenderness and love.
> Wide flush the fields; the softening air is balm;
> Echo the mountains round; the forest smiles;
> And every sense, and every heart, is joy.
> Then comes thy glory in the Summer-months,
> With light and heat refulgent. Then thy sun
> Shoots full perfection through the swelling year.

The poem continues through the other seasons, and through the farthest reaches of the universe, and ends with a restatement of ineffable power:

I cannot go
Where universal love smiles not around,
Sustaining all yon orbs and all their suns;
From seeming evil still educing good,
And better thence again, and better still,
In infinite progression. But I lose
Myself in him, in light ineffable!
Come then, expressive Silence, muse his praise.

In an early preface to his poem "Winter," 1726, Thomson wrote what he thought about the state of poetry in the early eighteenth century, and what should be done about it. After his own century, more American poets than English believed in him and followed his advice. He said,

> Let poetry once more be restored to her ancient truth and purity; let her be inspired from heaven, and in return her incense ascend thither; let her exchange her low, venal trifling subjects for such as are fair, useful, and magnificent. . . . Nothing can have a better influence towards the revival of poetry than the choosing of great and serious subjects, such as at once amuse the fancy, enlighten the head, and warm the heart. [Then he in effect anticipates and rejects the poetry of the Waste Land.] To be able to write on a dry, barren theme is looked upon by some as the sign of a happy, fruitful genius:—fruitful indeed! like one of the pendant gardens in Cheapside, watered every morning by the hand of the Alderman himself. . . . A genius fired with the charms of truth and nature is tuned to a sublimer pitch, and scorns to associate with such subjects. . . . I know no subject more elevating, more amusing; more ready to awake the poetical enthusiasm, the philosophical reflection, and the moral sentiment, than the works of Nature. Where can we meet with such variety, such beauty, such magnificence? All that enlarges and transports the soul! . . .

This was the belief which, though often in milder language, would prevail in American poetry, even into the work of the reformed Alderman of Cheapside, in the sublime passages of his *Four Quartets,* and into more youthful symbolic splendors of Ezra Pound, Hart Crane, and Richard Wilbur. It was a doctrine which met with tough opposition from English sceptics or even classicists from Dr. Samuel Johnson to Coleridge, Arnold, and Hulme; but it was a doctrine which found no great opposition on the new continent, rather a soil fertile for rich growth, with growing transcendentalism and modern imagism not stays but aids.

One might almost call it a doctrine native to America, because even a century before its enunciation by Thomson, it was practiced with enthusiasm by America's first muse, Anne Bradstreet. In her poem, "Contemplations," she writes the stiffer and simpler language of the seventeenth century and of Sylvester, but with the sweeping panegyric spirit of the century to come. Here are the first two stanzas:

Some time now past in the autumnal tide,
When Phoebus wanted but one hour to bed,
The trees all richly clad, yet void of pride,
Were gilded o'er by his rich golden head;
Their leaves and fruits seemed painted, but were true
Of green, of red, of yellow, mixed hue.
Rapt were my senses at this delectable view.

I wist not what to wish, yet sure, thought I,
If so much excellence abide below
How excellent is He that dwells on high,
Whose power and beauty by his works we know!
Sure He is goodness, wisdom, glory, light,
That hath this under world so richly dight.
More heaven than earth was here, no winter and no night.

Later in the poem Bradstreet devotes more famous lines to "I heard the merry grasshopper then sing. The black-clad cricket bear a second part"; but these are not so closely American as her general spirit of praise: "More heaven than earth was here, no winter and no night."

In time with the ringing of the Liberty Bell, the positives grew more superlative and competitive, as in Dwight's "Greenfield Hill" (I, 1-41).

As round me here I gaze, what prospects rise?
Etherial! matchless! such as Albion's sons,
Could Albion's isle an equal prospect boast,
In all the harmony of numerous song,
Had tun'd to rapture, and o'er Cooper's hill,
And Windsor's beauteous forest, high uprais'd,
And sent on fame's light wing to every clime.
Far inland, blended groves, and azure hills,
Skirting the broad horizon, lift their pride.
Beyond, a little chasm to view unfolds
Cerulean mountains, verging high on Heaven,
In misty grandeur.

Then there was, in early romanticism and late, free modulation of line-structure and implication—as in Lydia Sigourney's "Tomb of a Young Friend":

I do remember thee.
There was a strain
Of thrilling music, a soft breath of flowers

Telling of summer to a festive throng,
That fill'd the lighted halls. And the sweet smile
That spoke their welcome, the high warbled lay
Swelling with rapture through a parent's heart,
Were thine.
Time wav'd his noiseless wand awhile,
And in thy cherish'd home once more I stood,
Amid those twin'd and cluster'd sympathies
Where the rich blessing of thy heart sprang forth,
Like the moss rose. Where was the voice of song
Pouring out glad and glorious melody?—
But when I ask'd for thee, they took me where
A hallow'd mountain wrapt its verdant head
In changeful drapery of woods, and flowers,
And silver streams, and where thou erst didst love,
Musing to walk, and lend a serious ear
To the wild melody of birds that hung
Their unharm'd dwellings 'mid its woven bowers.
Yet here and there, involv'd in curtaining shades
Uprose those sculptur'd monuments that bear
The ponderous warnings of eternity.

Or Timrod's "The Cotton Boll":

Yonder bird,
Which floats, as if at rest,
In those blue tracts above the thunder, where
No vapors cloud the stainless air,
And never sound is heard,
Unless at such rare time
When, from the City of the Blest,
Rings down some golden chime,
Sees not from his high place
So vast a cirque of summer space
As widens round me in one mighty field,
Which, rimmed by seas and sands,
Doth hail its earliest daylight in the beams
Of gray Atlantic dawns;
And, broad as realms made up of many lands,
Is lost afar
Behind the crimson hills and purple lawns
Of sunset, among plains which roll their streams
Against the Evening Star!
And lo!
To the remotest point of sight,

Although I gaze upon no waste of snow,
The endless field is white;
And the whole landscape glows,
For many a shining league away,
With such accumulated light
As Polar lands would flash beneath a tropic day!

At the same time, a larger more social sweep: as in Thomas Holly Chivers' "The Rising of the Nations":

Millions of millions now are groaning, groaning
    Beneath the grinding weight of Despotism,
While bloody Anarchy, unmindful of their moaning,
    Plunges them deeper into Hell's unsunned Abyssum!
While Earth, now slimed beneath his vile pollution,
    Echoes the wailings of their desolation,
Until the remnant, ripe for revolution,
    Answers the music of their soul's salvation,
Uttered by Liberty upon th' immortal Mountains,
    From all the vallies, out of every habitation—
Coming, like many rills from new-born Fountains
    Fresh opened in the Earth from long-descending rains,
Which, gathering into one great onward rushing river,
    Distending, overflows its banks, till all the plains
Are inundated with its everspreading waters—
    Still gathering volume as it flows forever;—
So did they gather in one mighty multitude,
    As if the Nations from the four great quarters
Of all the earth had migrated in one great flood,
    With one great common sympathy, to overthrow
    This mighty Monarch of the world—this foe
To human greatness—this great Devil to the Free—
This damned Abaddon of the Sons of Anarchy!

The sublime poets were political poets; they were moved by vast social forces, and exercised a public rhetoric, as Pindar did, for public purposes. For all of them in America, from Barlow and Trumbull on, we may let John Greenleaf Whittier do the speaking, for he spoke from the civil-war torn middle of the century, with a passion we are still feeling. Here are some stanzas from his "Lines, Suggested by a Visit to Washington in the 12th Month of 1845":

With a cold and wintry noon-light,
    On its roofs and steeples shed,

Shadows weaving with the sunlight
    From the gray sky overhead,
Broadly, vaguely, all around me, lies the
    half-built town outspread.

Through this broad street, restless ever,
    Ebbs and flows a human tide,
Wave on wave a living river;
    Wealth and fashion side by side;
Toiler, idler, slave and master, in the same
    quick current glide.

Underneath yon dome, whose coping
    Springs above them, vast and tall,
Grave men in the dust are groping
    For the largess, base and small,
Which the hand of Power is scattering, crumbs
    which from its table fall.

Base of heart, they vilely barter
    Honor's wealth for party's place:
Step by step on Freedom's charter
    Leaving footprints of disgrace;
For to-day's poor pittance turning from the
    great hope of their race.

Then, after a vision of the South's anguish, and the nation's highest purposes, the final exhortation:

Let us then, uniting, bury
    All our idle feuds in dust,
And to future conflicts carry
    Mutual faith and common trust;
Always he who most forgiveth in his
    brother is most just.

From the eternal shadow rounding
    All our sun and starlight here,
Voices of our lost ones sounding
    Bid us be of heart and cheer,
Through the silence, down the spaces,
    falling on the inward ear.

Manifold traits of the sublime style are here: the visionary spirit and invocative tone, the irregular line length and harmonic use of sound, the sense of mankind as one great body, with personifiable characteristics, the exclamations and superlatives, and even the figures, of the restless river, the eternal shadow, and the voice of silence falling on the inward ear. I know none more directly representative of this whole American tradition than Whittier.

While in Whittier we have its representation, in Whitman we have its extreme. More visionary, more invocative, more adjectival, more cumulative and harmonic than any other poet in English, even more than Blake, Whitman is the great, and American, culmination of the sublime tradition. Each of us can recall a dozen or a hundred passages from *Leaves of Grass* which embody these traits we have been thinking of. To begin to quote is not to know where to end. But here is an early passage, "On Journeys through the States," with its free-swinging line and its all-encompassing attitude:

> On journeys through the States we start,
> (Ay through the world, urged by these songs,
> Sailing henceforth to every land, to every sea,)
> We willing learners of all, teachers of all, and lovers of all.
> We have watch'd the seasons dispensing themselves and passing on
> And have said, Why should not a man or woman do as much as the seasons, and effuse as much?
> We dwell a while in every city and town,
> We pass through Kanada, the North-east, the vast valley of the Mississippi, and the Southern States,
> We confer on equal terms with each of the States,
> We make trial of ourselves and invite men and women to hear,
> We say to ourselves, Remember, fear not, be candid, promulge the body and the soul,
> Dwell awhile and pass on, be copious, temperate, chaste, magnetic,
> And what you effuse may then return as the seasons return,
> And may be just as much as the seasons.

Every particular has its place in the list, every list its place in the whole poem, and every whole poem its place in geography and universe. Smallness and greatness are equal in this cycle of meaning. Through Whitman, Emily Dickinson, Marianne Moore and others, America has fostered the sense of size not only in greatness, but in smallness also, in the most minute and loving detail. As Whitman said in "Song of Myself,"

> I chant the chant of dilation or pride,
> We have had ducking and deprecating about enough,
> I show that size is only development.

And therefore the gamut, the interest in degree, of small to large and little to great, in the careful and fond details of the most sweeping verse.

In a particular way, Whitman naturalized the sublime: he located it in individual bodies and souls, not only by specifying the sublime, but by generalizing and expanding the human. Like his contemporaries in America, he fostered the Whig poetizing of earth, sea, and land—the expanses of nature—and then in his own way gave them a human presence, in woman, mother, child; in water, which could be both human and natural, and in the human, natural counterparts of hair and grass. This sharing of physical values, this passiveness of holding and beholding, sleeping and waiting, has been characteristic of much poetry since Whitman—of Pound, Eliot, Lawrence, Crane, Roethke—(See my *Renaissance, Eighteenth Century, and Modern Language in Poetry, 1960*). While for Blake, Keats, and others before Whitman, sublime figures were externalized, for Whitman and those after him they were internalized; earth felt through body, body through earth.

As the historian Bancroft wrote to Prescott in 1848, in terms like Whitman's, "Go forth, then, language of Milton and Hampden, language of my country, take possession of the North American Continent! Gladden the waste places with every tone that has been rightly struck on the English lyre, with every English word that has been spoken well for liberty and for man! . . . Utter boldly and spread widely through the world the thoughts of the coming apostles of liberty, till the sound that cheers the desert shall thrill through the heart of humanity . . ."

I have been making here a number of generalizations which run counter to some standard descriptions of American poetry. I have suggested first that the Protestant-democratic style is not the plain English but the high Biblical style; second, that of two major and almost opposite Romantic styles it was again not the dramatic one of Coleridge but the high one of Thomson and Blake that most affected American nineteenth century romanticism; third, that the prevalent balanced style in America, often called classical, represents a steady and conscious effort at compromise between extremes: between the lowly and plain in poetry, for which the country has so much affinity, and at the other extreme the sublime, the worshipful Sunday poetry early adopted and enthusiastically maintained; and fourth, that when the two nations separated politically at the end of the eighteenth century, it was America, not England, that carried on the eighteenth century poetic tradition, and it is now America which is taking the lead in returning this tradition to England, with an increasing consolidation of interests and powers.

The drama of O'Neill and the fiction of Faulkner each in its own way gives us again this vision of the mystery in the near at hand, and confirms in the sublime style of the prose of America the sublimity of its poetry. The importance of this sublimity will, I think, increase with time. Of all the modes it has been least consciously explored and defined, least critically championed. Yet Dylan Thomas in England and Hart Crane in America have spoken with this voice what Whitman spoke, what the prophets spoke, to the young poets—"Come then, expressive silence, muse his praise."

This American poetry of praise has a long free cadenced line, full of silences, symbols, and implications. It has a cumulative structure, building up to a height of force and feeling, whether in imprecation or in rhapsody. It has a phraseology of resounding sound and of warm responsive sense, suggestive of heights and depths beyond the reach of form or reason. As at its worst it can be dangerously loose, semi-conscious, and irresponsible, at its best it can be powerfully aware of moving forces and meanings. Strong as it was in England in the work of Keats, Tennyson, and Dylan Thomas, it has been more widespread and more central to tradition in America, with added impetus from poets of the Orient as well as of Europe. What can it mean to our future?

It can portend for our poetry a strong sense of ceremony and of public concern, strong personal and passionate comments on public issues, a highly vocal and expressive function of evaluation for the poet—comparable to the role played by Pindar, for example, in his celebration of the Olympic Games—a calling up and praising of great figures of our life—or perhaps of denouncing them, but at any rate of perceiving and portraying them, larger than life, in a great frame of human values and human concerns. It can be not only personal and ambiguous, but social and magnanimous, in the magnanimity of a poetry which transfigures what it values.

Chronology of Important Dates

1819	Walt Whitman born May 31, on a Long Island farm.
1823	Moved to Brooklyn, New York. Father worked as a builder.
1831-1841	Worked as a printer's devil, printer, reporter, schoolteacher, handyman.
1842-1846	Reporter, magazine-writer, small editor and politician in New York City. Published (1842) *Franklin Evans, or the Inebriate,* a tract.
1846	Editor of the Brooklyn *Daily Eagle.*
1848	Discharged from the *Eagle.* Visited New Orleans.
1849	Editor of the Brooklyn *Freeman,* a free-soil journal.
1850-1855	Part-time journalist and homebuilder with father.
1855	*Leaves of Grass,* first edition.
1856	*Leaves of Grass,* second edition—with which began the continuing expansion and revision of the book.
1860	*Leaves of Grass,* third edition.
1862-1864	Went first to Virginia to search for brother George, then to Washington as volunteer nurse in army hospitals. Worked in government offices.
1865	Fired from Department of the Interior on charge that *Leaves of Grass* was indecent. Rehired by Attorney General's office. *Drum-Taps* published.
1866	W. D. O'Connor's *Good Gray Poet,* the first major apologia for Whitman, marked the beginning of his international reputation. His health gradually deteriorating, demands on his time increasing, Whitman continued in Attorney General's office until 1873.
1867	*Leaves of Grass,* fourth edition.
1871	*Leaves of Grass,* fifth edition. *Democratic Vistas.*
1873	Partially paralyzed by mild stroke. Moved to Camden, N.J., where he lived out his life—to be finally at the center of the group of disciples which came to be known as "The Whitman Fellowship."

1876	*Author's Edition: Leaves of Grass* and *Two Rivulets.*
1881	Boston edition of *Leaves of Grass.*
1882	*Specimen Days and Collect.*
1888	*November Boughs.*
1891-1892	"Deathbed Edition" of *Leaves of Grass.*
1892	*Complete Prose Works.* Died March 26 at Camden.

Notes on the Editor and Contributors

Roy Harvey Pearce, the editor of this volume, is Professor of English at The Ohio State University. In addition to many articles and reviews on American Literature and Intellectual History, Professor Pearce has published *The Savages of America* (1953), *The Continuity of American Poetry* (1961), the Introduction to the Facsimile Edition of the 1860 *Leaves of Grass,* and is general editor with William Charvat of the Centennial Edition of the writings of Hawthorne.

Roger Asselineau is Professor of English at the Sorbonne. He is author of *L'Evolution de Walt Whitman* (1954).

Richard Chase is Professor of English at Columbia University. He is author of *Quest for Myth* (1949), *Walt Whitman Reconsidered* (1955), and *The American Novel and its Tradition* (1957).

Charles Feidelson, Jr. is Professor of English at Yale University. He is author of *Symbolism and American Literature* (1953).

John Kinnaird is Instructor in English at Vassar College.

D. H. Lawrence (1885-1930) was the British novelist, poet, and essayist who spent much of the later part of his life in the United States. In a way, *Studies in Classic American Literature* is the richest record of that part of his life.

R. W. B. Lewis is Professor of English at Yale University. He is author of *The American Adam* (1955) and *The Picaresque Saint* (1960).

F. O. Matthiessen (1902-1950) was Professor of English at Harvard University. He is author of *Sarah Orne Jewett* (1929), *The Achievement of T. S. Eliot* (1935), *American Renaissance* (1941), *Henry James: The Major Phase* (1944), *Theodore Dreiser* (1951).

Josephine Miles is Professor of English at the University of California, Berkeley. She is author of *Eras and Modes in English Poetry* (1957) and *Poems: 1930-1960* (1960).

James Miller, Jr. is Professor of English at the University of Nebraska. He is author of *A Critical Guide to Leaves of Grass* (1957) and *The Fictional Technique of Scott Fitzgerald* (1957).

Perry Miller is Professor of English at Harvard University. He is author of *The New England Mind: The Seventeenth Century* (1939), *The New England Mind: From Colony into Province* (1953), *Jonathan Edwards* (1949), *Errand into the Wilderness* (1956).

Ezra Pound now lives in Italy, where he works toward completion of his *Cantos.*

Walter Sutton is Professor of English at Syracuse University.

William Carlos Williams retired from his medical practice a few years ago and has increasingly assumed his rightful position as one of the grand old masters of American letters. His major achievement as a poet is *Paterson* (1946-1958), which is in effect his version of "Song of Myself."

Bibliography

Whitman's Text

The standard edition of Whitman is *The Complete Writings* (New York, 1902), 10 vols., ed. R. M. Bucke, T. H. Harned, and H. L. Traubel. It is, in fact, far from "complete" and is being superseded by *The Collected Writings of Walt Whitman,* ed. G. W. Allen and S. Bradley—of which the first two volumes (containing Whitman's early correspondence) have been issued (New York, 1961). The best among many editions of *Leaves of Grass* is the "Inclusive Edition" of Emory Holloway (New York, 1925 and frequently reprinted) which reproduces the variorum readings of *The Complete Writings. The Complete Poetry and Prose,* ed. M. Cowley (New York, 1948, reprinted 1954) is the most readily available edition of its kind. There are facsimile editions of the 1855 *Leaves of Grass,* ed. C. J. Furness (New York, 1939), and the 1860 *Leaves of Grass,* ed. R. H. Pearce (Ithaca, 1961). The 1855 *Leaves of Grass* has also been reprinted, ed. Malcolm Cowley (New York, 1960), and as a Dolphin paperback (New York, 1960). Fredson Bowers has edited *Whitman's Manuscripts, Leaves of Grass: 1860* (Chicago, 1955) and given us the best detailed view we have so far had of a stage in the growth of *Leaves of Grass.* One of the best critical introductions to Whitman's poetry, the text for which derives from the various editions of *Leaves of Grass,* is *Walt Whitman's Poems: Selections, with Critical Aids,* ed. G. W. Allen and C. T. Davis (New York, 1955—reprinted 1959 as an Evergreen paperback).

Biography and Criticism

The number of biographical and critical studies of Whitman is of course enormous. The most judicious recent survey of them is Williard Thorpe's essay in *Eight American Authors* (New York, 1956), pp. 271-318. Below are listed a small selection, representing, along with the essays in this volume, the most important and, from their various perspectives, the most soundly expounded twentieth-century views of Whitman.

Allen, Gay Wilson. *The Solitary Singer.* New York: The Macmillan Co., 1955. The definitive biography.

———. *Walt Whitman Handbook.* Chicago: Hendricks House, Inc., 1946. With its careful bibliographies, this remains the best introduction to the problems raised by Whitman's work.

———, ed. *Walt Whitman Abroad.* Syracuse, N. Y.: Syracuse University Press, 1955. A representative collection of foreign opinion of Whitman, in English translation.

Arvin, Newton. *Whitman.* New York: The Macmillan Co., 1938. The best politically-minded study of Whitman.

Asselineau, Roger. *L'Evolution de Walt Whitman.* Paris: Gregory Lounz, 1954. The first part of this close study of Whitman's "creation" of his biography has been published in English as *The Evolution of Walt Whitman,* Volume I, Cambridge, Mass.: The Belknap Press of Harvard University Press, 1960. Translation of the second part, a selection from which is printed herein, is forthcoming.

Bradley, Sculley. "The Fundamental Metrical Principle in Whitman's Poetry," *American Literature,* X (1938-39), 347-359. The best of the more "traditional" studies of Whitman's prosody.

Chapman, John Jay. "Whitman," in *Selected Writings,* J. Barzun, ed. New York: Farrar, Straus & Cudahy, Inc., 1959, pp. 157-164. Originally published in *Emerson and Other Essays* (New York: Charles Scribner's Sons, 1898), this is one of the earliest balanced assessments of Whitman as at once a threat to and a promise for American life.

Chase, Richard. " 'Go-Befores and Embryons': A Biographical Reprise," in *Leaves of Grass One Hundred Years After,* M. Hindus, ed., Stanford, Calif.: Stanford University Press, 1955, pp. 32-54. The best of the psychoanalytic accounts of the origins of Whitman's genius. Developed into a full-scale historical-critical study in Mr. Chase's *Walt Whitman Reconsidered* (New York: William Morrow & Co., Inc., 1955).

Coffman, Stanley K., Jr. "Form and Meaning in Whitman's 'Passage to India,' " *PMLA,* LXX (1955), 337-349. One of the surprisingly few good formalist explications of a Whitman poem.

Cox, James M. "Walt Whitman, Mark Twain, and the Civil War," *Sewanee Review,* LXIX (1961), 187-193. The best account on the significance of the Civil War for the achievement of Whitman's poetry.

Fiedler, Leslie. "Walt Whitman: Portrait of the Artist as a Middle-Aged Hero," in *No! in Thunder,* Boston: Beacon Press, 1960, pp. 61-75. Originally published as the introduction to the Laurel paperback *Whitman* (New York: Dell Publishing Co., Inc., 1959), this is a free-wheeling assessment of a shape-shifting Whitman who made sure that the joke was on his readers, not excluding Mr. Fiedler.

Foerster, Norman. "Whitman," in *American Criticism,* New York: Houghton Mifflin Company, 1928, pp. 157-222. An interested, cautionary, conservative account of the implications of Whitman's "creed" for modern literature.

Griffith, Clark. "Sex and Death: the Significance of Whitman's 'Calamus' Themes," *PQ,* XXXIX (1960), 18-38. Whitman's Civil War experiences and their role in the sublimation of his homosexuality, thus in the achievement of his poetry.

Holloway, Emory. *Whitman: An Interpretation in Narrative.* New York: Alfred A. Knopf, Inc., 1926. Though superseded by Allen's biography, this remains an exciting and excited account of the discovery of the "real" Whitman.

Jarrell, Randall. "Some Lines from Whitman," in *Poetry and the Age,* New York: Alfred A. Knopf, Inc., 1953. A strenuous Cook's tour through Whitman, marking his acceptance by one of a generation of American poets who heretofore had tended to shun him. In effect, an important "re-discovery."

Matthiessen, F. O. *American Renaissance.* New York: Oxford University Press, Inc., 1941. Both the discussion of Whitman, pp. 517-625 (part of which is reprinted herein) and the book at large are basic compendious studies, knowledge of which is by now a necessary condition to the comprehension of American literature and life in the nineteenth century.

Miller, James, Jr. *A Critical Guide to Leaves of Grass.* Chicago: University of Chicago Press, 1957. The best defense of the "prophetic" Whitman—which in effect mounts an offense, a section of which is printed herein.

Parrington, Vernon Louis. "The Afterglow of the Enlightenment: Walt Whitman," in *Main Currents in American Thought,* Volume III (New York: Harcourt, Brace & World, Inc., 1930), pp. 69-86. The principal "liberal" assessment of Whitman.

Pearce, Roy Harvey. *The Continuity of American Poetry.* Princeton, N. J.: Princeton University Press, 1961. On Whitman, see pp. 63-69, 164-174.

Santayana, George. "The Poetry of Barbarism," in *Interpretations of Poetry and Religion* (New York: Harper & Brothers, 1900, reprinted 1957), pp. 166-216. The "barbarians" are Browning and Whitman. One of the great attacks on Whitman, among other reasons, because Santayana can acknowledge his power. An influential essay, because it directly and indirectly gave rise to so many "defenses" of Whitman.

Saunders, H. S., ed. *Parodies of Walt Whitman,* New York: American Library Service, 1923. The best of these parodies are exercises in exorcism. See also Dwight MacDonald, ed. *Parodies* (New York: Random House, 1960), pp. 143-146, 324, 326, for some more recent examples.

Schyberg, Frederick. *Walt Whitman,* Evie Allison Allen, trans. New York: Columbia University Press, 1951. The best "internationalist" account of Whitman.

Shapiro, Karl. "The First White Aboriginal," in James E. Miller, Jr., *et al. Start with the Sun.* Lincoln, Neb.: University of Nebraska Press, 1960, pp. 57-70. An impassioned plea for the "prophetic" Whitman, coming from a full, frank, free confession of a recent convert.

Spencer, Benjamin T. "Walt Whitman," in *The Quest for Nationality,* Syracuse, N. Y.: Syracuse University Press, 1957, pp. 219-241. A masterful account of Whitman's role in the definition of an autochthonous American literature.

Stovall, Floyd. "Main Drifts in Whitman's Poetry," *American Literature,* IV (1932-33), 3-21. A careful survey of the shifting ideological components of Whitman's work—one of the most valuable of the many descriptive introductions.

Van Doren, Mark. "The Poet," in *Walt Whitman: Man, Poet, Philosopher,* Washington: Reference Department, Library of Congress, 1955, pp. 15-33. A balanced, ordered assessment. In its sweet calmness, one of the best recently written introductions to Whitman.

TWENTIETH CENTURY VIEWS

American Authors

AUDEN, edited by Monroe K. Spears (S-TC-38)
STEPHEN CRANE, edited by Maurice Bassan (S-TC-66)
EMILY DICKINSON, edited by Richard B. Sewall (S-TC-28)
EMERSON, edited by Milton R. Konvitz
and Stephen E. Whicher (S-TC-12)
FAULKNER, edited by Robert Penn Warren (S-TC-65)
F. SCOTT FITZGERALD, edited by Arthur Mizener (S-TC-27)
ROBERT FROST, edited by James M. Cox (S-TC-3)
HAWTHORNE, edited by A. N. Kaul (S-TC-55)
HEMINGWAY, edited by Robert P. Weeks (S-TC-8)
HENRY JAMES, edited by Leon Edel (S-TC-34)
SINCLAIR LEWIS, edited by Mark Schorer (S-TC-6)
ROBERT LOWELL, edited by Thomas Parkinson (S-TC-79)
MELVILLE, edited by Richard Chase (S-TC-13)
ARTHUR MILLER, edited by Robert W. Corrigan (S-TC-84)
MODERN AMERICAN DRAMATISTS, edited by Alvin B. Kernan (S-TC-69)
O'NEILL, edited by John Gassner (S-TC-39)
POE, edited by Robert Regan (S-TC-63)
EZRA POUND, edited by Walter Sutton (S-TC-29)
WALLACE STEVENS, edited by Marie Borroff (S-TC-33)
THOREAU, edited by Sherman Paul (S-TC-10)
MARK TWAIN, edited by Henry Nash Smith (S-TC-30)
EDITH WHARTON, edited by Irving Howe (S-TC-20)
WHITMAN, edited by Roy Harvey Pearce (S-TC-5)
W. C. WILLIAMS, edited by J. Hillis Miller (S-TC-61)

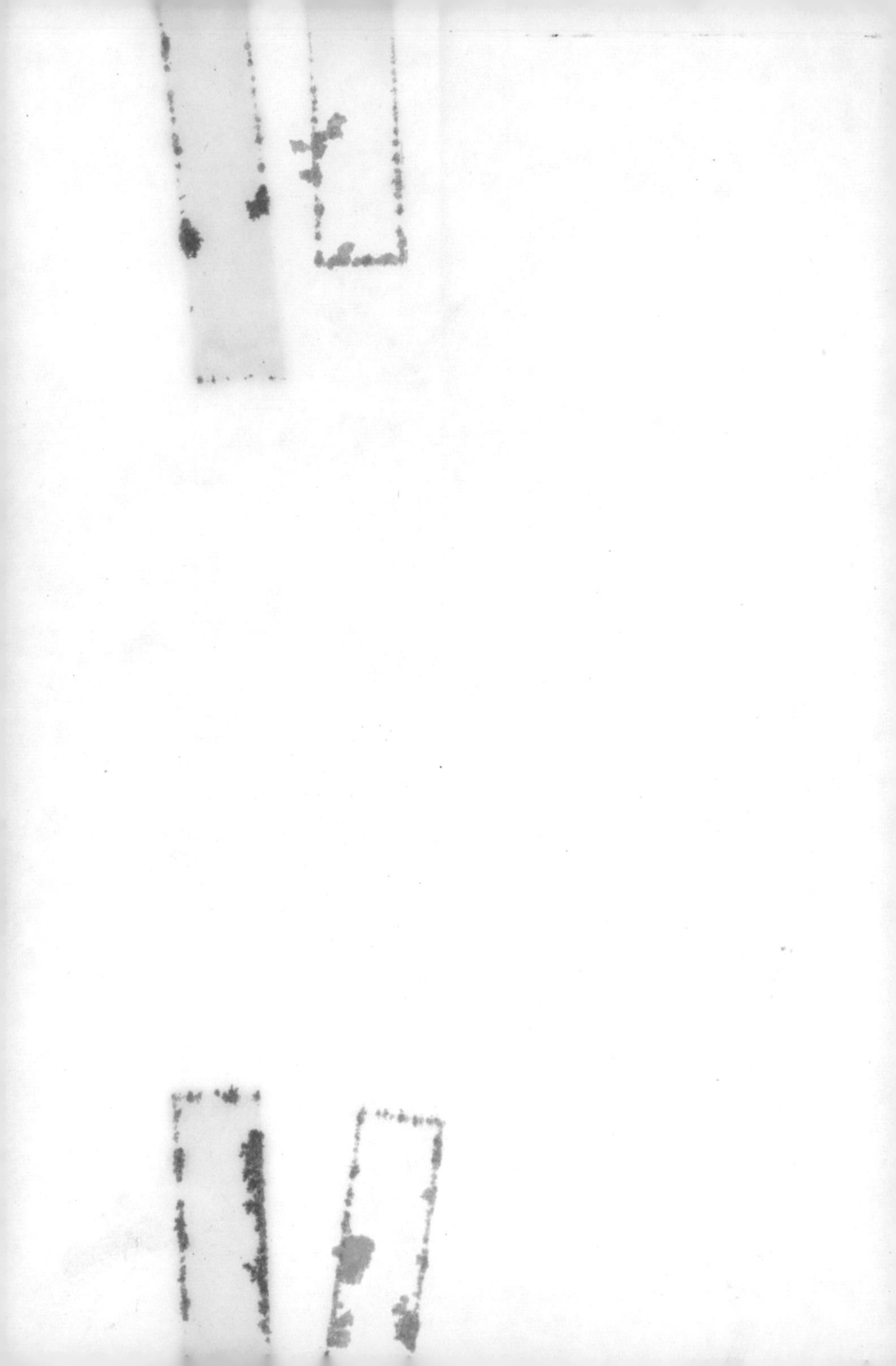